D1714785

THE SCIENCE OF SELF-CONTROL

53 Tips to stick to your diet, be more productive and excel in life

MENNO HENSELMANS

CONTENTS

CHAPTER 4: HOW TO STICK TO YOUR DIET   115

FOREWORD

Motivation books are a dime a dozen. Every other book promises to launch you from your seat and into your most productive life. Of course, most fail to work as intended, and that's often because they ask you to radically change who you are without concretely telling you how to do so. That big, life-altering change, which is both the premise and the requisite buy-in for most self-help books, is completely absent from *The Science of Self-Control*. Instead, you get lists of effective actions that can improve your ability to actually accomplish your goals. Many of them are so effortless, so simple, and require so little buy-in to pull off, that you might, as I did, read them and hit yourself over the head for not trying them sooner. In this book you'll find take-home strategies that work, not because of their miraculousness, but because of their simplicity and ease of implementation. The tips are insanely practical, down to matters like how to do your grocery shopping. If you end up integrating all the tips in this book on how to get things done, you'll become an unstoppable version of yourself. Even with a casual read, you'll be sure to pick up a few tips that will instantly make a big difference in your life, such as the use of the Zeigarnik effect. Yep, this book is that useful. Enjoy it!

- Mike Israetel, PhD, professor & professional athlete

INTRODUCTION

Our species has it made these days. Instead of facing frostbite during winter, we live in comfortably heated houses. Instead of being forced to hunt to avoid starvation, we can go to supermarkets, where our biggest problem is deciding which of the 50 brands of cereal to buy. Yet our conquest of nature has imposed on us new challenges of life. Rather than fight starvation, we now face an obesity pandemic. Without artificial diet and exercise programs, our health is threatened not by scarcity and war but by abundance and leisure. Without being forced to build shelter or find food, many people struggle to motivate themselves to work. More freedom brings with it more decisions. In making these decisions, we often encounter a conflict between our primal instincts and our conscious will. We intend to get some work done, but we end up procrastinating on Instagram. We intend to stick to our diet, but we end up eating pizza. Our intentions give way to hunger and other forms of instant gratification. We have difficulty enforcing our conscious will: our self-control fails us.

Self-control has been a unifying theme in my own life as well. I first started studying behavioral psychology and cognitive neurosciences at Utrecht University's honor's college, UCU, and then further at Warwick. While I learned a great deal about willpower and how our minds work, like most students, I personally still struggled enormously with procrastination. If I had known what I know now, I could have finished my studies in half the time. I still managed to graduate both with distinction and I started working as a business consultant. Like most office workers, there I struggled to stay motivated and productive during the whole workday. I realized I was on the career path that society and my parents expected of me but not the path I was most passionate about. So I traded in my company car to pursue my passion in fitness. I also started traveling the world as a digital nomad and have lived in over 50 countries since then. My career as an evidence-based fitness educator became more successful than I ever dreamed: I currently own a multinational Personal Training certification company with almost a thousand students per year across courses in 5 languages. I also work as a scientific researcher. While optimizing my own physique and productivity as an entrepreneur, I again realized how important willpower is. Whether I was grinding out that last rep in the gym, trying not to succumb to hunger before a photoshoot or optimizing my methods to answer over a hundred messages per day, it all came down to self-control. Self-control is key to self-improvement and success.

After over a decade of studying the science of self-control and improving my own self-control, I decided to write this book to share what I've learned. My goal is to help you take control of your body and mind to develop an iron will, top productivity, effortless diet adherence and ultimately excellence in life.

Ready?

To control something, you must first understand it. Before we can take control of our minds, we must first understand the brain.

CHAPTER 1: 2-SYSTEM THEORY

We like to think we are aware of everything that happens in our brain, but that is not always the case. For example, why are we sexually attracted to certain people? I'm sure you can come up with many reasons. Their personality, their body, maybe their bank account. But you probably didn't list circumstance. Yet the circumstances in which we meet someone significantly influence how attractive we find someone.

In 1974, a team of psychologists set up a clever experiment to demonstrate the importance of circumstance, and in doing so, taught us something very important about how our brains work [1]. An attractive woman approached men privately either on a high, shaky suspension bridge or on solid ground. She thought her task was to survey them. In reality, the researchers were interested in how attractive the men found her. As it turned out, high up on the shaky bridge, the men gave more sexually themed answers during the survey and were more likely to call the female interviewer for 'follow-up questions' than the men that were interviewed on solid ground. Replication of the experiment with a male interviewer showed no differences between footing conditions. Why were the men more attracted to the female interviewer on a shaky bridge than on solid ground?

This experiment demonstrates what psychologists call a 'misattribution effect'. Being on a suspension bridge makes us anxious. When we then meet a potential romantic partner, we misinterpret the arousal we feel as attraction. Other research shows similar misattribution effects. For example, men perceive women as more attractive when the men are exercising [2]. So if you're in the gym and 'love at first sight' hits you, you may want to hold off on buying a wedding ring until your heart rate has calmed down.

And no, it's not just men. Women rate men as more attractive and dateable when arousing music is playing during their encounter [3]. Misattribution effects are part of the success recipe of night clubs: arousing music, dim lights and alcohol all help stimulate attraction. Studies have reported similar misattribution effects by administering adrenaline to subjects and by giving them electric shocks. (Science is serious business.)

Misattribution effects tell us something profound about how our minds work: we often don't know why we feel what we feel. It's tempting to think most of our brain's activity happens within our consciousness, as we are by nature unaware of everything outside our consciousness, but a whole lot happens in our bodies that we are not aware of. We can't control many of our body's functions. We can't, for example, stop our own heartbeat or make our kidneys excrete more sodium. Most basic physiology is not under conscious control. And as you saw in the above experiments, our emotions are also under only limited control.

Even the brain activity of regions you may expect to obviously fall under conscious control, such as the auditory cortex, which we use for hearing, and the visual cortex, which we use for sight, occurs largely subconsciously. A classic demonstration about hearing is the 'cocktail effect' [4]. When you're at a noisy party, it can be difficult to make out what even someone right in front of you is saying, yet when somebody across the room mentions your name, you instantly hear it. The cocktail effect demonstrates our auditory cortex has in fact 'heard' most sounds in the room: the sound waves entered our ears and were analyzed by our brain. 'You' just didn't 'hear' them because your brain filtered out the information it deemed unimportant and it passed only the relevant information on to your consciousness.

The visual cortex operates similarly: what we see is not an uncensored picture of reality [5]. Our sight is the end result of the visual cortex's filtering and processing of all the light that entered our eyes. The brain turns these data into a 'most plausible scenario' and that is what we see. Visual illusions are testament to the limits of our brain's ability to turn data from light into a representative picture of reality. Have a look at the following optic illusion.

The squares A and B are the same color. Yes, really: see the following image where the 2 squares are connected.

How we perceive the world is a complex construction of our brain and sometimes our brain gets it wrong. As an extreme example, consider phantom limb pain [6]. As the name suggests, phantom limb pain means you experience pain in an amputated arm or leg. Obviously, people with this problem realize the limb is not there anymore, yet they still feel its pain.

We are also not privy to the going-on in our brain when it comes to self-control. People's self-reported self-control barely correlates with their objective performance on self-control tasks [7]. Why are we so clueless about what's going on in our own brains?

It's because we have 2 systems in our brain: a conscious and a subconscious part. The Nobel prize-winning psychologist Daniel Kahneman described system 1 as the intuitive system and system 2 as the reasoning system. System 1 operates rapidly and effortlessly and can process huge amounts of data, but it's fallible to errors resulting from its use of shortcuts and associative rather than causative reasoning. System 2 is the conscious part of our brain you probably identify mostly as 'you'. System 2 allows us to make rational decisions, understand logic and do math. While intellectually superior, system 2 is slow and its use is effortful. Therefore, system 1 first filters all information it registers from the environment and passes on only a fraction of it to system 2 for higher processing. In this sense, system 1 is like a company with system 2 as its director. The renowned psychologist Jonathan Haidt used the metaphor of a rider (system 2) sitting on top of an elephant (system 1). As the rider, system 2 is in control. In theory, that is. If the elephant insists on going left where you want to go right, you don't have a leg to stand on (no pun intended).

System 2 also literally sits on top of system 1. The human brain's structure roughly corresponds with the order in which it evolved over time, with the more sophisticated functions literally coming from the higher brain regions [8,

9]. The division of functions and regions isn't very neat within or across species, but we can roughly categorize brain regions from bottom to top as follows. At the very bottom on top of the spinal cord sits our brainstem, which oversees basic physiology like breathing. Neuroscientist Paul MacLean has coined this bottom area the 'reptile brain'. Built mostly on top of this area sits the limbic system with more complex functions, such as emotions, that we share with many mammals. Accordingly, the limbic system is also called the paleomammalian cortex. The third and top layer of evolution consists of the neocortex with the brain functions most unique to humans: this is where system 2 operates.

Understanding 2-system theory is crucial to understanding self-control. Michael Inzlicht, one of the world's experts on self-control, defined it as follows: "the mental processes that allow people to override thoughts and emotions." [10] In the perspective of the 2-system theory, self-control is the ability of your system 2 to control system 1. For example, system 1 produces the sensation of hunger, making you want to eat whatever's available, but system 2 allows you to make more deliberate choices in line with your dietary goals. Without system 2, you couldn't say no to the birthday cake at work to eat your own prepared lunch instead. In Haidt's metaphor, self-control failure is the rational rider losing control over the emotional elephant.

Now that we know what self-control is, we can turn to why it fails.

CHAPTER 2: THY WILL BE DONE

Starting in the 60s, a group of researchers performed what would later become known as the Stanford marshmallow experiment [1]. In one of the studies, researchers offered children a dilemma: you can have 1 marshmallow now or, if you can wait 15 minutes in this room and you don't eat the marshmallow now, you can have 2 marshmallows later. This simple test turned out to have remarkable predictive power about how the children's lives would unfold. About a third of the children managed to resist temptation and enjoy the double treat. These children ended up more successful in life with better grades in school, lower body fat levels and a better ability to cope with failure [2, 3].

What separated the children that immediately ate the marshmallow from the children that managed to delay gratification? In other words, what made system 2 fail to override the primitive urge of system 1?

The dominant theory on self-control is that of Roy Baumeister. Baumeister coined the term 'ego depletion' to describe the state of mind in which self-control is likely to fail. Briefly, the theory proposes that willpower is a limited resource that you tap into when you exert self-control. When the 'willpower container' is empty, you succumb to the temptations of your baser instincts. In 2-system theory parlance, system 2 is a finite resource that can control system 1. Once system 2 is depleted, system 1 has free reign to control your mind. The theory of willpower as a limited resource is well-known and seemingly supported by a number of scientific studies running into the triple digits. Here are some of the findings to illustrate situations of self-control failure as a result of 'ego depletion'.

- Resisting the temptation of eating tasty chocolates results in less perseverance afterwards during the completion of frustrating puzzles [4].
- Controlling your emotions while watching a movie results in snacking on more ice cream during a follow-up ice cream tasting task [5].
- Balancing an object while counting backwards from 1000 results in less perseverance during subsequent physical exercise, such as a push-up or sit-up challenge, even in competitive athletes [6].
- In general, cognitive effort and mentally demanding activities like puzzles and brain games result in more snacking and indulgence of our sweet tooth instead of sticking to our regular diet [7].

Supposing that our willpower is indeed like a glass that slowly empties as we use up its powers, we want to know how we can increase the size of the glass. Scientists have been looking for this 'glass' in our body for around 2 decades now and have not been able to find anything like it. Our brain's structure doesn't have vials with fluids or anything that seems like a 'willpower resource' that empties over time. It's just a bunch of neurons. Like a computer, there has to be a power supply – in our case oxygen and nutrients delivered via blood – but when the power is on, the computer functions and it can keep repeating the same task over and over. This line of thinking led scientists to suspect that glucose, more commonly known as blood sugar, is our willpower reserve. The scientists Matthew Gailliot and Roy Baumeister put this idea to the test and found drinking a sugary beverage can indeed increase our self-control [8]. Other research confirms this. Consuming glucose can increase our ability to control our aggression and improve our focus during memory games [9, 10].

Paradoxically, however, engaging in self-control does not reduce our blood sugar levels, at least no more than any other kind of brain activity does [11, 12].

Moreover, it doesn't need to be sugar that you drink to prevent willpower failure. An artificially sweetened beverage has the same effect as one with actual sugar [13].

These findings indicate that our willpower is not limited by our blood sugar level. So what is the willpower reserve that 2 decades of scientific research have been unable to find? The simplest answer is: willpower is not a limited resource. There is nothing that *physiologically* prevents you from having perfect willpower. The problem is *psychological.*

Modern research methods allow us to look into our brain to see what happens when our self-control fails, but in order to grasp this, we first have to understand 2 basic principles of how our brains work.

Principle 1: We instinctively approach pleasure and avoid pain [14].
Our brains are continuously monitoring what psychologists call our affect. It is our level of wellbeing, pleasure or contentment. Positive affect basically means we feel good; negative affect means we feel bad. For simplicity's sake, I'm often going to use the less scientific term enjoyment rather than affect.

Our brain does not stop at monitoring our affect: it continuously simulates future scenarios and their predicted level of enjoyment. Based on the predicted enjoyment, it sends a signal to either approach or avoid. This signal often comes in the form of an emotion. For example, when we look over the edge of a tall building, we may experience fear, driving us to move away from the edge. This is, in a nutshell, how we make decisions, whether consciously or subconsciously. We evaluate our options and pick the one we deem best. This is how we intuitively avoid things that may cause pain, like fire, and approach things that give us pleasure, like food.

Principle 2: Cognitive conflict is inherently unpleasant [15]. When we entertain 2 opposing thoughts, such as 2 opinions that contrast with each other, we experience cognitive conflict. When these thoughts take the forms of beliefs or behaviors, we call this conflict 'cognitive dissonance' and we are strongly motivated to solve this conflict. For example, if you see yourself as a trustworthy person, yet you broke a promise to a friend, you may experience cognitive conflict in the form of regret or shame.

Minimizing cognitive dissonance generally makes us pretty reasonable, as consistency of thought is a prerequisite of rationality. However, our brain is quite flexible in how it solves cognitive conflicts. In a classic demonstration of cognitive dissonance, a UFO cult called The Seekers believed the world would end in 1955. When the world didn't end even though they prepared for it, this required some serious cognitive dissonance solving. Some of the cult members reasonably concluded they were wrong and went on with their lives. Others, however, become *more* devoted to the cause. They had quit their jobs, broken up with their spouses and sold their apartments. The idea this was all for nothing was too painful, so their minds instead solved their cognitive conflict by believing their devotion had made God call off the apocalypse and they had saved the world.

With the previous 2 principles in mind, we can understand what happens in our brain when self-control fails [16]. Self-control is required when there is conflict between system 2 of our brain, the rational rider, and system 1, the emotional elephant. Say you're filing your taxes, but you're hungry and your Ramen noodles are beckoning you. System 2 says you should finish your work, but system 1 says it's time to ditch the numbers and down some noodles. Since conflict is inherently unpleasant, self-control is unpleasant as well. Our anterior cingulate cortex (ACC) plays a crucial role here, as it is active during conflict resolution and the location of our attentional focus. It is also sensitive to our wellbeing. When the ACC registers decreasing wellbeing, its activity during conflict resolution decreases and we gradually lose attentional focus. We also see decreased activation in other parts of system 2, such as the prefrontal cortex. We experience this change in brain activity as mental fatigue or boredom, which feel essentially the same way if you think about it. This is why ego depletion is sometimes also called 'task fatigue'.

In other words, when you are performing an effortful and unpleasurable activity with a conflict between systems 1 and 2, system 2 gradually shuts down, our attention shifts from have-to to want-to goals, we get bored and after a certain amount of time, system 1 wins, your self-control fails and you succumb to activities resulting in more instant gratification.

A 2017 study of self-control in students illustrates how our willpower fatigues [17]. Students generally will show signs of task fatigue within an hour of studying. Most students will be intimately aware of this as they'll find it difficult to maintain their attention on their work. However, this generally doesn't affect their self-control on other tasks across the day: the fatigue is task-specific. There was also no time-of-day effect on self-control: self-control didn't deplete across the day independent of study behavior.

These findings contrast with the idea that our willpower is like a vat in our brain that we drain. Instead, they support that engaging in prolonged have-to activities causes our brains to shift our attention to want-to activities.

When our inner emotional elephant has gotten bored with a task and our rational rider loses the reins, our attention shifts to things that offer more immediate gratification, such as food [18]. This is not merely a motivational change but also a cognitive one. For example, one study found that the change in brain activity causes us to see and process cues like a dollar sign ($) more readily than mathematical symbols like a percentage sign (%) [19]. Our inner elephants apparently like money but dislike math, not a good combination for economics. This sensitization for signs of instant enjoyment is also why a Facebook pop-up or notification on your phone while you're working can be so disastrous for your productivity.

Another study found that when task-fatigued dieters saw food, they experienced more brain activity in their reward centers and reduced connectivity with the top-down control centers of system 2 than non-fatigued dieters [20]. This is why it's difficult to stick to your diet after a long day at work. Throughout the day, you accumulate mental fatigue from all the have-to tasks at work and by the time you get home, all your brain wants is instant gratification. It just wants to watch TV and have ready-to-eat comfort food. (We'll get to how to solve this problem in the chapter on how to stick to your diet.)

The realization that self-control failure occurs not because your willpower is a limited resource but because your attention shifts from have-to to want-to goals, allows us to explain many things about self-control.

For one, self-control doesn't fail us when we're doing something we love. For example, I worked on this book for hours a day without pause. I read paper after paper, noting down my new findings in a trance-like state. My fiancée knows there's no point in even trying to talk to me when I'm immersed like this. Psychologists – and probably certain drug users too – call this 'flow' [21]. Now contrast this with office work. When I was a business consultant, like any employee, not all of my work was enjoyable. For example, when I worked for a major insurance company, I had to familiarize myself with their insurance policies. Now, this may come like an odd claim from someone who studied behavioral economics, but I'm bored to tears by finance topics outside of my own wallet. Whereas while writing this book, I sometimes forgot to eat, during finance research I looked for any chance at a coffee break I could get. When I had to go to a finance website and entered the letter F in my browser, it was hard to resist the urge not to accept the autocomplete to Facebook. That's procrastination and it's a classic case of self-control failure. Unrewarding tasks quickly cause our brain to set our sights to something more rewarding.

More generally, research has found that motivation for a task wards off mental fatigue and self-control failure [22]. You don't get bored easily when you're doing something you enjoy. As a less obvious example, people are more likely to persevere on a task when they believe it will help others [23].

Fortunately, we can motivate ourselves to do something unenjoyable. There just has to be a perceived reward at the end [22]. Then self-control allows us to forego immediate rewards and invest in the future with the aim of being better off in the end, like resisting 1 marshmallow to get 2 later.

The difficulty of the task also influences how soon our self-control fails during the task [24]. Remember that it's the inherently unpleasant conflict resolution taking place in the anterior cingulate cortex that causes your brain to shift attention away from the task to something more pleasant. During an easy task, by definition there isn't much cognitive conflict being registered by the brain. That's the essence of something being easy to understand: there's no cognitive conflict. A very difficult puzzle, on the other hand, can be a real brain breaker, as they say. This is one of the reasons why humans in general are averse to effort [25]. Given the choice, we naturally tend to prefer leisure over labor.

Third, self-control failure is less likely to occur during tasks we choose to do ourselves [26]. This is consistent with an abundance of psychological research showing autonomy is a key driver of intrinsic motivation and overall happiness. Think about reading a book you want to read compared to reading a book you have to read for work or school. A good book, even if it's not a simple one, can keep you engaged for hours on end, whereas it can be a struggle to even get to the next page of a boring book you have to read. Self-control only fails us during have-to tasks, not during want-to tasks.

Fourth, our self-control is intricately tied to our wellbeing [27]. People report greater self-control when they're happy and less when they feel poorly. The reason our attention shifts to something else is because our current attention is focused on something insufficiently rewarding: the purpose of the shift is to make us happier. We'll discuss many implications of this in later chapters.

Lastly, remember scientists thought glucose was our willpower reserve because drinking sugar improved self-control, but it turned out artificial sweetened drinks had the same effect? Well, in an attempt to address a different kind of 'spit or swallow' question, you don't need to actually drink the sugary beverage for it to improve your self-control: just rinsing it in your mouth is sufficient to improve your self-control [12, 28, 29, 30]. A carbohydrate mouth rinse can even improve endurance exercise performance [31, 32]. In fact, one recent study found that actual glucose consumption *decreased* cognitive performance compared to an artificially sweetened placebo [33]. Digestion of energy isn't required, because self-control failure is psychological in nature. It's the pleasure of the sweet taste, not the sugar's metabolic effects, that gives your brain a boost in how long it can ward off the shift of your attention.

The evolution of self-control

Why are our brains organized so that we experience loss of self-control? It may seem silly that our brains do not allow us perfect self-control while we're physically perfectly capable of it.

We can understand the limits on self-control from an evolutionary and economical point of view. The mental sensation of boredom and mental fatigue that causes us to abandon our current task can be understood as a mechanism to balance our options. Whenever you're pursuing one option, you are foregoing a different option. Economists call this the opportunity cost. It is equal to the value of what you could have gained from a different option. This is easy to understand for money and time. Both you can only spend once. So the most economical choice from any set of options is the one that maximizes the benefit you gain from the amount of time and money that you spend on it: a cost-benefit analysis, taking into account all your options. This is basically what the brain does when it produces ego depletion. Whenever you're engaging in a task, your brain is weighing the effort and reward obtained from the task. This is essentially a rudimentary cost-benefit analysis. When the cost (effort) of the task is relatively high and the benefit (reward) is low, our brain produces the sensation of boredom or fatigue. This sensation causes us to abandon our current activity choice in search for an alternative option with a better cost-benefit. From an evolutionary point of view, boredom in response to unrewarding work is a rational mechanism to have. It's just not as conscious and deliberate as an economist would perform the cost-benefit analysis, which means it doesn't always work as intended. And that is precisely why we have evolved self-control: the ability to consciously override the more primitive systems of our brain, a rational rider to tell the emotional elephant what to do when it's not acting in our best interest.

Specifically, self-control is fundamentally an ability that allows us to forego immediate rewards to reap greater future rewards. An economist would call self-control an investment strategy, in contrast to consumption. Animals don't always need to invest in the future. Take a cow on a grassland, for example. Food is readily available, so there is no point in delaying gratification: immediate consumption is consistently the optimal strategy for survival. Only when the grassland becomes depleted, does the cow have an incentive to migrate. Correspondingly, a cow doesn't need much self-control. A bigger cow brain would just be a needless source of energy expenditure, more likely to hinder survival than benefit it.

Humans are different for several reasons. For one, we evolved as omnivores. We don't consume just grass. Well, some people come close, but that's a different kind of grass. Evolutionarily speaking, humans have eaten pretty much everything we could get our hands on, except grass that is. Due to the breadth of our diet, we are faced with dilemmas such as: do we keep plucking berries or do we venture off to find meat? Do we try to keep living near our current campsite or do we move on to hopefully greener pastures? These are exploitation vs. exploration dilemmas. We often have to choose between either exploiting the environment and opting for the easily obtainable food source at hand or exploring new options. Exploring in this sense is the investment choice requiring more deliberate thought and self-control. We have to delay gratification now to get greater gratification later. Research throughout the animal kingdom has found that animals with more food options have better self-control and bigger brains [34].

Other evolutionary drives for humans to develop self-control included living in changing environments and consuming foods that require preparation, such as meat. Both incentivized us to invest in the future rather than just consume ready-to-eat foods. For example, marmosets and tamarins are 2 species of primates that are very much alike in almost every aspect, yet marmosets have significantly better self-control. Why? Marmosets feed on gum from trees, which they have to patiently wait for. Tamarins, on the other hand, opportunistically feed on insects that they grab whenever they encounter one [35].

In line with the number of different foods we eat and the many changes in our environment throughout our evolution, we as humans have evolved the greatest level of self-control in the animal kingdom. We have such a great capacity to pursue long-term have-to goals instead of short-term want-to goals that we have organized our societies into companies where we engage in have-to work in exchange for later payment so that later at home we can enjoy want-to activities. Labor vs. leisure. Shoulds vs. wants. Immediate vs. delayed gratification.

While our self-control may be great compared to other animals, you probably wouldn't mind having a bit more of it. We've discussed what self-control is and why it fails: self-control fails when task boredom sets in during unrewarding have-to tasks, causing us to experience mental fatigue and your attentional focus to shift to more rewarding want-to goals.

Now we can turn to how to improve our self-control. In the Stanford marshmallow experiment from the start of this chapter, the strategy used by the children was a significant predictor of success. While there is certainly a genetic component to self-control, as there is to virtually everything in life, this and other research demonstrates that how we deal with our self-control is of much greater relevance than how much innate self-control we have. Let's see how we can use this knowledge to level up your productivity.

CHAPTER 3: HOW TO BE MORE PRODUCTIVE

Our society's paragon of productivity is someone who foregoes sleep to work, works for 12 hours straight and skips meals: a robot. Indeed, industrialization is characterized by massive replacement of human labor with machines that can work tirelessly day-in day-out. Should the pursuit of self-control have the goal of becoming more robotic?

Why willpower is not like a muscle

The rationale for the dominant disciplinary approach to productivity is the idea that your willpower is like a muscle: if you train it, it gets bigger and stronger. The willpower-muscle concept was based on the outdated view that willpower is a limited resource. We now know that there is no 'willpower reserve' in your brain but rather self-control fails because of a shift in attentional focus to more immediate rewards. So there is no 'willpower tissue' that can undergo training adaptations and grow like a muscle does after strength training. This begs the question: can we train our self-control?

Early research looking at self-control training was promising. However, it suffered from several methodological problems, such as not having proper control groups and using highly artificial self-control tasks, like solving anagrams. Findings were mixed and it was highly questionable if any of these studies had 'real-world' practical applications. So a team of researchers recently teamed up to perform the ultimate study on whether self-control training results in improvements in self-control outside the lab [1]. One hundred and seventy-four students from UK universities enrolled in the study and were randomly allocated to 6 weeks of intensive self-control training or a control group not receiving this training. The self-control training consisted of a behavioral program, in which the participants had to perform daily tasks with their non-dominant hand, and a cognitive program, in which the participants had to perform difficult mental tasks. The mental tasks required the participants to override their impulses. One of the tasks was the famous Stroop task. Here's an example. What color is the following word? Be quick.

BLUE

It may seem easy to look at something and state its color, but since the word itself states a different color, this causes cognitive conflict. Our first impulse is often to simply read the word. This impulse has to be suppressed and that requires self-control.

After 6 weeks of training, the participants were tested on a battery of self-control tasks, including the following: handgrip perseverance after severe mental fatigue, resisting the temptation of chocolate, suppressing prejudice, success in translating good intentions into positive habits and outside-the-lab self-control success during studying, dieting and control of their emotions. The overall result was that the researchers "found no evidence that training led to any improvements in self-control."

An older meta-analysis and review of the literature did find a positive effect of self-control training on self-control ability, but it was a small effect and they primarily studied artificial laboratory tasks [2]. A more recent meta-analysis concluded any small benefits of self-control training for dieting are likely the result of better habit formation and different food associations from the sheer practice, not any actual improvement in self-control [3]. Overall, any benefits from self-control training for your day-to-day ability to stop procrastinating, stick to your diet or control your emotions are likely small, arguably trivial in comparison to the extensive training required for them.

The difficulty of improving your willpower is in line with several other lines of research on the brain. The general finding on cognitive task improvement is that all improvements are highly specific to the learned task and have limited transfer to other abilities [4]. For example, studying mathematics will surely make you a better mathematician. Many people would argue it makes you 'smarter', but that is a limited view of intelligence. Being better at math does not make you, for example, better at reading facial expressions or making multifaceted decisions under stress.

The function of the brain we can train that comes closest to 'fluid intelligence', as researchers call it, is working memory. Working memory ability refers to how good you are at remembering things while you do something else, like remembering the intermediate result of a math problem that you need for the final calculation. Or remembering a phone number while you find somewhere to note it down. Working memory has been intensely studied, because we need it for so many activities. Alas, working memory training results in little improvement in memory outside of tasks very closely related to the training [5]. If you have to keep a lot of names in working memory for your job, for example, you'll probably get quite good at that. But your working memory for numbers won't improve nearly as much, if at all.

More directly relevant to self-control is the research on executive functioning. Executive functioning is a term for the higher-order brain process of delegating which areas of the brain should be active and when. Working memory, self-inhibition and attentional control are all executive functions. Since self-control is directly related to your ability to inhibit system 1, keep system 2 active and keep your attention on the have-to task at hand, self-control is very much an executive function. Research here again finds we can improve our executive functioning with training of a specific task, but the improvements are highly specific to the trained task with little transfer to other tasks [6].

It's plausible that self-control training has no benefits for your cognitive ability itself at all: nothing in your brain gets stronger like a muscle. Rather, the improvements from any kind of training may only indirectly benefit you by teaching you hard work pays off, improving your self-confidence and increasing your motivation to dedicate yourself to something.

In any case, the whole issue of self-control training is moot in the first place. Since self-control is not a limited resource and there is nothing physically preventing you from maintaining control, cognitive training is not the solution. Self-control failure is a problem of our psyche, not one of inexperience. Unlimited self-control is already achievable by your brain: we just need to learn how to unleash it. This starts with changing your mindset.

Productivity tip 1: A lethal illusion

In 2006, a Mr. A approached his neighbor and told him he had taken an entire bottle of pills to commit suicide. He had been in a fight with his girlfriend, but he immediately regretted the decision and wanted to live [7]. His neighbor rushed him to the VA Medical Center in Jackson. There Mr. A collapsed. The nurses saw he indeed had an empty bottle of drugs in his pocket. Mr. A had extremely low blood pressure, so the doctors had to put him on an IV to stabilize him. They battled to stabilize Mr. A for 4 hours and were unable to take him off the IV without tanking his blood pressure. Mr. A repeatedly fainted. What worried the doctors most was that after running a battery of tests on Mr. A, they still couldn't figure out what was wrong with him and they couldn't identify the drug he had taken. After more research, they discovered Mr. A was participating in a clinical drug trial, so they had to get a scientist from the trial to the clinic to assist them. The drug Mr. A had overdosed on was no ordinary drug. It wasn't in the doctors' database...

Because it wasn't a drug at all. It was a sugar pill. Mr. A was in the placebo group of the trial. Upon hearing this, Mr. A spontaneously recovered and walked out of the clinic without any further problems.

What Mr. A had experienced was a nocebo effect, the opposite of a placebo effect. The word placebo comes from Latin, meaning "I shall please." A placebo effect is a phenomenon wherein the mere expectation of an effect causes the body to actually experience it. An example placebo effect is the carbohydrate mouth rinsing research we discussed. The effects of carbohydrate consumption on performance are often not because carbohydrates are needed as a fuel substrate but instead because the taste of a sweet beverage causes pleasure, which wards off mental fatigue and improves our willpower, motivation and perseverance during exercise. Just rinsing a sweet beverage in your mouth, even if it doesn't contain carbs but only sweeteners, can have the same effect as ingesting sugar. The **no**cebo effect is placebo's dark twin. It means "I shall harm."

Mr. A isn't some deranged idiot to suffer a nocebo effect. Nocebo effects are common in medical practice as well as everyday life. The effects range from easily imaginable 'in your head' complaints such as nausea, pain and erectile dysfunction to physical problems such as constipation, asthma attacks and allergic reactions [8, 9, 10, 11]. The effects are not exclusive to weak-minded people. We are all susceptible to placebo and nocebo effects to at least some degree. Personality traits and susceptibility to hypnosis, for example, have little to no effect on the likelihood of experiencing a placebo effect [12]. Nocebo effects are also common in all healthy individuals, though some research finds nocebo effects are more common in women and very neurotic and pessimistic individuals [13].

Placebo effects can be miraculously extreme and physical. In one study, giving advanced athletes fake steroids caused them to actually achieve steroid-like strength development in their training [14]. Compared to an average 2% strength development during 7 weeks without the placebo, the placebo resulted in strength gains of 8 to 15% in just 4 weeks. The placebo-juiced athletes ended up with an average 214-pound military press and 333-pound bench press. As group averages for natural athletes, those strength levels are what you'd expect in international powerlifting teams, not university athletes. As the researchers put it: "Taking the placebo apparently supplied the psychological inducement to increase strength gains above and beyond reasonable progression."

Another study tested whether you can increase your IQ with a placebo effect [15]. One group performed an hour of brain training without instructions. They showed no improvement in IQ as expected: you can't increase your brain's IQ all that much and certainly not with a mere hour of training. Yet participants that were led to believe this training would improve their IQ showed an improvement in IQ of up to 10 points. That's a huge increase. For reference, there's only a 20-point IQ difference between average intelligence (100) and intellectual disability (80 or lower) on common scales. It's likely that the placebo expectation of doing well on the test made people work harder for it.

Miraculous as placebo effects can be, so insidious nocebo effects can be. Arguably the most extreme expectation effect of all time was documented by Dr. Erich Menninger von Lerchenthal [16]. One of his assistants was highly unpopular. To teach him a lesson, his colleagues orchestrated an extremely morbid prank for him. They jumped him, blindfolded him and told him they'd decapitate him. They put his head on a chopping block, bid him farewell and slapped the back of his neck with a wet cloth to mimic the sensation of the executioner's axe. But the joke was on them. The assistant, overcome with terror, actually physically died.

Compared to such extreme cases, it shouldn't be hard to imagine our self-control also suffers from nocebo effects. Scientists Veronika Job, Carol Dweck and Gregory Walton conducted a series of studies on how to cultivate an indomitable will [17]. They replicated earlier studies on self-control while taking into account what the participants' beliefs about willpower were. They found self-control failure after mentally demanding tasks only occurred in people who believed their willpower was limited. Participants that did not share this pessimistic view of our inner limitations did not show any diminished self-control during the follow-up tasks.

Let me reiterate: people who simply *believe* they have unlimited willpower *actually* show no signs of willpower failure.

This isn't just a weird lab phenomenon. Out in the 'real world', people who are not concerned with their willpower manage their time better, procrastinate less, eat healthier, spend their money more wisely and achieve better grades at school than people who believe their willpower is limited [18].

If you don't believe you can persevere or control yourself any further, you have already lost the battle. You have subconsciously already decided you're going to have that extra slice of pizza or go to the coffee machine instead of continuing your work. On the other hand, if you believe what I just told you, and you should – you can check the scientific references for yourself and I in fact highly encourage you to do so – you should already have better self-control from now on. By realizing your mind is capable of unlimited self-control without a hard physical limit, you should hereby have rid yourself of the nocebo belief of limited willpower.

Well, at least partly. Truly internalizing a belief is not that simple and it's wishful thinking that everyone reading this suddenly has perfect self-control now. While the powers of belief and motivation are strong and can significantly improve self-control, they do not make you fully immune to self-control failure [19]. I didn't just turn you into a robot. It takes some experience to internalize the confidence that your willpower is not a limited resource. Physiologically, your willpower isn't limited. However, your perception is what matters, not your physical capacity. It is primarily your perception of being mentally depleted, not the amount of actual effort that you have expanded, that determines how well you can maintain your self-control [20]. So you have to learn to prevent your inner voice from being a nocebo. Change your perception. Cultivate an indomitable will.

At first, you'll have to constantly remind yourself that mental fatigue is just a feeling. It's an attempt by your brain to shift your focus of attention. There is nothing physically being fatigued like an exercised muscle that is now damaged and low on fuel substrate. Mental energy, a subjective feeling, has nothing to do with physical energy, objectively measured in joules. When you are mentally exhausted from work, keep in mind you are essentially just bored. It's the same sensation you get when you spend a long time in a car, when you spend a lot of time in a waiting room with nothing to do or when you've had to be nice to people you don't really like all day at a formal event. Your brain is fine. Your feelings of fatigue are just that: feelings. It is up to you what you do with them.

Productivity tip 2: The locus of control

You're not the only person that can talk yourself down. In a series of studies, people were informed they were working on paper with a specific color tone that causes mental exhaustion [21]. It was a deception. The color had no such effect. Others worked with the same paper but were not told anything about this magical energy draining color. The people who were told the color drained their mind were less capable of resisting a persuasive message, did not persevere as long on a problem-solving task and did not sustain their attention for as long as the nocebo-free group.

To prevent yourself from being talked into fatigue you don't actually have, it can help to cultivate an 'internal locus of control', as psychologists call it. It means you believe *you* are in control of your actions. Your environment is just a set of stimuli. They enter your brain, but it's up to you what you do with them. Words and information do not affect your body. Only your perception of them does. People with an internal locus of control are more productive and have a higher level of job satisfaction [22].

Importantly, your locus of control is not genetically fixed. You can learn to adopt an internal locus of control [23]. For example, say you come into the office and someone says: "Hey, you look tired! Are you ok?" You may see this as a sign you're indeed tired and so you may be tempted to apologetically respond with: "Ah yeah, I didn't sleep very well." Don't let their perception influence yours. Just respond with: "Yes, I'm fine!" Nobody likes a whiner anyway. A positive atmosphere in companies predicts high productivity levels [24]. If you do feel the need to apologize for your allegedly tired look, add: "I just didn't sleep very well, but I feel fine."

Productivity tip 3: Framing for self-efficacy

To break out of your self-imposed willpower chains, you need to not only change your perception of yourself and others, but also your perception of the work you do. Specifically, you have to learn how to frame your tasks.

Research has looked at the effect of perceived task difficulty on performance [25]. Across 2 experiments, one group served as the control group. In the other group, self-control depletion was induced by having the participants think of anything but a white bear or by having them write an essay without the letters U and K. As expected, subsequent performance during negotiations and a creative Unusual Uses Task was objectively worse in the mentally depleted group compared to the control group. This is a classic demonstration of mental fatigue. More interestingly, the researchers added a second level to the experiments. The participants could choose a strategy framed as easy-but-suboptimal or difficult-but-optimal to complete their tasks. In reality, the strategies didn't differ in difficulty. The researchers just wanted to know if mental depletion changed people's attitude to their work. Indeed, depleted individuals were more likely to choose the easy strategy, in line with people's general unwillingness to exert effort when mentally fatigued. Here's the kicker. Despite there not being any objective difference in difficulty, depleted individuals performed just as well as the non-depleted individuals when they performed the task with the 'easy' strategy. In other words, just believing their work was easy enabled them to get rid of the effects of mental fatigue.

It doesn't matter as much how difficult the work you do is by any objective standard. What really matters is how difficult you *think* it is. Ever heard someone say: "Just thinking about that makes me tired?" There is profound truth in this. Mental fatigue really is primarily the result of your perception of how difficult the work you're going to do is. If you think something is easy, that cultivates what psychologists call self-efficacy: belief in your own ability. Self-efficacy is a strong predictor of good performance in almost everything we do [26].

To cultivate self-efficacy, think of the following steps before any difficult task.
1. Have you done something like this before? If so, great. That means you can do it. Now go do it!
2. If not, who has done something like this before? Are they that much smarter or more capable than you are? At work or at school, all your colleagues or

class mates should be roughly equally qualified, so you should be able to do most things they did.

I used the above mindset a lot as a business consultant to cope with unknown challenges. A defining feature of good consultants is that you can get sent out to any company with minimal training and you have to make do. Could I learn this new programming language? I really couldn't say, but I knew some of my colleagues could, so I should be able to as well.

You can also use this strategy for many daily life activities. Can you get your driver's license? Sure, basically everyone gets their license, so you should be able to as well. The day before writing this I received a new IKEA office chair and a fan. After unpacking both, I saw they had many more components than I expected. Just from the components you could barely imagine how it could all fit together and turn into a chair and a fan. Both sets looked really complicated, but I knew manufacturers make these things so any random person is supposed to be able to put them together. So I got to work and it indeed wasn't nearly as difficult as I feared.

For larger or more difficult projects, it can also help a lot to break down the task into action steps. Many projects can seem overwhelming at first, but when you break them down into separate steps, they're really not that difficult. Organizing the project into an action plan helps you see what needs to be done. Then you start working through your plan one step at a time. For example, I did not spend today 'writing my book'. That would be overwhelming and I wouldn't know where to start. Instead, I spent today writing productivity tip 3 about framing and compartmentalizing tasks. I had written down basically this book's entire table of contents before I started writing out any full chapters. For every chapter and tip, I had the research and bullet points ready, so I knew exactly what to do. This greatly decreased my perceived task difficulty.

In sum, relativizing a task's difficulty and breaking it down into simple action steps can prevent your willpower from waning during even the most complex work. It can also help you get started, which brings us to the next tip.

Productivity tip 4: How to use the Zeigarnik effect to stop procrastinating

The biggest barrier for many projects is getting started. We often end up procrastinating on a task for a longer time than it takes to finish the actual task. Think of writing a letter. Most letters, even formal ones, don't need to take more than a few minutes to write, yet many people face a large mental barrier to get themselves to start writing.

You already learned one tip to overcome this: create an action plan with the concrete step required to finish the project. But you still have to get started. Your brain registers the perceived effort of the project. It uses that to determine when to shift your attention to something else that may be more rewarding and requires less effort. To prevent your brain from going into procrastination mode in search of more immediately gratifying things to do, you can start by making only a small commitment. Tell yourself you're going to start the project and complete step 1 but not necessarily finish the whole project in one go. Even if you abandon the project after only having completed step 1, you will most likely finish the project later anyway. Humans have a natural tendency to finish what we started. This is called the Zeigarnik effect [27, 28, 29]. Not finishing what we started triggers cognitive dissonance: we started for a reason, right? German psychologist Bluma Zeigarnik first documented the effect as far back as 1927 based on the observation that waiters were more likely to remember unpaid orders than paid ones.

By making only small commitments, it's easier to get started and avoid procrastination. Start with a baby step and let the Zeigarnik effect help you to the finish.

Productivity tip 5: There's no sin without temptation

To finish your tasks and attain your goals, many people believe self-control is key: achieving your goals requires actively fighting temptation and keeping your mind on the task. A recent large-scale study suggests otherwise [30]. Researchers followed the lives of 159 students throughout a college semester. They monitored the pursuit of their goals in life, acts of self-control and the experience of temptations and mental exhaustion (ego depletion) along the way.

In contrast to popular belief, the researchers found strong evidence that there was no relation between acts of self-control and goal achievement. People that engaged in more self-control were no more successful in achieving their life goals than others. The researchers concluded: "contrary to conventional wisdom, self-control was unimportant in accomplishing one's goals." [30]

Instead, the strongest determinant, or rather saboteur, of successful goal achievement was temptation – and this relation was explained entirely by mental depletion. People that were exposed to more temptations experienced greater mental depletion and this prevented them from pursuing their goals. Their ability to control themselves when faced with temptation didn't matter much. This suggests it's not the case that some people have better self-control than others and are therefore more successful. Rather, some people are more successful because they experience less temptation during the pursuit of their goals.

The key to success then is not to resist temptation but to avoid it in the first place. Got a particularly chatty colleague at work? Go sit next to someone else when you have to focus on your work. Don't want to be tempted to go on Facebook at work? Consider blocking Facebook on your computer. There are many apps and browser extensions that make it easy to restrict your time on social media or other procrastination websites, such as Offtime (iOS and Android), Stay Focusd (Chrome), LeechBlock (Firefox) and ColdTurkey (Windows). You can also use the website x.minutes.at to put a timer on any website.

A more insidious distractor is your homepage. Many office computers by default start up to a news page. Unless you're a journalist or politician, this is just another distraction your mind has to suppress. Instead, I recommend you make Google.com your homepage or you have your browser reload the last page you were on when you exited the browser.

In sum, an ounce of prevention is worth a pound of self-control.

Productivity tip 6: How to do more work while working less

So far I've argued the robotic approach to productivity is bound to fail. Humans can't just sit at a desk for 8 hours straight and be productive the entire time just because they have to. Moreover, your ability to maintain focus on have-to tasks doesn't improve over time. Self-control cannot be developed much. But if we can't just productively push ourselves through an 8-hour workday, what's the alternative?

Success leaves clues, so let's look at some of the most productive people on the planet. Dr. K. Anders Ericsson has made it his career to study expert performance. He has analyzed what it takes to acquire eminent mastery in a variety of domains, particularly elite violinists [31, 69]. The central conclusion of Ericsson's research is that expert performance is greatly determined by the amount of deliberate practice. It shouldn't come as a shock that becoming a world class musician requires a ton of practice. Common rules of thumb are that it requires 10 years and 10.000 hours of practice to become a master musician (a number erroneously extrapolated to becoming an expert in different fields).

Importantly, only *deliberate* practice time, not *total* practice time, distinguishes the good from the great. In many instances, good and great performers practice for a comparable amount of time across the week. The great ones just practice more deliberately.

What does deliberate practice mean, precisely? It means you're not just going through the motions but actively focusing on your task to the extent that it's effortful and no longer always enjoyable. In other words, deliberate practice requires self-control.

Without effortful focus, most people reach a plateau in performance at any task. There's only so much you can learn from messing about. By actively focusing on improving your performance, you can break this plateau and reach a new level. This has been found even in experts with years of experience at jobs you may think aren't that skillful, such as Morse Code operators and typesetters. Crucially, elite musicians recognize that effortful performance cannot be sustained indefinitely. A commonly employed rule is to limit any practice session to 90 minutes tops, after which you need a break of ideally a full hour.

The 90-minute attention concept is also found in various other fields. Neurophysiologists have found that throughout the day, our alertness comes and goes in roughly 100-minute intervals [32]. Military research has found the alertness ultra-rhythm is approximately 90 minutes [33]. In Hollywood, 90 minutes is the traditional movie length to keep viewers interested. Many schools also keep classes below 90 minutes in length.

The exact maximum attention span most likely varies per person and per activity based on how motivated someone is for the task and how difficult the task is. However, it's not a bad rule of thumb to limit effortful have-to work to 90-minute sessions.

Psychological research also strongly supports the need for breaks during effortful work. In a review of over 40 studies on strategies to improve self-control, one of the 2 most successful strategies was resting in between activities that require self-control [34]. (We'll get to the other one later.)

It may seem almost too good to be true, but sometimes less is more. By planning pleasurable break activities throughout the day, you can be more productive during the rest of the day. Rather than wait until your self-control fails and your attention wanders, take a pre-emptive break. Win-win.

Employers reading this may be reluctant to offer their workers more breaks or reduced work hours. Can this really be done without sacrificing overall work output? In my personal experience as a lecturer and consultant for various top companies, I can confidently say yes. Most highly successful entrepreneurs I've talked to agree that most people cannot be truly productive for more than about 4 hours a day if the work is at all effortful. This figure is in line with a survey of nearly 2000 office workers [35]. The workers admitted to only being truly productive for an average of 2 hours and 53 minutes a day. In other words, most people with an 8-hour office day could probably achieve the same work output in 2 focused 90-minute work stints. Most of the remaining time each workday was spent on the following, listed as the percentage of workers who admitted to spending a lot of time on the listed activity:

1. Checking social media – 47%
2. Reading news websites – 45%
3. Discussing out of work activities with colleagues – 38%
4. Making hot drinks – 31%
5. Smoking breaks – 28%
6. Text/instant messaging – 27%
7. Eating snacks – 25%
8. Making food in office – 24%

9. Making calls to partner/friends – 24%
10. Searching for new jobs – 19% (my favorite finding)

Other research finds managers are unable to tell which workers actually work long hours and who just pretend to work extra hours to pass off as ideal workers [36]. The current business culture of working over 8 hours a day is a mistake that has been made before in history. Even non-intellectual jobs typically don't benefit from chronically working over 8 hours a day. As far back as 1848, England passed a law to cap work to 10 hours a day and there was a widespread *increase* in productivity per worker. The same productivity boost occurred in the US in 1937 during the New Deal when the 40-hour workweek was adopted. Multiple in-house studies in between these dates, the most famous of which by Ford, found that average productivity progressively increased or stayed the same when decreasing weekly work hours from 80 to 40 [37].

Even the elite violinists in Ericsson's research were found to engage in an average of 4 hours of pure leisure time throughout the midweek, going up to 5 hours during the weekends.

As a more extreme example of the detrimental effects of overworking people, what if failure to sustain your attention at work resulted in not just a waste of your time but a loss of lives? The overworking of nurses in hospitals poses a serious risk to patient safety: when nurses work overtime or work more than 40 hours per week, they make significantly more errors at work [38]. The Federal Aviation Administration has similarly cautioned against overworking pilots: when pilots do not get sufficient breaks to eat or nap, their operational performance suffers [39].

Ericsson concluded the following about productivity in his research on elite performers: "In virtually all domains, there is evidence that the most important activity – practice, thinking or writing – requires considerable effort and is scheduled for a fixed period during the day. For those exceptional individuals who sustain this regular activity months and years, its duration is limited to 2-4 hours a day, which is a fraction of their time awake." [40]

In short, optimal productivity requires relatively short bouts of highly focused work interspersed with breaks.

The following break activities are particularly effective.

Exercise

Many people associate taking a break with rest. Intuitively, it may feel like your 'willpower reserves' need to be refueled like a car that ran out of gas. Or your mind needs rest like a fatigued muscle. However, as you learned, both analogies are wrong. You don't have willpower reserves that deplete and the fatigue you feel is not physical wear-and-tear but rather boredom. Your system 1 is trying to shift your attention to more enjoyable matters than what you're doing right now. In that sense, your mind wants the opposite of rest: it craves excitement. A great way to give your body literal physical excitement is to exercise. Exercise is more reinvigorating than quiet rest [41]. If you can't take your mind off work, there's nothing quite like heavy iron on your back to shift your attention to more pressing matters (no pun intended).

In addition to forcing you to take your mind off what you were doing before, exercise has numerous mental health benefits: brain gains, if you will. A wide range of studies have demonstrated exercise improves brain functioning and cognitive performance [42]. Among other mechanisms, exercise stimulates the release of brain-derived neurotrophic factor (BDNF). BDNF keeps your brain cells healthy and improves your ability to learn, remember and cope with stress. Aerobic exercise or 'cardio' is particularly effective to increase BDNF levels, but strength training can be beneficial as well [43]. The benefits of exercise become even more impressive as you get older [44].

Among all the benefits of exercise, one of the most striking ones is perhaps its ability to improve creativity. Exercise is uniquely potent at boosting creative thinking [45]. I can personally attest to this. My training journals are always riddled with notes, because I have some of my best ideas in the gym.

Even if your work doesn't tax your memory or creativity, exercise is still a great break option, because it improves your mood [46].

If you don't work from home, it's worth discussing with your employer if you can have an extended lunch break to fit in a workout.

Hydrotherapy

Need a quick 'refresher'? Try hydrotherapy, specifically ice-cold showers. Yes, I know a cold shower is probably the last thing you want when you're exhausted, but give it a try. The benefits are immediate. No matter how drained you felt beforehand, afterwards you feel energetic. Taking a cold shower is like giving yourself a shot of adrenaline: "Exposure to cold is known to activate the sympathetic nervous system and increase the blood level of beta-endorphin and noradrenaline and to increase synaptic release of noradrenaline in the brain as well." [47]

Hydrotherapy in general is an ancient and now evidence-based therapy for a wide range of problems, including depression [48]. While daunting, in my experience many people come to greatly appreciate this strategy to freshen up not just their body but also their mind. If a pure cold shower is too much for you, you could try a warm shower followed by a minute of cold at the end, or a contrast shower in which you alternate between warm and cold.

Cold showers can be a great habit to get into when you come home from work. You'll need to make it a habit to get under the shower rather than plump down on the couch, but afterwards you can spend your evening much more energetically.

Not into exercise and cold showers? Fortunately, you can also take more leisurely breaks.

Work hard, play hard

Many people are under the impression that being a productive person requires cracking the whip on yourself non-stop, but the age of factory work is over. Not only can breaks in between focused work improve your productivity, they can also be fun. When your brain is getting fed up with the have-to task you're doing, a win-win solution is to do a want-to task. This allows you to re-engage self-control afterwards while you're having fun. For example, watching your favorite television program is effective to restore your self-control [49]. Research finds this is particularly effective when the break involves positive social interactions, so a comedy show may be more effective than watching a documentary on the Texas Chainsaw Massacre.

In general, pretty much anything you enjoy is effective as a work break. If you like playing video games, play a level or match of your favorite game in between work bouts. Video games may actually be particularly effective as a break due to their high level of immersion. Just make sure it's a game that's delineated by time. Games with single matches, like a racing match or a shooter, lend themselves much better to being break activities than more addictive, never-ending games, like World of Warcraft.

Power napping

Short naps can give you most of the 'brain rebooting' benefits of a night's rest. An abundance of scientific research supports the use of napping to increase productivity in i.a. office workers, pilots, firefighters, air traffic controllers and nurses [50, 51, 52, 53, 54, 55]. Particularly interesting findings include the following.

- Napping can be more effective than caffeine use or the same amount of extra nighttime sleep.

- As little as 6 minutes of napping can improve memory retention.

To prevent the grogginess that comes from waking up after entering deeper sleep stages, limit your naps to 20-30 minutes. After that, you would go into deeper sleep stages and in this case it would be best to finish a full sleep cycle of about 90 minutes. If your alarm wakes you up in a deep sleep stage before the end of a full sleep cycle, you may feel like you got teleported from another dimension into a foreign body and you don't know what planet you're on (read: not well-rested).

Many of the more forward-thinking companies in the world are already actively promoting what was once grounds for dismissal: sleeping at work. Google even has specially installed 'nap pods'.

Meditation

If you're not allowed to nap at work or you're not the type of person that can just take a nap at will, you can get many of the same benefits with meditation. And by meditation, I mean the scientific practice of mindfulness therapy, not necessarily sitting in a lotus position in a room filled with incense and chanting monks. Mindfulness therapy simply comes down to focusing intensely on something that does not evoke any emotional reactions, like a cube, for several minutes, or to focus on absolutely nothing and just experience your bodily sensations. Mindfulness training like this can alleviate mental fatigue and improve cognitive functioning [56, 57]. It may be one of the few ways you can actually improve your self-control over the long run [58]. For those into computer metaphors, I tend to see meditation as 'cleaning your brain's cache'. Meditation empties your mind and 'resets' your mental state.

Prayer

If you're religious, prayer is a very effective break activity that functions much like meditation [59].

"That's great and all, but I'm not allowed to do any of this stuff at work." Unfortunately, many traditional companies still essentially prohibit any form of leisure at work. Even then, there's always the most magical of breaks: the imaginary break.

The imaginary break

Yes, really. In line with the purely psychological nature of self-control failure, it can help to simply *imagine* taking a break. The key to making an imaginary break successful is to visualize yourself or someone you can empathize with engaging in some restorative activity, like a power nap or massage, in great detail [60]. You're not just leaning back in your office chair with your eyes closed. You're on the beach in the Bahamas and the sun's shutting your eyes. That's not the air conditioning chafing your skin. It's the gentle ocean breeze. What you hear is not the radio. It's a live music festival at your all-inclusive resort. A little retreat into your own mind palace never hurt anyone, and it functions similarly to meditation.

There are many more successful break (in)activities you can do. Basically anything that is very enjoyable or very immersive should get the job done.

Productivity tip 7: How (not) to incentivize yourself and others

Taking a break from work is not always possible, nor is it necessary. The cause of self-control failure is essentially boredom. When your current activity is not rewarding enough, your brain starts searching for more rewarding activities. The solution: you must keep your brain happy. A happy brain is a productive brain. Remember I mentioned a scientific review of 40 strategies on self-control management? Two strategies stood out like a new Ferrari at a junkyard. The first was rest, as you read earlier.

The second strategy was having a reward structure. Rewards by definition increase how rewarding your work is and thereby prevent your brain from searching for something more rewarding to do. Many types of rewards have been found to be effective in research, but one of the most common types of rewards often backfires: the non-competitive, performance-contingent reward [61]. For example, a sales worker may be told she'll get a $100 bonus if she calls 100 potential customers. This type of pure performance reward is generally only motivating for the most unfulfilling tasks that people have no intrinsic motivation for. It also needs to be sufficiently large to warrant the effort it takes to obtain the reward. A reward like this motivates people only rationally: people will only strive to obtain it if the expected time and effort warrant the probable benefit.

What's worse, for tasks that people have at least some intrinsic motivation for, which should include sales if you're a salesman, a performance goal makes a task seem even more like something you *have* to do rather than something you choose to do. The less autonomous a task feels, the greater the mental fatigue it induces, because it increases cognitive conflict between systems 2 (have-to) and 1 (want-to) in the brain. A performance reward can hereby result in what psychologists call the overjustification effect: your intrinsic motivation for the task gets replaced by the extrinsic motivation of the reward [62]. Rather than focus on the task's enjoyment, its purpose or how it helps others, the performance reward makes you determine your level of effort for the task more as a rational cost-benefit analysis.

A famous example of the overjustification effect happened in an Israeli daycare center [63]. Parents were often late to pick up their kids, so the daycare center implemented a small fine to motivate parents a bit more to be on time. The fine had the complete opposite effect: parents were on average significantly later afterwards, because the fine justified them being late. Before the fine was implemented, they were intrinsically motivated not to be late – being late is bad manners and a sign of being a bad parent – but with the fine they could tell themselves they were basically just paying longer for the service to take care of their kid. Their intrinsic motivation was replaced with a weaker extrinsic motivation.

A better approach to performance rewards is to make them contingent on competence [64]. Most people are intrinsically motivated to become good at what they do. Even if the work itself isn't exciting, you can take pride in a job well done. So rather than give a $100 reward for contacting 100 customers, it would likely be more effective to give the reward for 10 successful sales.

Even more effective is making the reward not just competence-based but also competitive: "This month's top biller gets a $100 bonus." Competition adds social standing to the reward, and as tribal animals, we humans are intrinsically motivated to obtain status within our social network.

Even the most ideal performance rewards have limited motivational power, however. Many other types of rewards are generally more motivating than performance awards

[65]. Social rewards are particularly effective. People placed in leadership positions do not show nearly as much mental fatigue as subordinates. So it can help to take charge at work. Assume responsibility and actively coordinate with your colleagues. Become a beacon of productivity.

Being watched by an audience is similarly effective to maintain attentional focus. To increase your productivity, it can help to inform others what you're doing. Get all eyes on you.

Of course, the classic pat on the back and "Good work!" from a colleague can help too. While you cannot give that to yourself, what you can do is think of how your work is helping others. Helping others is inherently motivating and can thereby reduce task fatigue. Research finds that directly rewarding others can be effective to keep mental fatigue at bay as well. Even if you're doing something boring like filing a cabinet, remind yourself of how useful this will be for anyone using the cabinet.

It can also help to remind yourself of the values and goals linked to your work. Logging recycling receipts may be boring, but your work is helping the environment.

More physical rewards can prevent mental fatigue too if they function as pleasurable mini-breaks. We have already seen one such effective reward: consuming a sweet beverage (or even just rinsing it in your mouth). It's not surprising that the coffee machine at work is so popular: it's not only an attractive procrastination option but also an effective productivity boosting mini-break. If you find yourself using breaks too much as procrastination rather than refreshers, frame them more as rewards. Don't go get coffee because you don't want to finish that email. Allow yourself to get coffee if you finish the email.

Speaking of physically enjoyable mini-breaks, smoking cigarettes has also been found to buffer against mental depletion. Of course, I don't endorse smoking cigarettes, so in the chapter on how to stick to your diet, you'll find a section with healthier comfort food snacks to self-medicate on.

A more uncommon way to reward yourself and restore your motivation is to affirm your core values [66]. This means you reflect on what's good about yourself or your life. You may think about how happy you are with your colleagues, how you're achieving your life goals, what a creative person you are or anything else that makes you feel good about yourself. Practicing gratitude is a well-established strategy to improve your wellbeing. Remember: the bane of continued focus and productivity is essentially insufficient pleasure being registered by your brain. Anything that makes you feel good can thereby boost your productivity.

Productivity tip 8: Vary up your stimulus modalities

Variety is the spice of life, it's said. I don't know about that, but I do know variation is the spice of productivity. It doesn't always take a reward or a break to stay productive. You've probably experienced yourself that highly monotonous tasks are particularly susceptible to task fatigue: your attention quickly wanders off to something more enjoyable. You can thus increase your productivity by rotating between different kinds of tasks: by rotating I do not mean multitasking in the sense of doing multiple things at once, which we'll get to later, but rather switching between tasks over time.

Switching to a task with a different presentation modality is most effective [67]. The presentation modality is either light, sound, pressure, taste, smell or temperature. It's also called the stimulus modality or the sensory modality. These different stimuli activate different sensory receptors in our body and this information is processed by different parts of the brain. For our purposes, there are 3 key modalities and associated brain areas: light and sight (visual cortex), hearing (auditory cortex) and physical feeling, such as touching (somatosensory cortex). These areas process information largely individually: your auditory cortex isn't of much use to process visual information. As such, task fatigue is modality-specific. By switching to a task with a different modality, you effectively reset the build-up of task fatigue that would otherwise result in self-control failure.

For example, say you're an analyst. Your job is to read sales statistics from graphs and listen to customer feedback and make reports of your findings. Reading graphs has a visual presentation modality: you rely on your sight to process the information. Listening to customer feedback has an auditory presentation modality: you hear what the customers say. You may be tempted to schedule all your graph analysis work in the mornings and schedule the customer feedback reporting to the afternoons after lunch. Since then you'd be working on the same task for about 4 consecutive hours, mental depletion would be high. Instead, you'd probably be more productive by alternating between 60–90-minute blocks of both tasks.

Varying up your workload can be so effective that your performance on the second task doesn't just suffer less but can even improve [68]. The key to successful variation seems to lie in the timing: you need to switch tasks before you become very fatigued/bored. Be preemptive and keep your brain happy. Once you are mentally exhausted, it's more difficult to engage in any further acts of self-control to restore productivity.

Interestingly, the auditory cortex appears to be relatively resistant to mental fatigue [67]. From an evolutionary view, this makes sense. Humans are highly social animals with a remarkable ability to communicate with each other in the form of language. As such, we rely on our auditory cortex a great deal to process information. This part of our brain may have therefore become most resilient to task fatigue. Since social interaction is often inherently motivating as well, this means you don't have to worry as much about mental fatigue in group settings. You can take advantage of this by planning your group work when you'd otherwise be too mentally depleted to be very productive anyway. In the office, the ideal meeting times are thus arguably right before lunchtime and at the end of the day. I also personally plan my interviews and consultations around lunchtime and in the evenings whenever possible. I've found that long interviews in the morning hamper my productivity the rest of the day, whereas a long work day doesn't considerably reduce the quality of my interviews.

Productivity tip 9: To multitask or not to multitask?

If variation is good, is multitasking then best for performance? Common wisdom says no, but what does the science say?

Common wisdom is correct here. While variation is good to ward off boredom, performing multiple tasks at the same time greatly reduces productivity, because our brains are very poorly equipped to multitask. Specifically, system 2 has serial processing. Like older computers, the conscious part of your brain can only attend to 1 thing at a time. You should experience this yourself all the time: you can keep a thought in working memory while you attend to something else, but you cannot have 2 entirely different lines of thought going on in your mind at the same time. Think of a math problem like 5 x 8 + 8 x 3. You first multiply 5 by 8 to get 40, then you store 40 in working memory. Then you multiply 8 by 3 and you store 24 in working memory. Then you add 40 to 24 to get 64.

Unfortunately, our working memory is very limited. You may have heard that you can only store 7 items in working memory. That number comes from a famous paper from 1956: "The magical number seven, plus or minus two:

some limits on our capacity for processing information."
[70] More recent research has demonstrated that the
number 7 isn't so magical after all: working memory
capacity can vary greatly per person and per task. However,
the core idea still stands: your working memory storage
room is small.

Accordingly, an abundance of research has found that
trying to tax your working memory with 2 tasks at the same
time is a bad idea for productivity [71, 72]. Humans are
simply not good multitaskers. For example, in one set of
studies, people had to make financial decisions for the
future while they had to keep numbers in working memory
[73]. Future financial decisions are a classical self-control
task, because they require system 2, which can calculate the
most economical option, to override system 1, which only
cares about immediate gratification. When you are hungry,
system 1 will readily eat all the fruits from a plant,
destroying it in the process. It requires system 2 to carefully
cultivate the plant so you can reap its fruits for a long time.
It's no surprise then that our species could only start the
Agricultural Revolution after evolving enough self-control.
In the experiments, there was a strong, direct relation
between working memory load and impulsivity. The greater
the strain on working memory, the less influence system 2
has on decision making and the more system 1 will opt for

instant gratification, even if it comes with considerable losses in the future.

And yes, this includes you, ladies. Common wisdom holds that women are better at multitasking than men [74]. The classic rationale for this comes from evolutionary psychology: men evolved primarily to be hunters, whereas women had to attend to more different tasks in the household when distracted by their children. However, there is surprisingly little scientific research to support this alleged gender difference of multitasking ability. Some research has found that women are indeed better at multitasking than men, but it seems to depend on the task at hand, because in other studies there is no sex difference and in one study, men outperformed women [75, 76]. In any case, while the battle of the sexes is sure to continue, the important take-home message for productivity management is that we're all very poor multitaskers, some maybe just less terrible than others.

Multitasking also increases our sensitivity to food cues [77]. Multitasking is stressful for the brain and this internal discomfort makes the brain more sensitive to instant gratification, which can make us more likely to deviate from our planned diet and succumb to impulsive snacking.

Not multitasking requires more than not starting two different tasks at the same time. You have to actively fight your urge to multitask, because when task boredom sets in, you'll be tempted to multitask by, for example, continuing your work while you're chatting with a colleague or browsing the internet while you're attending a lecture at school. Problematically, it is exactly the individuals who are worst at multitasking who most commonly engage in multitasking [78]. The most impulsive individuals are most strongly tempted to multitask, yet they tend to have the worst working memory, so of all people they should most refrain from multitasking. They also tend to overestimate their own multitasking ability even more than others. So don't trust your instincts when it comes to multitasking. If you are strongly tempted to do multiple things at once, that is a strong indication you need to develop your ability to focus your attention on one specific task at a time.

Here are some more productivity tips to avoid the pitfalls of multitasking.

Productivity tip 9.1: "Do not disturb"

If aliens were to observe modern humans, they would surely be baffled by one specific device in our lives. They would see us go through our entire lives with something in our pocket. Throughout the day, the device repeatedly makes a sound that seems to prompt us to look at it. As you can probably guess, the device that constantly activates us is our mobile phone. It constantly bombards us with notifications from Facebook, Instagram, Snapchat, WhatsApp, TikTok, WeChat, LINE, etc. (Tangentially, depending on which of these apps you use, I can probably tell you roughly from which generation you come and on which continent you live.)

As long as that phone is on, you are not in control of what's in your mind and you are constantly multitasking. New thoughts enter your memory and you get distracted from what you were doing.

If you need to get stuff done, turn off or completely mute your phone. Also consider disabling the notification access of most of your apps. The same goes for your computer's email and social media notifications.

Productivity tip 9.2: No peeking

If you can't shield yourself from ongoing notifications, because you, for example, need email for your work, create the following golden rule for yourself: if you're not going to answer it, don't read it. Opening an email makes its contents enter your memory. Your mind will then be spending cognitive resources on processing the information. Even worse, the information often remains in the back of your mind, clogging up your working memory.

Ignore all messages unless you're going to reply to them. In addition to improving your productivity, you'll also be shielded from the social pressure of others having seen you read their message while you haven't responded yet. Making it visible if someone saw your message is a clever invention from social media to keep you even more bound to them.

If you really can't answer the message now for whatever reason, make sure you mark the email as Unread so you don't forget about it.

Productivity tip 9.3: Batching

When you're going to answer your email or any sort of inbox, put some time aside for it and answer a whole batch of messages at once. On many days I answer over 100 messages from my online clients, my team, my subscribers, social media and personal matters. If I were to do that as they came in randomly across the day, I would on average have to answer a message every 14 minutes. Including at night. Even though most messages only require a single-sentence answer, that's clearly not feasible. I couldn't possibly get any productive writing or research done.

However, if you answer your messages in batches, your productivity can increase manifold. Since I can answer all those 1-sentence messages in a minute, I can reply to the first 60 of my 100 daily messages in a single hour of focused work.

I personally choose to reply to my paying clients virtually every day, but I know several entrepreneurs and professors that only reply to their email once a week. Unless you regularly receive urgent messages, you can probably do this as well. If you just thought: "Well, I do receive many urgent messages", think carefully: how urgent are they really? Would anything happen if you answered them tomorrow instead of today, or even next week? Most messages can wait. Most phone calls too.

Productivity tip 9.4: The right number of projects to take on

Based on the previous tips, you want to be able to switch between different kinds of tasks, preferably those with a different presentation modality, across the day. However, you generally do not want to engage in multitasking.

In order to satisfy our need for variation without juggling too many balls at the same time, there is an optimum number of projects we should work on at any time [84]. The exact number will be highly individual, but it's generally not 1 and it's also not a large number. For most people it should probably be a low single digit number, say 2-5. You want enough different projects in your work to enjoy variation, but you don't want to overwhelm your working memory and limit your ability to engage in deliberate, single-minded work. If you are constantly bored with the monotony of your work, you'll probably benefit from starting a new project in your life or work. Yet if you constantly feel overwhelmed by the variety of different things you have to do, or if you feel unable to devote yourself to 1 task at a time, it's probably time to reduce your project load.

To know when you're going to work on which project, you need a to-do list, which brings us to our next tip.

Productivity tip 10: How to optimize your to-do list

Since your (working) memory is limited, you want to minimize the number of things you have to save in it. Thus, a to-do list is crucial for most people. A to-do list is exactly what it says: a place where you note down all the things you have to do, so that you don't have to remember it.

Outlook and Google have good calendars with lots of fancy functions that integrate nicely with your email, so those are good to use if you email a lot. Rainlender is a highly efficient and top-rated desktop app calendar that doesn't require an internet connection to use. To-do lists needn't be fancy though. All you really need is a list of dates and room for text next to each date. You can easily create your own to-do list in a spreadsheet. This way, you have maximal flexibility with its design. Even a simple text file can work well. A to-do list seems like the simplest tool in the world, but we can optimize it to take your productivity to the next level.

Productivity tip 10.1: Beware of overuse

When I was in high school, I got reprimanded by one of my teachers because I didn't have a day planner. I told her day planners were inefficient: I just performed all my homework on the day I received it. When I got home, I opened my books, looked at the next assignment and promptly did the work. My teacher understood that this practice won't work when you have a high workload: you can't always finish your work on the very day you receive it and some tasks must be performed at a certain date. That's why a day planner or agenda, which is basically a to-do list with dates, is important.

However, my younger self was on to something. To-do lists should be a tool to make you more productive, but any time spent on creating them is a loss of productivity. If you can be just as productive without a list as with one, creating a to-do list is simply a waste of time. When you have a to-do list, it's tempting to put any new task that comes your way on there. Don't. It will fill up with endless lists of small stuff. Rather than serving as a working memory aid, your to-do list will turn into a procrastination dump and you'll end up dreading doing even the smallest task on there.

Instead, before you put anything on your to-do list, always ask yourself: can I do this in a few minutes? If the task is so simple it doesn't require an action plan, do it right now. In extreme cases, like sending a simple email, it can take as much work to put something on your agenda as it takes to actually perform the task. So don't use your to-do list for tasks you can easily perform on the spot. Create the following rule for yourself: if you can do something very quickly, do it right now.

Productivity tip 10.2: How to structure your to-do list

A to-do list sounds like a simple list of things you want to do, but that is not how you should structure it. Note how all the recommended software options I gave earlier are calendars. There's a good reason for that. Your to-do list should be something you look at so that you immediately know what to do. If you have to think about which of the tasks to complete, your brain has to use executive functioning and this means you'll use self-control, which risks mental fatigue and falling into procrastination. You've probably experienced this: you look at a whole list of tasks to complete and you end up not doing a single one of them over the next 30 minutes because you're paralyzed by choice.

You should therefore assign a date and preferably even a time to all the tasks on your list. If the task is not time sensitive and doesn't have a deadline, schedule it at the earliest time there's open space in your agenda. Research supports that people are more productive when they give themselves a deadline [79]. Even factory workers, a job classically regarded as the ultimate "I'm just here to get paid" job, are 11-15% more productive when they have a concrete production or quality goal planned [80]. Most work on our to-do list is have-to work, not want-to work, which means intrinsic motivation is low. As such, we benefit from some extra extrinsic motivation to push ourselves.

Productivity tip 10.3: How to set deadlines

A good to-do list has dates assigned to each task. When a task has an imposed deadline, it's relatively straightforward to assign a date to it in your agenda. However, how do you decide when to do tasks without a pre-set deadline?

Research has found that most people do not set optimal deadlines instinctively [79]. Setting a deadline helps compared to not planning ahead, but we tend to give ourselves too much time. This phenomenon is now known as Parkinson's Law, not to be confused with Parkinson's Disease. Parkinson's Law states: "Work expands to fill the time available for its completion." This was originally a semi-tongue-in-cheek remark made in a 1955 issue of The Economist, but it contained deep truth supported by several subsequent studies [81, 82]. People don't take as much time as they *need* for a task. They take as much time as they *have*. The available time sets the expectation of how much time the task should take, so when we are given excess time for any task, we just do it more slowly than needed. Think of how long it takes you to get up and have breakfast before a workday compared to in the weekend or on holiday. Many workers are in their car on the way to work within an hour after getting up, yet in the weekend getting up takes so long breakfast and lunch merge into the now famous Sunday brunch.

One study leveraged Parkinson's Law in a real IT office workplace over a period of 6 months [83]. Could we make people more productive by giving them less time than they think they need? To test this, the workers were given 33% less time for all their tasks than they estimated they needed. It worked. Work output increased by over 15% without loss of quality.

You can use this study's findings as a guide for your own work. When you allocate time to any task, first think of how quickly you could feasibly complete the task. Then take off 33% from your estimate and schedule that amount of time in your agenda. This goes in particular for meetings.

As Milton Berle famously said: "A committee is a group that keeps minutes and loses hours."

Productivity tip 10.4: The most important time to consult your to-do list

The most beneficial time to consult your to-do list is often at the end of your work day. It requires no mental effort, because you don't have to commit to do anything, only look at it. The next day, you'll know exactly what to start working on. This prevents procrastination and as we discussed in the section on the Zeigarnik effect, getting started is one of the most important barriers to break for any task. So make sure you know what your first task of any day is and get started on it without delay.

Productivity tip 11: Wipe the bureaucracy from your mind

A few years ago, I went on a trip through Northern Thailand's beautiful nature that took much longer than expected. By the end I was ravenous. Unfortunately, most shops were closed in the area. There were only some food stalls and convenience shops with junk food around. One of the stalls made fresh banana milkshakes and had multiple hands of bananas hanging around it. I didn't want a milkshake, but I could do with a banana or two. So I approached the middle-aged Thai man behind the counter and greeted him with the Thai wai, which is a slight bow with the hands in a prayer-like position, and asked him: "Sawasdee khrap ['hello' in Thai], I see you sell milkshakes with 2 bananas for 15 Baht. How about I give you 15 Baht and you just give me the bananas and you don't have to make the milkshake?"

He replied: "Sawasdee khrap, sir. I don't sell bananas."

Me: "Why not?"

Thai man: "I only sell milkshakes."

Me: "Ok, but they have the bananas in them, and you can make the same money by giving me the bananas without even having to make the milkshake. What if I give you 100 Baht for the 2 bananas? You can buy loads of bananas with that at any market."

Thai man: "I only sell milkshakes."

Me: "..."

I grudgingly went home hangry, murmuring stuff about the irrationality of not having a transaction with such a difference in reservation prices.

The Thai man fell into the classic trap of bureaucracies: enforcement of rules and regulations (selling a milkshake for 15 Baht) without regard for why those regulations are there in the first place (to make money). Einstein said: "Bureaucracy is the death of all sound work." Our brains inherently share Einstein's brain's view of bureaucracy, in particular the forsaking of purpose. Remember that mental depletion and willpower failure occur in response to high perceived fatigue, not necessarily actual task difficulty. When we focus on rules and regulations, we are focusing on what psychologists call low-level construals: a narrow view of the task and what we have to do for it. This focus on instrumental work makes the brain register task fatigue very saliently. Conversely, when we focus on the task's higher-level construals, namely the task's purpose, this reduces the perceived task fatigue. As a result, in scientific experiments where people focus on the goal of the task, they suffer less loss of self-control than when they focus on the task's requirements [85]. This may be why lawyers, who spend their lives focusing on rules and regulations, report remarkably low job satisfaction for their income and education level [86, 87].

In other words, work without a higher purpose is exhausting. Always keep your purpose in mind. Don't lose sight of your goals. Everything else is just the means to those ends.

Productivity tip 12: Schedule your work in line with your circadian rhythm

Remember Ericsson's research on how the best in the world attain their expertise? He observed a striking pattern in the time of day they chose to perform their work. "Scientists and authors consistently chose to use mornings for demanding writing, and athletes prefer afternoons for their most strenuous practice sessions." [88]

Success leaves cues, they say, and these particular cues have now been validated by scientific research on our body's circadian rhythm. Your circadian (sir-kay-dee-an) rhythm is a daily cycle of biological activity. The biological activity with the most obvious circadian rhythm is your sleep-wake cycle. Think of your body as having an internal clock that regulates when to activate every system. In fact, the part of your brain called the suprachiasmatic nucleus (SCN) has built-in molecular oscillators that function very much like a pacemaker. That's why the SCN is often called your internal or biological clock. The SCN interacts with virtually every major system in your body, including hormone production and central nervous system activity. Look at the following image from Wikipedia for examples of biochemical and physiological events with a 24-hour biorhythm.

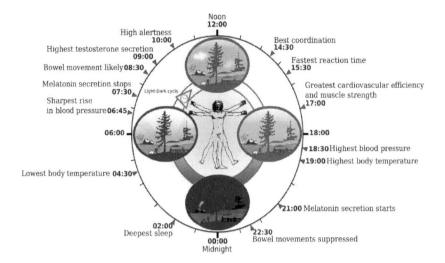

Our brain functioning also has a circadian rhythm. In the morning, our brain runs at peak performance and cognitive performance is highest. Mental performance then gradually decreases during the afternoon and reaches a low before bedtime. See the following image for several studied tasks [89].

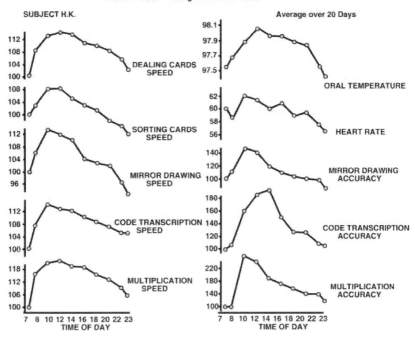

Physical tasks have a different circadian rhythm, as they are influenced by different bodily processes than your brain, in particular core body temperature. As a result, physical performance tends to peak in the afternoon or early evening. This is the period when most world records are broken. Trainees that exercise at this time may also gain muscle mass faster based on some research, though your body can adapt very well to training at different times if you do so consistently [90].

The 'lunch dip' is also a real phenomenon, though its magnitude varies per person and per task. The loss of focus around lunchtime occurs even in individuals who haven't eaten lunch and don't know what time it is. It appears to be a physiological effect related to our circadian rhythm, not merely a psychological effect [91]. So there may be something to the Siesta, the practice of napping around lunchtime that is common in many Spanish speaking countries.

Based on our natural biorhythm, it is best to schedule your most intellectually demanding work in the mornings. Lunchtime is a good time for a break, such as a Siesta or some recreation. Then later in the afternoon is an ideal time to have a break from work in the form of exercise. Since exercise stimulates creative thinking and the end of the work day is a good time to consult your to-do list, brainstorming and planning can be scheduled at the end of the day. This would also be a good time to have meetings, as auditory stimuli are relatively resistant against mental depletion, as you read earlier.

Here's a template I often use to schedule my own days. I work from home, but most office workers and students can employ a similar set-up.

- Morning: scientific research and writing
- Lunch: extensive meal with my fiancée
- Afternoon: answer client emails

- Early evening: training session
- Evening: video calls, interviews
- Late evening: create my agenda for tomorrow

Productivity tip 13: Why Obama only wore 2 colors of suits

Former president of the United States of America, Barack Obama always wore a gray or blue suit [92]. This was very intentional. Obama was aware of the phenomenon of decision fatigue and didn't want to waste any willpower on relatively trivial decisions.

Decision fatigue is a specific form of mental fatigue caused by making decisions. Decisions require forsaking something over something else and this causes mental conflict, just like cognitive dissonance. This makes decisions inherently unpleasant. Unpleasantness makes our brain look for pleasure. We experience this as fatigue or boredom with the unpleasant task we're doing now, which motivates us to find something more enjoyable to do. In short, making decisions reduces our self-control [93]. You should thus try to minimize trivial decisions in your life. Free up your mind to focus on the important matters in your life.

Have a look at your wardrobe and see if you can learn from Obama. And yes, I realize these tips may be heresy for many people.

- When you find a piece of clothing you like, considering buying it in several colors.
- For greater variation, get matching clothing. If you have 4 pants and 4 t-shirts that all only fit in 1 specific combination, that's a hassle. If all 4 pants match with all 4 t-shirts, you can just grab one of each at any day to wear.
- For greater variation still, you could order your wardrobe. You could rotate through a set of matching clothes or have a set of clothes for each day of the week.
- Only buy 1 or 2 colors of socks, such as black and white. This saves a lot of time finding and folding matching socks when doing the laundry.

We'll go into more examples later, such as why you should not decide how you travel to work or what you're going to eat.

Housekeeping also shouldn't take too much of your attention. If you make more money than cleaners, you should consider getting a cleaner or housekeeper. For fit individuals, there are also more and more services that prepare and cook meals for you based on your specified macronutrients.

If you're financially well off, consider getting a personal assistant (PA). PAs aren't just for executives anymore. You can get digital personal assistants from Asian countries for a modest fee. They can help do your online groceries and other online purchases, make restaurant reservations, help filter your inbox, prepare some of your tax administration (your much more expensive accountant doesn't have to do everything), etc.

In short, try to simplify your life so you can spend most of your attention on your most important decisions.

Productivity tip 14: The optimal work environment

Jay has a neat desk with only the essentials on it. His computer desktop similarly has only the links to his most frequently used programs on it without a background. Bob's desk is filled with pens and documents, a plant and other personal items. His computer desktop has more icons than free space with an extravagant wallpaper. Who do you think is more productive: neat Jay or messy Bob?

Trick question. It depends.

We intuitively know being organized is a sign of control, and research suggests an organized environment is not just a symptom of being in control as a person but also a potential cause of it. Or rather, seeing clutter around us is distracting and stressful. According to Statistics from the National Association of Productivity & Organizing, office workers report that cluttered desks negatively affect their productivity. They spend a significant amount of time dealing with the clutter and searching for stuff rather than doing actual work. Scientific research similarly finds a cluttered work environment is a strong predictor of procrastination behavior [94]. In many settings, chaos around us causes stress and reduces our productivity.

- Children in messy homes have poorer attentional focus, higher stress and more learned helplessness, than those living in tidier houses, even after controlling for sociodemographic factors, such as family income, and parenting style [95, 96].
- Similarly, parents report lower parental efficacy in more crowded homes [97].
- Women experimentally put in chaotic vs. organized kitchens snack more on cookies but not carrots, and other research confirms a tidy environment increases healthy food choices [98, 99].
- Women in messier homes have higher levels of the stress hormone cortisol and more depressive feelings, even after controlling for their level of neuroticism [100].

Even if you may feel unfazed by working in a chaotic environment, at a very primitive level you'll still be distracted. Cognitive neuroscientific research shows that visual stimuli interfere with attentional modulation [101]. Having many different things in sight makes our brain process those, even if they're not passed on to our consciousness.

These findings have led many companies to institute a 'clean desk policy'. While this may help increase productivity by forcing us to stay organized, it can also backfire by decreasing personal expression and creating a colder, more depressing work environment. A series of modern research experiments have found that plants and personal decorations increase not only worker wellbeing but also productivity [102, 103].

Moreover, increased organization is not always desirable. While an organized work space generally helps us stay organized for our work, it can also suppress our creativity [99]. The first study showing a messy desk could increase our creativity went viral as the proof a messy desk is a good thing after all, but that's a misguided conclusion for most people. For most work output, creativity is not that important, whereas being organized is. We need creativity to come up with new ideas and solutions, but after we found those, the hard part is seeing the project through to the end. Most people don't lack ideas to do new things, or need to do new things in the first place. The more common problem is finishing familiar work. Completing projects requires being organized and working through stress without distraction, not more creativity.

When creativity is actually important for productivity, you probably shouldn't be working from an office space to begin with. If you're a graphics designer looking for a new logo idea, don't sit around in a neat cubicle and stare at a white wall. You should scroll through lists of similar logos for inspiration or start putting your thoughts on paper. If you're a programmer and you just can't see how to code the next step of your algorithm, go for a walk. Modern companies tend to have lounge rooms for exactly this reason: traditional office space is not an ideal place to take breaks or be inspired. Personally, I tend to get my best ideas in the gym and in the shower, rarely at my desk.

So what should you keep and what should you remove from your work space? The golden rule seems to be to keep items and objects with positive associations and remove items you don't need with negative associations. Personal decorations and plants should make you feel calm, not stressed, so keep those or put them in. Newspapers, left-over documents from previous work and stuff you 'think you may need to use at some point' should all be archived or thrown away. They will only distract or stress you.

The same applies for your computer, perhaps even more strongly so.

- Remove all icons from your desktop you don't regularly use, but get a nice wallpaper background that doesn't obstruct your sight. It's hard to go wrong with scenic nature views.

- Optimize your internet browser.
  - o Remove all add-ins, bookmarks and icons that you don't use daily from your browser's main task bar.
  - o Consider a custom theme, but only use one that has great readability: large enough text and icons and high contrast for all text, preferably black text on white background.
  - o Get into the habit of closing all browser tabs and windows you don't need anymore.
  - o Stick to Google.com for your starting page, or load previously closed tabs upon start-up. Don't use a news page as your starting page, unless you need that for your work.
- If you work with a customizable email agent like Gmail, as you probably should, enable its minimalist design and go to your settings to implement the following.
  - o Remove all inbox labels you don't actively use. Most people don't need any labels.
  - o Remove all categories you don't need. Google's great search function typically makes even archiving categories redundant, so most people shouldn't need any categories at all.
  - o Disable the chat, unless you use it daily.

o   Make emails show only the title, not any
    text, in your main inbox. (Remember the tip
    about only opening emails you're going to
    answer!)

If you have trouble staying organized and you find your
work space and desktop clutter up over time, schedule a
moment in your agenda each week for a clean-up.

Productivity tip 15: The Yerkes–Dodson law

"Whatever the problem, caffeine is the solution." That could be the mantra of many officer workers and students these days. Caffeine is well-known for its energizing effect and caffeine is by many standards the most popular drug on the planet. However, as with most drugs, it's easy to take too much of it because it feels so good at first. While caffeine is relatively benign in side-effects with overconsumption in comparison to, say, cocaine, many people arguably abuse caffeine all the same. For productivity, more caffeine is certainly not always better. Caffeine only helps for certain tasks and only up to a certain dosage, as it improves certain brain functions but hampers others [104]. (Not to mention the anxiety you get from overstimulation at a certain point and the tolerance and withdrawal you accumulate.)

Caffeine's effects on productivity are like that of external motivation, and often stress in general: stress can effectively boost our willpower by making system 1, our inner emotional elephant, focus on a have-to task that otherwise only system 2 would be concerned with. For example, if you have to write up something boring for your job or studies, you may care about that task rationally but not emotionally. As a result, you're likely to procrastinate on it because forcing yourself to focus on it requires your system 2 to suppress system 1. You then experience cognitive conflict, which we perceive as an unpleasant feeling. Meanwhile system 1 is looking for instant gratification and when system 2 fails to suppress your system 1, your attention dwindles from the have-to activity to a want-to activity. The right amount of stress can make system 1 pay attention to the have-to task. You may not care about your paper's topic, but you do care about missing your deadline tomorrow. Stress effectively cracks the whip on our inner emotional elephant.

Of course, too much anxiety can be debilitating. More generally, there is an optimum level of stimulation for every task. This optimum generally decreases with task difficulty so that simple tasks benefit from a lot of external stimulation, whereas for complex tasks, too much external stimulation can backfire. These findings are called the Yerkes-Dodson law, first studied by Harvard professors Yerkes & Dodson in 1908 [105]. A great deal of research since has generally supported that there's an optimum level of external stimulation for most tasks, and the optimum is generally higher for simpler tasks, although how far we can generalize the law has been contested [106, 107, 108]. The following graph from a great review by Diamond et al. summarizes the Yerkes-Dodson law [109].

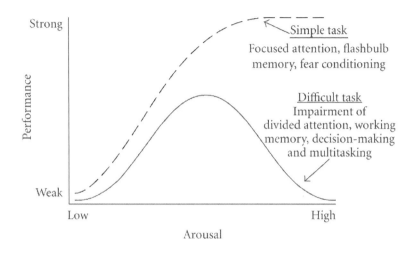

You can take advantage of the Yerkes-Dodson law in several ways to boost your productivity. To maximize your performance on simple tasks, like administrative work or cleaning your house, you want to be in a state of high external stimulation or arousal. You can create this stimulation with caffeine or music. If you have a set deadline for the task, you can also take advantage of the arousal you get from being near this deadline: defer the task to just before the deadline. This works best for time-intensive but braindead work, especially administrative matters that you'd otherwise just procrastinate on. You can drag around it for hours or you can get it done in 30 minutes of focused work close to the deadline.

If you're into nootropics ('brain boosting supplements') and you're not susceptible to addiction, nicotine gum (1-4 mg) is surprisingly effective and safe to enhance simple task performance [110]. Nicotine acts as a mild stimulant and potent attention enhancer. It also reduces your appetite and slightly increases your metabolic rate, so it dual-functions as a mild fat loss aid.

It's crucial to stick to gum for nicotine, because during oral consumption the rate of nicotine uptake in the brain is slow enough that addiction is not a concern for most people, unlike with smoking tobacco. Nicotine gum is also self-limiting in its reinforcing effect for most people by 'virtue' of being nauseating in large amounts. First-time users should stick to 1 mg gums and chew them very slowly, parking them in the mouth before it starts causing throat pain or nausea. At the risk of sounding like an affiliate sales talk, most people I know find Nicotinell Mint the best-tasting brand.

Nicotine may sound dangerous, but it's found to be safe in research for healthy people. I also don't know anyone who's experienced any side-effects on it or gotten addicted to it on dosages up to 12 mg a day. Nicotine gum and smoking tobacco are physiologically completely different things, as demonstrated by the fact the gum is prescribed to help people quit smoking.

For complex tasks, especially creative work, nicotine gum is not your friend. I believe many people routinely overstimulate themselves for intellectual work, in particular with caffeine. While intuitively it may seem effective to 'energize' yourself when you don't feel like working, research decisively shows overarousal can harm your performance on complex tasks. High stress and emotionality seem to interfere with certain higher order brain functions, especially in the hippocampus [111]. Being too focused can also backfire by creating tunnel vision and harming your ability to divide your attention and multitask. For example, an experiment on the game of chess found that even powerful nootropics like caffeine, methylphenidate (commonly known as Ritalin, similar to Adderall) and modafinil failed to enhance overall performance [112]. The stimulants caused over-reflection: the players made better moves but with an excessive time investment per move, therefore they lost more games on time.

My general recommendation for complex, intellectual tasks is to perform them in a quiet, unstimulating environment without time pressure or distractions. If you want to use any stimulants, especially caffeine, be mindful of the dosage and consider adding an equal dosage of l-theanine, such as 100 mg each, or get your caffeine from green tea. L-theanine is a non-dietary amino acid that's in large part responsible for the difference in how you feel on coffee vs. green tea. Both have caffeine, but green tea also has l-theanine, which preserves the attention enhancing effects while moderating the stimulant effect [113]. Basically, you get the focus without the jitters. Without caffeine, l-theanine only has very mild effects, but if you suffer from trouble concentrating, it may be worth supplementing on its own 30-60 minutes before tasks that require high focus but not high arousal.

Productivity tip 16: *Mens sana in corpore sano*

If you want your brain to function at maximum capacity, you must take care of your body. A healthy mind requires a healthy body and a healthy body requires a healthy diet. Avoiding neuro-inflammation is specifically relevant for your cognitive functioning or 'brain power' [114].

Diets lacking in vegetables, fruits and fish but rich in processed foods, sugars and trans fats can cause chronic and systemic inflammation by elevating blood sugar levels, forming advanced glycation end products (AGEs), increasing low-density lipoprotein cholesterol (LDL or 'bad' cholesterol) and potentially causing leaky gut and a leaky blood-brain barrier. Having chronically high inflammation affects many bodily functions, including your brain. While it's difficult and arguably unethical to conduct very long-term experiments in humans with diets that result in brain damage, research in rats clearly shows diets rich in sugars and processed fats impair memory functioning [114]. The experiments in humans also trend in the direction that energy restriction improves some measures of cognitive functioning, especially memory and executive function [115].

Neuro-inflammation seems to effectively degrade the functions of the hippocampus, which is crucial for learning and memory, and the prefrontal cortex, which is crucial for self-control.

Maintaining a healthy diet can thus likely improve your cognitive functioning and your self-control, but to maintain a healthy diet in the first place, you also need self-control. That brings us to our next chapter.

CHAPTER 4: HOW TO STICK TO YOUR DIET

To get lean, you have to understand what your primary objective is. It is not to detox. It is not to be in ketosis. It is not to eat healthily. Your food choices are in fact largely irrelevant, in theory at least, as long as you do this one thing: create an energy deficit. Obesity is fundamentally an energy balance problem [1]. If you are fatter than you'd like, your energy intake over time is too high relative to your energy expenditure. Physical law, specifically thermodynamics, dictates that energy cannot be destroyed. When it enters your body, it must either be stored, such as in the form of body fat, or the energy has to be used as fuel. When energy intake exceeds energy expenditure, the surplus is stored in your body. At a physical level, that is all there is to it and losing weight is as simple as creating an energy deficit.

Together with Cambridge PhD Anastasia Zinchenko, I have extensively reviewed the scientific litcrature on how your metabolism adapts to prevent further fat loss [2]. All anti-starvation mechanisms ultimately culminate into 2 effects:

they either stimulate increased energy intake by increasing your appetite or they decrease your energy expenditure.

At this point in nutritional sciences, anyone who tells you fat loss is not primarily dictated by energy balance is either ignorant or a quack.

Thermodynamics dictate that no one is so genetically screwed that they cannot get lean. Some have a greater appetite or slower metabolism, making it more difficult to create an energy deficit, but an energy deficit will always result in energy loss from the body, which normally means fat loss. In other words, everyone can get sixpack lean. Physically, it is as simple as creating an energy deficit for a long enough time.

Mentally, however, fat loss is much easier said than done. Telling someone to 'reduce your calorie intake' is a lot like telling someone to 'just quit smoking'. It's not the physical execution of the task that is the problem. It's the mental journey that comes before it. Let's go into how we can make this journey easier.

Diet tip 1: The flesh is strong, but the mind is weak

The reason dieting is difficult mentally may seem obvious. Low energy levels, the inability to muster up energy to do something, a mental fog, these problems occur because of a low energy intake, right?

A team of researchers led by Harris Lieberman designed a clever experiment to test what the mental effects of energy deprivation are without having people know they're dieting [3]. The researchers took a group of healthy individuals and gave them gel-based diets. The gel structure allowed the researchers to greatly manipulate the energy content of the food without altering the physical appearance, taste or texture of the food. The study subjects were then given either a maintenance diet of 2294 Calories per day or a starvation diet of 313 Calories per day to eat for 2 days. The researchers compared the groups on a battery of cognitive, physiological and psychological tests. How big do you think the difference between the groups was?

There was *no difference*, except that the subjects were predictably hungrier when eating next to nothing. Their mood, sleep quality and mental performance were not affected by the 2 days of practical starvation. In fact, after the study, the subjects were informed of the study design and asked if they thought they were in the starvation or the maintenance group. The subjects couldn't tell.

The similarity between dietary energy intake – how many calories we consume – and mental energy is largely metaphorical.

- A calorie is a measurement unit to quantify chemical reactions, officially "the approximate amount of energy needed to raise the temperature of one gram of water by one degree Celsius at a pressure of one atmosphere".
  Technically, the nutritional Calorie should be spelled with a capital C, because it's a kilocalorie, but few people adhere to this rule.
- Mental energy is a vague, unscientific term used to refer to psychological or cognitive capacity, frequently motivation or arousal. For example, after dinner, you may be in a massive dietary energy surplus and still not have mental energy to do the dishes (read: not be motivated to do the dishes).

As the above experiment demonstrated, there is very little inherent relation between dietary energy intake and mental energy intake. They are fundamentally different concepts. Multiple lines of research consistently demonstrate that being in an energy deficit has practically no physiological effect on your brain's ability to function or your mood.

The oldest study I've been able to find on the mental effects of energy restriction is a 1987 trial on crash diets by the University of Pennsylvania School of Medicine [4]. In this study, participants were assigned to either a 500- or 1200-Calorie protein-sparing modified fast (PSMF) for 2 months. The dieters didn't feel any different on the different diets: "There were no significant differences between conditions in subjects' ratings of their preoccupation with eating or in their ratings of the acceptability or disruptiveness of their diets." Remarkably, the 500-Calorie diet did in fact result in overt hypothyroidism symptoms: their thyroids, the centers of their metabolism, were shutting down. So not only are we generally unable to blindly tell what energy intake we're consuming or if we're in energy deficit, we may not even be aware of it when our body is actually suffering from our diet. I've seen this myself in many people starting vegan and carnivore diets. When not properly implemented, these diets quickly result in significant nutritional deficiencies, yet people that try them are often convinced their diet is the stairway to heaven. So some people report feeling 'better than ever', yet when you look at their bloodwork, things are going downhill fast.

One of the most carefully controlled studies we have on the mental effects of dieting is a 2015 metabolic ward study [5]. Metabolic ward studies are the scientific gold standard for many nutritional interventions, because the subjects are kept in a lab and they're continuously monitored while all the food they eat is prepared for them. In this study, non-obese individuals in a massive 40% energy deficit experienced an initial dip in their mood during the transition from maintenance, but in the subsequent weeks there was no longer any effect on mood, sleep quality or mental performance compared to when eating a maintenance diet. The participants were exercising 3-4x a week. In fact, 10% of the deficit was achieved by increasing the amount of exercise they did. So the subjects could notice a difference in how they felt when suddenly going into a massive energy deficit and starting to exercise more, but they quickly habituated to 'the new normal'.

We have very long-term studies as well. Grigolon et al. (2020) [6] and Leclerc et al. (2019) [7] analyzed the cognitive performance of 220 non-obese adults over a 2-year diet. They found that the diets improved cognitive performance, in particular working memory, whereas energy intake per se had no effect on cognitive functioning.

Another line of research comes from the military. During a month-long field exercise, being in a massive 40% deficit compared to a moderate 14% deficit did not affect mood, psychological health or reaction time in soldiers [8].

Research has also specifically investigated how energy intake affects our sleep quality. It doesn't [9].

Additionally, we can learn from research on Ramadan fasting and fasting in general. Ramadan fasting does not impair brain functioning [10]. It's not nearly enough of a stress for our bodies. It takes 24 hours of total food deprivation before mental performance starts to deteriorate in some research and this most likely due to dehydration, not lack of energy intake [11]. Multiple studies confirm that even severe energy deficits or complete fasting up to 48 hours do not impair cognitive functioning, our mood, brain activity or motor performance [12, 13, 14].

In fact, some aspects of mental functioning **improve** after missing a meal and when dieting [15]. A 2015 systematic review concluded cognitive functioning is not consistently affected by our diet, but there was a trend for long-term energy restriction to improve some measures of cognitive functioning, especially memory [16]. Energy restriction and healthier diets may improve brain functioning by reducing neuro-inflammation. From an evolutionary perspective, it makes sense that energy restriction sharpens our brain. When you run out of food, you need to become active and stay alert to obtain new food. If you collapse whenever you venture out of walking distance from a McDonald's, your genes don't stand a very good chance of making it to the next century.

But what about blood sugar?

So how does this all jive with what we know about blood sugar? Everyone knows that after a meal, you feel better, and when your blood sugar levels fall again, you experience a dip, right?

Wrong. This conventional wisdom was debunked back in 1980. Johnson et al. studied symptoms of hypoglycemia in 192 men and women during an oral glucose challenge: monitoring blood sugar levels after consuming a lot of sugar [17]. While many participants did indeed experience symptoms similar to hypoglycemia (light-headedness, shakiness, diaphoresis, weakness, and fatigue), in the vast majority of cases there was no actual hypoglycemia at the time of the symptoms. In fact, there was no correlation between symptoms and blood sugar levels at all. More research since has consistently demonstrated there's no clear correlation between blood sugar levels and mood, appetite and symptoms of alleged hypoglycemia [18].

So what caused the symptoms? The researchers tested the personality types of the participants and found that they scored high on measures of conversion V, a personality trait that in theory makes people susceptible to psychosomatic symptoms. In other words, the symptoms were nocebo effects: in their head, self-induced.

Several other studies have confirmed that alleged subjective symptoms of hypoglycemia after meals generally do not coincide with actual hypoglycemia [19] and that relief of symptoms after eating does not correlate with an increase in blood sugar [20, 21]. In fact, there was a decrease in blood sugar levels during symptom relief in many participants. How about when you're *not* eating? Green et al. (1997) studied the effect of food deprivation – not allowing people to eat – on how they felt and mentally functioned during a set of cognitive performance tests [15]. Food deprivation did not generally affect brain functioning with one exception: memory *improved*. They also related glucose levels to cognitive performance: there was no relation. They concluded: "...the brain is relatively invulnerable to short food deprivation."

Blood sugar levels are tightly controlled within a narrow range in healthy individuals. The waves of 'spikes and crashes' after meals are normally more like the gentle lapping of the sea at the beach.

Nevertheless, food and carbohydrate intake can acutely impact how we feel. Conventional wisdom says carbs give you a 'sugar rush', but all-you-can-eat sushi veterans can attest that all you'll be rushing to after 5k Calories of rice is your bed. A 2019 meta-analysis firmly concluded carbohydrates do not improve our overall mood and generally make us drowsy: "Analysis of 176 effect sizes (31 studies, 1259 participants) revealed no positive effect of carbohydrates on any aspect of mood at any time-point following their consumption. However, carbohydrate administration was associated with higher levels of fatigue and less alertness compared with placebo within the first hour post-ingestion." [22] This sleepiness occurs not because of our blood sugar, but because of our nervous system's response to food intake, a phenomenon called postprandial somnolence.

Postprandial somnolence

The idea that food gives you mental energy is fundamentally misguided. It is based on the notion that food has energy, so surely it must give you mental energy. The problem here is semantic, as you learned: despite the similar words, mental energy and food energy are entirely different concepts. Food energy is physical energy, akin to heat and movement. Mental energy is a vague term informally used to refer to either cognitive functioning – how well the brain objectively performs mental tasks – or psychological motivation.

Rather than becoming more energetic after a meal, most people become sleepier. This phenomenon is called postprandial somnolence. Postprandial means 'after eating'. Somnolence means 'sleepiness'. From an evolutionary perspective, this sleepiness makes a lot of sense. Hunter gatherer populations had to be alert when food was scarce but could relax more when there was ample food available. To quote Vanitallie (2006): "the neurophysiologic and metabolic mechanisms responsible for the control of food-seeking behavior and the control of sleep and wakefulness are coordinated so that hunger and vigilance are paired during the daylight hours, and satiety and sleep are paired during darkness." [23]

The classic explanation for postprandial somnolence is that during digestion blood flow gets shuttled to the digestive system with greater priority, leaving less blood available for the brain. It was a plausible theory, but it turned out to be incorrect. Much like blood sugar, an abundance of evidence shows the body strictly controls blood flow and oxygenation in the brain [24]. Even when exercising, your body maintains cerebral (brain) oxygenation [25]. Turns out, your brain's kind of important, so if it didn't get enough oxygen and blood every time you ate, that would be kind of bad.

Another explanation was that the feel-good-but-sedating neurotransmitter serotonin was responsible for postprandial somnolence [26]. Carbohydrate-rich meals can promote serotonin production, while protein rich meals can decrease it, by influencing which amino acids enter our brain [27]. The theory was that it's thus specifically the carbohydrate content of the meal that influences postprandial somnolence ('carb knockout'). However, the macronutrient composition of a meal does not reliably affect its resulting postprandial somnolence [28].

The currently most well supported theory is that the central nervous system's state is altered by hunger [29]. Hunger motivates you to become active and search for food via activation of the sympathetic 'fight or flight' state, whereas satiety activates the parasympathetic 'rest and digest' state. Specifically, the hypothalamus – the area in your brain that controls vegetative functions such as eating, sleeping, bowel function and sex – registers satiety in the form of metabolites from the food we eat, peptides in our gut and signals from the vagus nerve, the biggest nerve of your parasympathetic nervous system. These signals of satiety can stimulate our brain's sleep centers, thereby causing postprandial somnolence. Satiety as the key driving force of postprandial somnolence explains why solid meals are more sleep-inducing than liquid meals [28]. It also explains why larger meals generally result in greater postprandial somnolence than smaller meals [30].

From an evolutionary point of view, the nervous system's reaction to satiety makes perfect sense. When you're hungry, you're stimulated to be active and go find food. When your belly is full, the nervous system sees: "Mission accomplished. The threat of starvation is gone. Now it's time to chill and go find a partner to make babies with... Maybe take a nap first."

In conclusion, you don't need food to be mentally energized. Being in a physical energy deficit does not inherently affect your cognition, mood or sleep quality based on numerous studies. I would add the caveat that this probably changes at very low body fat levels, such as during preparation for a physique contest or actual starvation, but even then it's uncertain if it's energy balance per se or the low body fat level that causes the problems.

If you're like most people and you have any experience dieting, at this point you probably feel like you're Neo that got red-pilled in the Nutrition Matrix and you protest: "I don't know about these studies, but I can definitely tell when I'm on a diet and it doesn't feel good!" And that's probably true. Because the participants in most of these studies share a crucial commonality that we commonly do not share. What do people eating nothing but gels or liquids, soldiers and people in metabolic wards have in common? Blissful ignorance. These study participants were not aware they were on fat loss diets. They didn't feel restricted. The soldiers just ate their provisions, the metabolic ward crowd just ate what the cafeteria made and Lieberman's human guinea pigs just ate the provided gels. You, on the other hand, must consciously restrict yourself. Restricting yourself causes 2 large problems in your mind.

The first problem with restricting yourself to go on a diet is the dreaded nocebo effect. As you saw in the studies on fake low blood sugar symptoms, the expectation of feeling poorly on a diet can actually make you feel poorly. This preoccupation with dieting makes it much harder than it needs to be. A 2018 meta-analysis of studies supports that diet-induced psychological stress is unrelated to how much weight you're losing [31]. In fact, the researchers found that people that aren't losing any weight on their diet, which means they are in fact still consuming maintenance energy intake, often experience just as much stress from their diet as people that are actually losing weight. In other words, the stress comes from the idea of 'being on a diet', not from the psychological state of negative energy balance.

A large body of research indicates that our brains do not react to caloric intake per se at all but rather use contextual cues to estimate our perceived food intake. When the energy density of food is secretly reduced in research, unaware people still eat approximately the same amount of total food volume and thus consume significantly fewer calories [32]. Moreover, hunger, fullness, desire to eat and prospective consumption ratings are the same, showing that you can be just as satiated with less, as long as you're not obsessing over the fact that you're restricting your caloric intake.

In a study by Crum et al. (2011), researchers told their participants that they were drinking a high-calorie 'indulgent' milkshake or a low-calorie 'sensible' milkshake, when in fact it was the same milkshake in both groups [33]. The participants consuming the supposedly indulgent milkshake reported higher satiety and they even experienced a greater decrease in levels of the hunger hormone ghrelin.

In sum, it's the feeling of deprivation and the expectation of suffering, not the actual energy restriction, that causes most problems when dieting. To counter these effects, it's good to realize that in terms of physical health, our bodies actually thrive in an energy deficit (at least until you get close to essential body fat levels, like during a bodybuilding contest). It's well-known that obesity is causally related to virtually all leading causes of death [34]. Being lean protects against diabetes, reduces chronic inflammation levels and corrects hormonal imbalances [35, 36]. Fat tissue, especially visceral fat, negatively influences all of these systems in the body. In research, losing body fat has very strong and consistent positive effects on almost every health biomarker, including blood sugar, heart rate, cholesterol levels and systemic inflammation markers. The rate of weight loss and even diet quality often do not matter as much for our health as the loss of body fat [37, 38]. Energy restriction, or rather staying lean throughout your life, increases the lifespan of various animals, including primates [39, 40, 41, 42]. Studies on humans have also found improvements in biomarkers of longevity and many health biomarkers, suggesting we too can live longer if we stay lean [43, 44, 45, 46, 47]. Energy restriction decreases inflammation and oxidative damage, which can decrease the rate at which our DNA degrades over time. Centenarians – people that live over 100 years old – are rarely overweight and have been found to have a metabolic profile very similar to that of people in an energy deficit [48]. Calorie restriction is currently the most likely candidate to delay the health defects of age. Exercise is contender number 2, but exercise seems to primarily reduce the symptoms associated with aging rather than truly prevent the aging process [49]. While it's certainly possible to be overweight but healthy, many people who appear to be 'metabolically healthy overweight' by certain standards actually have considerable subclinical health problems [50]. 'Healthy overweight' individuals are also still at greater risk than leaner individuals of developing metabolic risk factors [51, 52]. As such, being 'healthy obese' is often basically a timebomb and fat loss is still advisable [53, 54].

The knowledge that the side-effects of dieting are largely in your head and that your body is getting healthier is the first step to get rid of the nocebo effects of energy restriction. Whenever you're inclined to blame a lack of energy intake for not feeling motivated, remind yourself this is a mental issue, not a physical one. Your body is strong and your battle is psychological. You shouldn't need food to feel good.

Diet tip 2: Hustle

Did you ever think you would read a book that tells you it's going to help you not by giving you more knowledge but by making you more ignorant? Well, that's what you're doing right now. Ignorance is bliss when it comes to dieting: if you don't realize you're dieting, you don't suffer from its nocebo effects. The best way to not realize you're on a diet is to be busy with something else. Get work done. Do something with your friends. Create a website that tracks the number of funny cat videos on YouTube. Anything productive or fun will do the trick. Focusing on a task you're doing reduces food cravings [55, 56]. More generally speaking, actively thinking about anything other than food helps reduce food cravings and it doesn't seem to matter what else you think about [57]. Keeping yourself occupied prevents you from obsessing over the fact you're on a diet. Whatever you do, don't sit around and think about food. Distraction is your friend.

Diet tip 3: Why 'trying harder' doesn't work

To lower your energy intake, you have to restrict your food choices or portion sizes. This causes two problems in your mind. We already discussed the first problem: the nocebo effect. The second problem is that restriction requires self-control. The goal of losing fat is exclusively a goal from the rational and deliberate part of your brain, system 2: you have formulated this goal consciously and deliberately. The more primitive part of your brain, system 1, is never motivated to lose fat, because it has no foresight. It sure is motivated for some tasty ice cream though. System 1 just registers hunger and the pleasure of eating. So dieting, like virtually any type of investment into the future, poses an inherent conflict between systems 1 and 2 in our brain. Only as long as your rational system 2 can override system 1, can you deliberately choose to eat only foods that are in line with your diet. You could even choose not to eat any food at all.

Since consciously restricting yourself is essentially a battle of willpower, many people see dieting as a period of suffering they must endure to achieve their desired physique. Discipline is regarded as the key to success: you must force yourself through these periods. When you stumble, you must double up on your efforts and be stricter. Research, however, finds self-restraint does not significantly improve weight loss success and the degree of restraint doesn't matter [58]. Just look around you to see how successful the traditional disciplinary approach is. Over 2 out of 3 people in the US are overweight and over 1 in 3 is obese [59]. Even with help, most people don't lose more than a few percent of their body weight after years of dieting. And then, over time the majority of people gain back most of the weight they lost: the dreaded yo-yo dieting phenomenon [60].

Part of the rationale for the disciplinary approach to fat loss is the idea that your willpower is like a muscle and gets stronger over time as it is taxed. Yet as we discussed, this idea is fundamentally wrong. There is no 'willpower tissue' that you can make stronger. Nor do you need to. Your willpower capacity is not limited. Instead, self-control failure during dieting occurs when your brain perceives your current goals to be insufficiently rewarding relative to their required efforts. Your attention then shifts from system 2's goals to those of system 1, which invariably result in greater instant gratification. It's not like your 'brain fuel' has run out: your brain has just shifted its priorities. Your inner emotional elephant takes the rational rider's reins into its own... trunk. As a result, you choose to eat the want-to pizza instead of the have-to salad.

Unfortunately, relying on sheer will to prevent yourself from eating is bound to fail eventually, because your body has homeostatic mechanisms in place to prevent starvation. Specifically, fat mass has a negative feedback loop to your appetite via various mechanisms, including directly by secreting leptin [61]. Leptin is an appetite suppressing hormone. So the less fat mass you have, the less leptin you produce, and the greater your appetite. Appetite is a potent system 1 sensation, so as you get leaner, it becomes progressively harder for system 2 to keep suppressing system 1. We feel this cognitive conflict between our inner rational rider and emotional elephant as mental fatigue and unhappiness. These negative feelings motivate us to self-medicate on comfort foods to make us feel better [62]. As a result, exerting willpower increases the chance we'll later deviate from our diet [63]. For example, people that try to control their emotions while watching a movie subsequently snack more ice cream during other tasks [64]. In other words, as our inner rational rider forces our inner elephant not to eat what it wants, it becomes progressively unhappier, until it eventually becomes impossible to control the reins. Some people can maintain control for longer than others, but everyone has a breaking point. Even if you can maintain control, it's not a pleasant way to diet, as the conflict between systems 1 and 2 makes you feel unhappy.

How do we prevent self-control failure? Well, in a laboratory, researchers can put a magnetic prod near the right part of your brain. This device creates a magnetic field that sends an electrical current to your prefrontal cortex, the part of your brain that governs self-control, your system 2. It sounds like science fiction, but it works. This method, called transcranial magnetic stimulation (TMS), can help reduce energy intake, appetite, cravings and snacking behavior [65]. It's currently not available or practically usable for consumers, but it illustrates that the challenge with dieting is essentially staying rational. If system 2 was always in charge, dieting would simply be a matter of choice without any internal conflict.

So your dieting mindset should not be to rely on sheer willpower and discipline. You will need self-control many times, but it should be a last resort. Rather than double up on your willpower efforts, your goal should be to minimize the amount of willpower you need to stay on your diet. In the rest of this chapter, we'll go into many strategies to make it easier to lose fat without feeling constrained. Let's start with how to set up your diet in terms of macronutrients.

Diet tip 4: The best macros for adherence

A key feature of any diet is its macronutrient split: how much protein, carbohydrate and fat you're supposed to eat. What's the best macronutrient split for dietary adherence: high carb or low carb? In multiple of the studies from the section explaining many dieting side-effects are nocebo, the macronutrient split of the diet was also manipulated. Different groups consumed different macronutrient splits, so we can look at which groups did best. However, there was no effect of the macronutrient split in any of the studies on how the participants felt or mentally performed. This is in agreement with much of the literature that the macronutrient composition of your diet will only have a slight, highly situational effect on your brain and mood if you're healthy [66, 67, 68]. High- and low-carb diets have similar effects on cognitive functioning [69]. One study found switching from a 41% fat intake to a 25% fat intake resulted in a poorer mood, but since there was no group switching in the opposite direction, it's likely that the change in diet rather than the decrease in fat intake per se was the culprit for the adverse mood effects [70].

Research has also found that low-carb and low-fat diets are equally effective at improving health-related quality of life, given the same fat loss [71]. It's mostly fat loss, not your diet composition, that improves your health, and as you learned, high- and low-carb diets are generally equally effective for fat loss for carb-tolerant individuals, given the same total energy and protein intake.

For dietary adherence, low-carb diets seem to perform better than higher-carb diets, but these effects may largely be the result of higher protein intakes in the lower-carbohydrate groups. A systematic review with a total sample size of 1222 people found that low-carb diets have a significantly better attrition rate (fewer drop-outs) than low-fat diets [72]. Another meta-analysis by Nordmann et al. (2016) compared carbohydrate-restricted diets to fat- and energy-restricted diets [73]. Six months into the diets, the low-carb diets had greater weight loss with a 70% vs. 57% success rate compared to the low-fat diets. At 12 months, there was no significant difference in either measure anymore, though the success rate was still 62% vs. 54% in favor of low-carb diets. In non-isocaloric weight loss interventions, low-fat diets also tend to result in poorer outcomes than higher-fat diets according to a large meta-analysis from 2015 by Tobias et al. [74].

All in all, you should consume enough protein and fat to make your diet healthy and sustainable. Beyond that, the precise macronutrient ratio of your diet doesn't matter much for most healthy people not involved in any exercise other than strength training. Any benefits of a specific carb-to-fat ratio are likely individual. For example, strength-endurance athletes like tennis players will typically perform and thereby feel better on higher-carbohydrate diets, whereas someone with type II diabetes or genetic carb intolerance will typically feel better on a lower-carb diet.

Diet tip 5: How to interpret your personal preference

Since the exact ratio of carbs to fats often doesn't matter, as long as you're not too low in fat or protein, it may seem intuitive to let personal preference decide whether you go higher or lower in carbs. If you personally prefer higher-carb diets, you'll likely adhere better to a high-carb diet, right?

Wrong. Allowing people to self-select a low vs. high carb diet based on personal preference does not improve dietary adherence in research [75]. In fact, giving people the choice of which diet to follow can reduce weight loss success [76]. A 2018 meta-analysis looked at all studies in which participants were either put in a certain diet group by the researchers or they were allowed to choose which diet to follow [77]. People that dieted based on their personal preference on average lost significantly **less** weight than people without a choice. Diet attrition rates were similar between groups.

Clinical psychologists have long known that choice is overrated. Choice of treatment has only a small and inconsistent effect on treatment success in clinical psychology [78]. Difficulty with diet adherence is in essence very similar to many psychological disorders: they're behavioral problems and their solution is to change your behavior. Unfortunately, there can be a substantial difference between what you *prefer* to do and what you *need* to do to improve. People with a strong preference for a certain treatment, such as a diet, may be more inflexible and unwilling to change. Being unwilling to change means being unwilling to improve. If you keep doing what you're currently doing, you'll keep getting the results you're currently getting.

There's a good reason why for diet adherence in particular, choice is even less likely to be beneficial than for behavioral therapy in general. People tend to choose their diets based on which foods they like, not the diet characteristics that are objectively best for their results [79]. If you love eating starches, a high-carb diet may be good for you in the sense that it allows you to keep eating them, but perhaps eating too many starches is exactly your problem. Palatability is a strong determinant of energy intake: people eat more of foods they enjoy. The key to losing weight for you may be in large part to learn to reduce your starch intake, not find ways to keep eating it.

In conclusion, most people don't intuitively know what's best for them and you and me are probably no different. So how then do we decide which macronutrient split to use? You generally shouldn't *decide*. You should find out. Experiment with high- and low-carb meals. Cook different recipes and see where you end up. Focus on making enjoyable meals and then tweak those to ensure you get enough protein and fat without going over your calories. Excessive preoccupation with macros is how many people end up with meals like 1 egg, 270 g of cottage cheese, half an apple and 3 walnuts. That's not a meal and eating like that is no way to live. Focus on food first, macros second. If you really need a new diet experience, a ketogenic diet for at least 2 weeks is an excellent learning experience for many people, as it forces you to prepare new recipes and rethink your food choices, assuming you haven't done a ketogenic diet before. Even if you hate going low-carb despite giving it an honest try, that's highly valuable knowledge. Learning how to be lean year-round is a self-discovery journey. Others can provide you with a map, but you'll have to find your own path.

Diet tip 6: How empty rewards can help us stick to our diet

Artificial sweeteners like aspartame and sucralose (common brand name Splenda) have a bad reputation. Many people fear that zero-calorie products like Coca Cola Zero do more harm than their sugary counterparts. To see if zero-calorie sweeteners sabotage our fat loss efforts, a large team of researchers compared the effects of water vs. water sweetened with zero-calorie artificial sweeteners on weight-related outcomes over a 12-week weight loss period, followed by a 40-week weight maintenance period over a full-year study [80]. Both groups had to consume a minimum of 720 ml of water with or without sweeteners every day. The water group was not allowed to consume sweeteners.

Can you guess what happened? Not only did the artificial sweeteners not sabotage fat loss, the sweetener group lost **more** fat and did not regain as much fat after the weight loss diet. In contrast to what you might expect, the sweetener group was less hungry overall during the diet. Most importantly, they had better dietary compliance (evidently).

Many other studies have established the safety and usefulness of zero-calorie sweeteners. In contrast to the media's fear mongering, there is widespread consensus among official health authorities and research groups that currently available artificial sweeteners like those found in diet sodas are safe for human consumption up to larger amounts than most people would ever consume [81, 82, 83].

However, previous research had generally found that artificial sweeteners are simply neutral: not harmful but not beneficial in any way either. How could allowing use of sweeteners result in better fat loss?

When we become mentally depleted from sticking to our diets and not giving in to our hunger and food cravings, remember that our brains shift our attention to goals that seem to offer more instant gratification. In our current society where food is almost always readily available, that gratification often comes in the form of food. Mental depletion can cause us to eat even when we are not hungry. Sometimes we eat not to satisfy our hunger but to satisfy our brain's need for pleasure. This is where the term 'comfort food' comes from. It's nutritional self-medication, food-form anti-depressants [62].

Therefore, to satisfy our cravings, we do not necessarily have to consume any actual energy. We just need pleasure. Recall that to boost our self-control, a sweet beverage without calories has the same effect as one with actual sugar [84]. In fact, you don't even need to actually drink the beverage for it to improve your self-control: just rinsing it in your mouth can be sufficient [85, 86, 87].

So when you're craving comfort food due to mental fatigue, you can indulge yourself guilt-free with a zero-calorie treat like a diet soda. Coffee and tea also work well. A personal favorite of mine is decaf cappuccino. With skimmed milk, a good milk foamer and sucralose to sweeten it, you can make a big cappuccino with only ~30 kcal in it. A manual milk foamer, the type that looks like a sealed jar with a plunger, works best in my experience. With one of those, you only need about 30 ml of skimmed milk to create a full glass of milk foam. If you're craving something a little sexier, here you can find several of my favorite very-low-calorie snacks: www.MennoHenselmans.com/Zero-Snacks

Diet tip 7: How not taking breaks can break your diet

Have you noticed how much more difficult it is to stick to your diet when you're stressed at work or at school? It's not just preparation. During finals weeks in college, I felt like there was an invisible hand that constantly pushed me towards snacks. I like to pace up and down the room when I'm thinking and somehow my path always crossed with dried fruit or nuts. When you snack like this while working or studying, you barely realize you're eating. I saw the same thing frequently in the office when people had a pack of nuts on their desk: I think I noticed their eating more than they did, but at the end of the day, the pack would be empty.

Snacking like this is the result of mental depletion from the have-to tasks you're doing. This mental depletion can cause us to crave comfort food. However, satisfying this craving doesn't need to involve any food or drinks. The craving is for pleasure in the broadest sense of the word, positive stimulation of the brain. As such, all the productivity breaks we discussed in the previous chapter can satisfy this purpose and satisfy your craving. You're not truly hungry: your brain is just bored. So an effective solution is to reset your mental state with anything restorative or enjoyable: a power nap, a video game, meditation, prayer, a cold shower, a workout or even an imaginary break. See the previous chapter for details and more ideas on productivity breaks.

For dieting, your breaks should be timelier than for productivity. If you get bored with work, you can do something else for 20 minutes and then resume your work afterwards. When dieting, however, you should ideally be a little further ahead of major mental fatigue. When you experience mental fatigue and your attention starts shifting to instant gratification, you're at risk of eating stuff you – your system 2 at least – don't want to eat.

You should especially avoid the level of mental fatigue that basically means full self-control shutdown. You may have experienced this at a party, especially if you had some alcohol. You intended to have only a few bites at the barbeque and have your regular dinner at home afterwards, but after a long day at work, you're hungrier than you thought. You find yourself repeatedly eyeballing the food and may realize you're looking for a justification to eat it. "The meat does have a lot of protein…"
"Carrot cake has carrots in it and those are healthy, right..?"
What's really happening is that your system 2 is constantly overriding system 1's impulse to eat. This is bound to fail at

some point. After you get tired of others telling you to 'live a little', you 'try a bite'. Then you may feel a slight hesitation, a voice in the back of your head. The voice fades and you eat the whole plate, another plate shortly after and then dessert and another drink. I call this the 'fuck it effect'. After a certain level of mental fatigue, your self-control basically fully shuts down and you just eat. No more deliberate decision making takes place. You have no idea of how many calories you're consuming and you exercise almost no self-restraint. Everyone has this point. People with binge eating disorders experience it much sooner than others. It has no effective cure, as with system 2 on sleep mode, you couldn't implement any strategy that would be a cure.

There is but one way to prevent your mind from shifting to food: prevent excessive depletion. Don't let yourself experience major mental fatigue. Learn to realize when it's happening and take a break or have a low-calorie reward from the previous tip.

Diet tip 8: "Don't bind bacon to the cat's back"

Science is the answer to all of life's profound questions. For example, what determines the chocolate snacking behavior of secretaries? We have just the study to answer this [88]. The researchers placed chocolate candies in the office of secretaries at different places and in different bowls for 4 weeks and measured how many were consumed. The results showed a clear pattern. When the candies were placed within arm's reach compared to 2 meters away, the secretaries ate 1.8 times as many candies. When the candies were placed in an open bowl compared to a closed, opaque bowl, the secretaries ate 2.2 times as many candies.

We're much more likely to snack on food when it's visible and easily accessible. For your diet, just like for your productivity, avoiding temptation makes things much easier. It's easier to avoid temptation altogether than to have to suppress it. An ounce of prevention is worth a pound of cure. If there are any high-calorie foods available in your house or workplace, hide them from sight and put them somewhere out of easy reach. And for the love of your abs, never place a bag of nuts on your desk. It's a quadruple-digit calorie-bomb that's bound to be empty by the end of the day.

Food on your kitchen counter is both visible and within easy reach, so you'll be strongly tempted by whatever's there. People in households with junk food visible on the kitchen counter are on average over 30 pounds heavier than people in households with a clean kitchen counter [89]. The easiest solution is to not have any food on your kitchen counter. However, if you struggle to consume enough fruit, you can take advantage of the kitchen counter's prominent position and put fruit there. Any other ready-to-eat food that doesn't spoil outside of the fridge could work too, but most such convenience foods are not very conducive to your health and fat loss.

Even better than hiding your snacks and indulgences is not having them in the house in the first place. If you think about it, many people have food in their house that they don't rationally plan on eating. In the Netherlands they have a saying for this, which we can liberally translate as: "Don't bind bacon to the cat's back." It means you shouldn't tempt people with things they can't have, and this goes in particular for foods in your own diet. All that junk food you bought at some point but aren't planning on eating, throw it away. It's not a waste to throw away food you don't want to eat, because this food has negative value. A temptation-free house will make losing fat much easier.

If you live with family or house mates that don't eat as healthily or lean as you do, you probably cannot just empty all the junk food from the kitchen cupboards. In this case I recommend dividing the cupboards. Get your own private cupboard and use only that one.

At the office, you have to be extra careful. At home you can relax and enjoy yourself, so it's easy to take breaks. At work, your willpower is constantly taxed by engaging in have-to activities rather than want-to activities and your break options are more limited. The most willpower-taxing activities are those with a high 'cognitive load', such as multitasking, making complicated decisions and mathematics [90, 91]. When your brain's system 2 is focused on other stuff, it can't regulate system 1's impulses well anymore. In other words, when your rational rider is occupied, your inner emotional elephant is free to go ape, no pun intended. So to avoid mindless snacking, keep food out of sight and out of reach from wherever you work or study.

During social occasions, you cannot always remove food from your view. Then you should remove your view from the food. Remember the famous Marshmallow Experiment in which children had to delay the gratification of 1 marshmallow to receive 2 later? The successful children used exactly this strategy: they averted their eyes and tried to think about the pleasures of life beyond marshmallows.

Subsequent research on the ability to delay gratification further investigated the children's clues of success [92]. A series of experiments resulted in the following conclusions, starting with the least surprising ones.

1. It's more difficult not to succumb to the temptation of food when it's right in front of you.
2. It's easier to resist the temptation of food when you are distracted.
3. It doesn't matter whether you distract yourself by actively thinking about other things or you are distracted by the environment.
4. Actively thinking about something to distract yourself only works if it's a positive thought and it's not related to food. Saddening thoughts and thinking of food make you *more* likely to give in to immediate gratification. This makes sense from the perspective of eating comfort food as a means of self-medication.

With a little planning, avoiding temptation is often not difficult when you have control of the environment, such as in your own house. Most people experience problems in social situations when they cannot control the environment and there's an incessant temptation of food. Here are 2 tips to deal with temptation in social situations.

First, make sure you have something to snack on or eat. Bringing your own food is ideal, but even just drinking a lot of water or some of the low-calorie snacks I gave you earlier can work very well. When you have something in your hand, you won't be tempted as much to mindlessly grab food with it.

Second, when food you don't want to eat is put right in front of you, actively push it away out of arm's reach. Socially, it may be even better to offer it to people on the other side of the table and, importantly, put it there before they've responded so you can't be rejected. This helps not only to reduce temptation, it also serves as an active psychological affirmation of your rejection of the food.

Diet tip 9: Make a meal plan

Jim wakes up. After having hit the snooze button on his alarm 3 times, he has only 1 hour left to get to work. It's a 45-minute drive, leaving him with just 15 minutes to get up and driving. He wants to eat his regular oatmeal bowl with Greek yogurt, but the bowl's in the dishwasher and he doesn't have time to unload it, so he quickly scavenges through his kitchen cabinet. He finds 2 peanut butter & chocolate bars, so he puts those in his pocket to eat in the car on his way to work.

By lunchtime he's ravenous and he realizes he didn't bring his lean lunch with fruit and chicken breast. There aren't many great options in the cafeteria, he's already behind on his diet's planned protein intake and it's burger day, so he gets a double burger. It turns out his burger is served with French fries on the side. He figures his colleagues will eat those, but they don't. So one by one during lunch hour, he ends up finishing all the French fries as well.

After a long day at work, he comes home. He figured he'd prepare his low-calorie chili dish with lean beef, but he's exhausted. He wants tasty food pronto. There's a good Thai take-away place right around the corner, so he goes there and gets the family box. It's too large, but he figures he'll only eat the meat to get his protein in and then just eat a little bit of the other dishes. He ends up eating the whole box in front of the TV at home. Jim's planned energy intake: 2000 kcal. Jim's actual energy intake: 4000 kcal.

In all the above situations, Jim's primary problem was planning. If Jim had thought about his upcoming meals and prepared them in advance, there likely wouldn't have been a problem. As Benjamin Franklin famously said: "By failing to prepare, you are preparing to fail." Deciding what to eat when you're mentally depleted or hungry is doomed to fail. The solution is already having made the decision earlier when you weren't fatigued yet. If you come home from work, when you already have a meal prepared you can easily reheat, it doesn't matter if you're too exhausted to cook. When you bring your own lunch to work, it doesn't matter if they only serve burgers and French fries.

The best plan is a full meal plan: a complete plan of exactly what you're going to eat and when. This can be as simple as the recipes you eat in a single day that you then eat every day. In research we see meal plans are so effective that they work even when you don't create your own meal plan. Many scientific studies find people on pre-set meal plans have more success restricting their energy intake, lose more fat, achieve better health and are happier than when they have to decide what to eat themselves [93, 94, 95, 96, 97, 98, 99, 100, 101, 102, 103]. Meal plans often beat self-selected diets even when the self-guided dieters receive counseling or support from a nutritionist and even when the meal plans aren't customized to someone's individual preferences. Taking the decisions out of dieting with a concrete plan, even if it's not a very good plan, is overwhelmingly helpful for dieting success.

Concretely, this is the diet success formula.

1. Make one day of the week your meal planning day. Sunday works well for most people.
2. Create a meal plan for the upcoming week, filling in each meal of the week with exactly what you're going to eat. If it's a good plan, you can repeat this plan every week. Don't fix what isn't broken.
3. Create a grocery list and do your shopping for the whole week, if possible.
4. Prepare your meals in bulk. Cook large batches and store whole meals in your fridge or freezer. Tupperware containers come in handy here.

Another less obvious benefit of having a meal plan is that you can often eat without having prepared food. Research finds that people eat more of meals that they prepared themselves right before [104]. In general, thinking about food increases motivation to eat, so ideally we don't want to spend too much time thinking about food that we can't eat right away. If you already had the meal prepared, you can effectively skip the 'food foreplay' and this should help prevent you from overeating.

Even ignoring the enormous diet adherence improvement most people experience from meal planning like this, the time you save alone is already worth it compared to figuring out each day anew what to eat and having to do groceries. Meal plans are efficient, they're effective, they're diettastic.

Don't worry about variety. Variety and flexibility are cool buzzwords, but in practice they often become euphemisms for being disorganized. It's perfectly fine to stick to a narrow selection of meals that you enjoy, as long as they cover all your nutritional requirements. However, if you insist on variety or flexibility, you can build that into your meal plan by having 2 or more options for each meal, rather than just 1. For example, you can create an omelet and a pasta-based meal with the same macros and choose which one you want when it's time to eat the meal. Assuming you consume the same macros on different days, you can also switch meals from different days around. For example, you can switch Monday's and Tuesday's dinners.

If you have trouble getting your meal planning and bulk food prep organized, meal replacement products like protein shakes can be a quick-fix stand-in for more wholesome meals. However, meal replacement products such as Slim-Fast have a poor track record for adherence, though they still often produce better results than diets without meal plans [102, 105, 106, 335]. My experience is that protein bars are almost as bad and people that rely a lot on protein supplements in their diet rarely manage to stay very lean long-term. Nutritionally speaking, many protein bars are no better than a Mars bar with some added protein. The often-added artificial fibers typically do more harm than good for your digestion. Personally, if I eat a Quest bar on an empty stomach, I quickly start to feel like I'm having contractions and there's a protein baby on the way. Plus, even the best protein bars are generally quite caloric compared to how small and unsatiating they are. Many people can eat a whole box of them and still be hungry for more, at least for the ones that don't taste like their second ingredient is rubber. At best, meal replacement products are an acceptable band-aid until you get your meal planning skills up to par to do without them. Ultimately, you'll want to build your physique chiefly on minimally-processed foods.

In conclusion, mental fatigue causes you to make bad decisions, but you can't make a bad decision if you already decided in advance. With a meal plan and bulk food prep, all you have to do is follow the plan you laid out for yourself. The road to success is easy to follow when it's the path of least resistance.

Diet tip 10: Eat in line with your circadian rhythm

Not only should you ideally plan what you're going to eat, you should also plan when to eat it. In the chapter on productivity, we introduced the concept of your biorhythm, an approximately 24-hour activity schedule of your body set by your biological clock. The biorhythm of your physical and cognitive functions generally means it's best to do your most intellectually demanding work in the morning and your workouts in the afternoons or evenings.

Your digestive and metabolic processes also have a pronounced biorhythm. This is why you generally don't have to go to the bathroom for number 2 at night, for example. More importantly, the biorhythm of your metabolism means your body 'expects' food at certain times of day and not others. When your body is not prepared for food, the metabolism of the meal is impaired. Eating out of sync with your biorhythm has been found to result in a multitude of negative effects for your health and wellbeing. While none are major, altogether they can be considerable.

- Higher fasting total and LDL ('bad') cholesterol [107].

- Decreased postprandial insulin sensitivity [107]. When you eat at a time your body is not accustomed to, you produce more insulin than normally.

- A disruption in the circadian rhythm of your appetite leading to more hunger [108, 109].

- A disruption in the circadian rhythm of cortisol ('stress hormone') production and an increase in total cortisol production across the day [110].

- Higher blood pressure [110].

- A lower thermic effect of food (TEF) as a result of decreased insulin sensitivity [109, 111]. When you eat at irregular times, your body burns less of it. In one study the thermic effect of food decreased almost 50% during the 2-week transition from a regular to an irregular meal pattern. That means if your TEF is normally on the high end of 25%, an irregular meal pattern could drop that close to 12.5% and thereby decrease your total daily energy expenditure by 12.5%.

Moreover, skipping meals tends to result in complete energy compensation afterwards [112, 113]. This means that you will be hungry to make up for the decreased energy intake later in the day and often end up consuming the same total amount of energy as if you had eaten the meal anyway, or you go hungry. Hunger puts you at risk for self-control failure, so you risk ending up binging on comfort foods, because you're starving and too fatigued to make a calculated decision about what you're going to eat.

In short, for your health, wellbeing and appetite management it's best to maintain regular meal times. You should eat your meals at roughly the same time of day. People that eat at consistent times and don't snack throughout the day have significantly more success sustaining their weight loss [114]. People that eat and snack whenever they feel like it often end up yoyo-dieting.

You don't have to be anal about your meal times though. You're not going to burst a blood vessel if you eat lunch at 12:10 h instead of 12:00 h one day. Based on the literature and my experience, 2-hour meal windows are strict enough, so if you normally have lunch at noon, any time from 11 AM to 1 PM is perfectly fine.

Eating in sync with your biorhythm is part of the reason why people that eat breakfast are generally leaner than people that don't [115]. However, conventional wisdom got it wrong that 'breakfast is the most important meal of the day'. This is a classic case of mistaking correlation for causation [116]. It's not about whether you **break** your overnight **fast** shortly after awakening or have **breakfast** several hours after awakening. It's about whether your meal timing is consistent. Given the same daily macronutrient intake, a multitude of scientific experiments have demonstrated that breakfast skipping has no negative effect on your body composition compared to always having an early breakfast, as long as you eat your first meal of the day at a consistent time [117].

You can readily experience this yourself. If you're currently eating breakfast regularly, try postponing your breakfast to lunchtime and having 'brunch' instead. You'll probably be hungry in the morning the first few days. If not, that's a good indication you should try an intermittent fasting diet, but even if you were really hungry in the morning at first, once your biorhythm has adjusted to your new meal pattern and meal entrainment has occurred, your morning appetite will largely disappear and you'll instead be hungrier later in the day. In contrast, people that are used to morning intermittent fasting tend to have no problem fasting through the morning hours, yet in the evening they struggle with controlling their appetite.

Diet tip 11: Constant macros

Your brain thrives on routine. While there is no such thing as 'the ideal macro ratio', *changing* the macronutrient composition of your diet can significantly affect brain functioning. In one study, participants were given a lunch consisting of a cheese sandwich and a milkshake [118]. By slightly tweaking the ratios of the ingredients, particularly the amount of cream and maltodextrin, the researchers could significantly change the macronutrient composition of the meal without it being visible and without changing total energy intake. Despite the participants not knowing the lunches varied in macronutrient composition, consuming a lunch meal with a different macronutrient composition than the participants were used to resulted in a worse mood and slower reaction times. The participants reported being more drowsy, uncertain and muddled and less cheerful. Crucially, the detrimental effects were the same for the higher-carbohydrate, lower-fat lunch and the higher-fat, lower-carbohydrate lunch. So it was the deviation from their habitual intake that caused the negative effects, not the macronutrient ratio per se.

A similar study performed at breakfast found no effect on actual cognitive performance, as measured by a battery of mental tests, but it replicated the negative effect on mood state of consuming a meal with a non-normal macronutrient composition [119]. The participants reported being less fatigued when they consumed a breakfast with their habitual macronutrient intake than when they consumed a breakfast with a different carbohydrate-to-fat ratio.

The size of the meal we're used to seems to matter too. One study found that a heavy afternoon meal impaired cognitive performance compared to a light meal in individuals that were used to a light meal but not in individuals that habitually consumed a heavy meal in the afternoon [120]. Consuming a much larger meal than we're used to may slightly impair brain functioning. We might expect based on this study that consuming a smaller than normal meal would have similar detrimental effects on our mind, but that may not be the case if we consider that fasting has minimal acute detrimental effects.

Arguably the highest-quality study in the literature on this topic looked at the effect of switching over from a month on a 41% fat diet to a 25% fat diet for the next month [70]. The diets were carefully controlled to be similarly enjoyable and have the same protein and total energy contents. Indeed, the participants rated the diets as equally enjoyable and satiating. Nonetheless, the group reducing their fat intake experienced a deterioration in their mood compared to the group maintaining the higher fat intake. Switching to the lower fat intake made them slightly more aggressive and hostile. There was also a strong trend for an increase in feelings of depression and a weaker trend for increased anxiety and tension. Importantly, the results were similar for participants regardless of whether the participants believed the diet affected their mood, indicating these results were not a nocebo effect.

Unfortunately, since we have no long-term research of people making the opposite dietary switch – going from a higher to a lower carb diet – we don't know if these negative effects on our mood are an inherent result of low-fat diets or if they're the result of simply not consuming our regular diet. Some other research finds that lipid-lowering drugs increase aggression, suggesting that a high fat intake is beneficial to reduce aggression, but the mechanisms for such an effect are still unclear and the effect may only occur in women [121, 122, 123].

How the brain adapts to your diet's habitual diet composition is still debated. The traditional theory was that deviating from your habitual diet may cause larger than normal fluctuations in blood glucose and insulin levels, but outside of individuals with diabetes and metabolic syndrome, research has not found consistent relations between blood glucose levels and mental performance or mood. Blood glucose levels in healthy individuals are tightly regulated within a very narrow range even after high-carbohydrate meals. Many individuals that complain of alleged low blood sugar levels are actually not hypoglycemic when tested [66].

Modern research points towards a larger role of neurotransmitters. Amino acids are the building blocks of various neurotransmitters in the brain, notably serotonin. Serotonin is the 'liking' neurotransmitter. It makes you feel calm, content and sleepy. Meals causing a larger release of insulin with more of the amino acid tryptophan would theoretically be expected to increase serotonin production and thereby calmness, happiness and drowsiness. However, the evidence for this is again mixed and there is certainly no linear relationship between these variables. The majority of research finds that the macronutrient composition of the diet per se, in healthy individuals used to this diet, does not affect cognitive functioning [67].

Regardless of how or why your brain adapts, changing the macronutrient composition of your diet can make you feel worse. This effect can occur even when you are unaware of it and when you cannot see or smell any difference in the meals you're consuming. Since a poorer mood will hamper your self-control (remember: self-control fails when the brain doesn't experience enough gratification), a stable diet routine is likcly optimal for your wellbeing as well as your diet adherence.

So after you've set up a good meal plan, embrace its routine. Feel free to experiment with different meals, but don't change a winning recipe.

Diet tip 12: Projection bias

A little over 10 years ago, Dan Ariely and George Loewenstein performed a scientific study that would probably never be approved by an ethics committee anymore [124]. The researchers asked a group of men to fill in extensive questionnaires about sex on 2 occasions. Once when not doing anything. Once when jerking off to pornography on their computer. When aroused, the answer to "Can you imagine being attracted to a 12-year-old girl?" went from 23 to almost 50 on a scale of 1 to 100 (1 = no chance, 100 = absolutely yes).

"Would you slip a woman a drug to increase the chance she would have sex with you?" went from 5 to 26.

"Would you keep trying to have sex after your date says 'no'?" went from 20 to almost 50.

In other words, when aroused, the men essentially admitted that the chance they could resist trying to engage in behaviors close to rape and pedophilia was little better than a coin toss. Crucially, the men were unaware their answers changed so much when aroused.

This study doesn't just show that men are pigs. It shows that humans are fundamentally incapable of ignoring their current feelings when trying to predict their future feelings, even if the reason for their current feelings is literally staring them in the face on their computer. We make decisions pretending to know how we act when we're aroused, but when we actually get aroused, we change.

Psychologists call this problem projection bias. We project our current feelings onto the future. We intuitively think we can predict accurately how we'll feel in the future, but our predictions are strongly colored by our current feelings. It is a form of the more general affective forecasting bias, our difficulty in predicting how we'll feel in the future [125]. For example, research has found that our current mood causes us to make systematic errors in predicting how happy we'll be when we receive a certain grade, when the president we voted for wins the election, when we win the lottery or when we lose a limb (the latter two have surprisingly small long-term effects: you can get used to almost anything).

Projection bias is also why smokers so often say they'll quit smoking yet end up lighting a cigarette again that very same day. When we don't feel the urge to smoke right now, we consistently underestimate how badly we'll want to when the craving starts [126]. For our diet, the same principle applies to hunger and food. We systematically underappreciate the effect a ravenous appetite can have on our decision making. And so we overly optimistically put ourselves in positions where we have to resist temptation in the face of hunger. We think we'll be fine at that birthday party. We think we'll be able to stick to our diet at that business lunch. Easier said when satiated than done when starving.

To avoid suffering from projection bias, planning ahead is crucial. I already emphasized the importance of having a meal plan. A paramount piece of advice I'd add to that is: never go grocery shopping when you're hungry. When you're hungry, you're likely to buy stuff that's not conducive to achieving your ideal physique. Let your rational rider do your grocery shopping, not your emotional elephant.

If you have a meal plan and you do all your groceries when you're satiated, you should have a relatively easy time sticking to your diet at home. Things get much trickier when you're out of your own house. When you have a trip or social event coming up, I find it helps to plan ahead in a very specific manner.

1. Think about a time you were extremely hungry: try to emulate exactly how you felt.
2. Now visualize the trip or event in detail. Actively simulate the whole period of time from the

beginning to the end, door-to-door in the case of trips from A to B.

3. Assume the worst: do you foresee yourself easily sticking with your diet? If not, plan ahead. If you're going to a restaurant, check the menu. If you're going to friends, ask what they're making. If you're staying somewhere, check Google Maps for nearby supermarkets. Bring your own food if needed. Make the necessary arrangements for future success now.

4. Make as many possible decisions ahead of time. Are you going to have cake at the birthday party? Are you going to have dessert at the restaurant? Will you eat the snacks served aboard the plane? Making these decisions now when you're not distracted, hungry or fatigued will greatly help you in the moment. Sticking to the default plan is much easier than having to make decisions in a state of decision fatigue.

We'll get to more specific tips for traveling and eating out in restaurants later in the book, but in all cases, the above framework is a crucial starting point for success.

Diet tip 13: Don't try to be a robot

Many people think maintaining a muscular, sixpack lean physique year requires active suffering, an enormous amount of discipline and a rigidly controlled lifestyle. There is truth to this in the sense that a lot of planning, experience and hard work in the gym are invariably required for a person with average genetics to achieve the body of their dreams. However, the idea that successful dieters have a robotically rigid approach to their nutrition is completely wrong. Research finds that flexible control, not rigidity, is predictive of successful fat loss and diet satisfaction [127, 128, 129, 130]. People with a rigid, all-or-nothing mindset often end up yoyo-dieting, regaining any fat they lost [114].

Emphasis on flexible *control*. Flexibility here does not mean you eat whatever you want, whenever you want. Excessive flexibility predicts poor diet adherence [129]. That's how people get fat. They don't have a plan and just eat. In our times of abundance and highly-caloric processed food, our ancestral drive to eat whatever's readily available to prevent starvation can rapidly result in overshooting our energy requirements. Voila, an obesity epidemic.

Research has categorized dietary control into 2 styles: rigid and flexible control [131]. The styles are not necessarily mutually exclusive or even strictly opposites on the same continuum, but they provide a useful framework of thought. Before we can understand the difference between the 2 forms of control, we must first understand the difference between control itself and the attitude towards this control. Control of a diet generally comes in one of the following 2 forms.

1. Restriction of food choices. Paleo diets, for example, typically limit non-paleo foods like dairy and bread.

2. Restriction of macronutrient or calorie intake. You have a schedule to eat X grams of fat, Y grams of carbohydrate and Z grams of protein for the day or per meal, or at least a calorie limit. Weight Watchers is a modified/simplified form of this with 'points' rather than 'calories' that you track, but the principle is the same.

Fully rigid control is characterized by high disinhibition, restraint and dichotomous thinking. This means you see foods outside of your planned diet as 'bad' and other foods as 'good'. You never eat the bad foods, only the good foods. This is an all-or-nothing mindset. If your diet says you can't eat gluten, you also cannot drink normal beer or dip your sushi into soy sauce with trace elements of wheat. If your diet specifies macronutrient targets, you must hit those regardless of whether you have a family dinner, a business lunch or you're having a meal by yourself at home. You must abide by the rules of the diet. No exceptions.

The other mindset has flexible control. With this view, the prescriptions of the diet are seen as guidelines or targets, not do-or-die rules to live by. Disinhibition and restraint are low, meaning you accept 'diet failure' when it just so happens to pan out. For example, research by Smith et al. (1999) found that a successful form of flexible calorie control is to set a daily quota or 'budget' of calories, but when you exceed your target, there is no need to despair or aggressively compensate for it afterwards [127]. You just continue with your diet as planned the next day and focus on the long run.

People with a flexible diet control strategy have been found to be more successful at getting and staying lean than people with a rigid diet control strategy, at least in the long run. Moreover, high dietary restraint is associated with binge eating and eating disorders [128].

As an example of a rigid dieting mindset, one study investigated how not being allowed to eat bread affected diet adherence [132]. Turning bread into a forbidden fruit (no pun intended) increased the diet drop-out rate by over 3-fold compared to an otherwise identical diet with bread on the menu. These results are particularly striking considering bread is not exactly a good fat loss food. Bread is quite caloric and not very satiating, so it's very easy to overeat on bread for most people. Many people have noticed it's easier to get lean when not eating bread, which is the main reason for the whole 'Wheat Belly' craze a few years ago and many people's positive experience with paleo and keto diets. There is 1 crucial difference between these diets and the no-bread diet group: choice. *Choosing* not to eat bread instead of not being *allowed* to eat bread makes all the difference. One is a rigid dieting mindset with poor chances of success. The other is deliberate, goal-directed behavior.

Another example of a rigid control mindset is the 'clean eating' practice of bodybuilders. Many bodybuilders have been taught that their diet for a physique competition should consist of practically nothing but unseasoned white rice, chicken breast, broccoli and oatmeal without dairy. This can be an effective way to keep hunger at bay: you forego the pleasure of eating for the sake of having a simple but effective diet. Food becomes nothing but fuel. In the long run, however, this mindset almost inevitably backfires. Just look at the unhinged binge eating episodes that typically occur shortly after a physique competition. Like most rigid diet control strategies, 'clean eating' has only short-term effectiveness. It is generally only somewhat sustainable as a lifestyle for pro bodybuilders who literally make bodybuilding their life.

The positive findings on flexible control have led many people in the evidence-based fitness community to embrace 'flexible dieting' as the ideal dieting method. While this is certainly a major improvement over the 'clean eating' days, the name 'flexible dieting' misrepresents the underlying psychological science. The flexibility in flexible control refers to the mindset of the dieter, not the diet itself. It is crucial to distinguish between the extent of control in the diet and the individual dieter's attitude towards this control.

- The extent of control is an objective characteristic of the diet: a more controlled diet has a more detailed specification of the macronutrient targets to hit or it limits more food choices.
- In contrast to the objective nature of the diet's restrictions, flexible control refers to someone's subjective attitude towards the diet's restrictions: their dieting mindset.

Psychologically, your mindset is the far more important issue. The relation between restrained eating, rigid control and difficulty with keeping off the weight that you lost is fully mediated by dichotomous thinking [133]. It's not the restrictions of the diet itself but the all-or-nothing approach to dieting and the black-or-white view of food as either 'good' or 'bad' that is the problem. When you can keep the big picture of the diet in perspective, notably long-term energy balance, control is not a bad thing. In fact, if you want to get sixpack lean, a considerable amount of control *will* be required. Not having any food restrictions for yourself is associated with unhealthier food choices and higher self-selected energy intakes [134]. A 2019 systematic review strongly supports that people that don't cut out unhealthy food choices from their diet often have great difficulty maintaining their weight loss [135]. Conversely, fruit and vegetable consumption is strongly predictive of sustainable weight loss. This shouldn't come as a shock to anyone but the most misguided flexible dieting proponents, but healthy diets make fat loss much easier. Some foods are much more diet-friendly than others. The problems arise when dietary control turns into obsession.

A flexible mindset teaches you that your diet is a tool, not the goal. You shouldn't blindly follow your diet when it's not contributing to your goals. For example, many people that 'do flexible dieting' try to hit their daily macros with very high precision. If they haven't hit their macros by the end of the day, they force-feed to make sure they hit their macros. The very point of the diet is to reduce energy intake, so force-feeding is practically always counterproductive in the short term, as it increases energy intake, as well as in the long term, as it reduces your ability to intuitively stop eating when you're full. Similarly, if you always compensate for overeating one day by undereating the next, that is not a flexible control mindset. The flexible solution is, generally, to proceed as planned and focus on the long run. The term flexible dieting puts the emphasis on the diet and this creates the opposite of a flexible control mindset.

Tangentially, excessive focus on the rules instead of the underlying principles to achieve a goal is also the fundamental problem of bureaucracy. We get lost in the system when we start enforcing rules without remembering what they're there for.

You'll also need *psychological* flexibility rather than diet flexibility when things don't go as planned. Life has a way of messing up our neat diet plans. A flexible mindset significantly improves coping success in unfamiliar situations [136]. To adopt a flexible control mindset, here are several concrete tips.

Diet tip 13.1: Failure is a learning experience

Whenever you deviate from your fitness lifestyle, don't focus on its failure. Consider it a learning experience. Reflect on why you failed. What does this teach you that you can change in the future? For example, if you find yourself often skipping workouts after dinner, you may be inclined to think: "I was weak, but I'll put in more effort and tomorrow I'll work out for sure." That's a nice thought, but it's not a plan and more importantly, it doesn't change that you'll end up in this same scenario again in the future. Instead, you should acknowledge that you evidently don't end up working out if you already had dinner. By that time, you're in a rest-and-digest mindset and you just want to relax – remember the section on postprandial somnolence. Thus, you'll probably be better off training straight after work before you've had dinner.

Diet tip 13.2: Adopt a sustainable lifestyle perspective

Think long-term. If you exceeded your planned calorie target for the day, focusing on what you can learn from this is more important than correcting the damage immediately.

Correcting the damage is nice if you can make it work with low effort, but don't let it disrupt your routines, habits and meal plan. If you already prepped food for the coming days, stick with the plan. It's often risky and not worth the effort to revisit the plan. Instead, think of why you ended up overeating and move on. One day of overeating that teaches you how not to overeat in the future is a big win, not a failure.

The use of cardio is also something to consider with a lifestyle perspective. If you rely on cardio to get lean, is it something you enjoy, something you're going to continue doing for the rest of your life? If not, how are you going to stay lean? This goes for everything you do in a fitness lifestyle. Don't think of its short-term use. Think of whether it fits into a sustainable lifestyle.

Diet tip 13.3: View your calories as a budget

Think of your calories as money. You get a certain number of calories every day: your energy expenditure plus/minus your desired energy deficit or surplus. You can spend these calories on foods you like at your discretion, or you can invest in the future by not spending all your calories and achieving some fat loss. Over the long run, you can't keep accumulating debt, as you'd get fat. A good diet that makes you happy involves making smart consumption and investment decisions.

Diet tip 13.4: You don't always have to spend everything

Many people that learned to track their macros fall into this trap: tunnel vision on hitting their macros. It's rarely ever problematic to undereat when your goal is fat loss. If you're full and you got your protein and essential nutrients in for the day, stop eating, at least if you're trying to lose fat. This generally doesn't apply to a bulk where you're trying to put on weight. When you're trying to lose fat, you should take any 'free deficit' you can get. Very few people systematically undereat and if this happens, you'll notice it soon enough and you can correct for it then. Learning to eat intuitively and to stop eating when you're satiated is a strong predictor of diet adherence, maintenance of a lower body fat level and higher wellbeing [137]. Intuitive eating is an even better predictor of diet adherence and wellbeing than a flexible mindset [129]. Force-feeding yourself to hit your daily targets is thus a very bad habit to get into.

Diet tip 13.5: Think outside the lunchbox

When I worked at a client as a business consultant, I always brought my own lunch and it was generally a hot meal, such as the chicken in Asian sweet-sour sauce or the Tex-Mex bowl on my website [138, 139]. Having a big plate of warm food for lunch, especially exotic recipes by Dutch standards, was considered highly irregular, not to say frowned upon, by many of my colleagues. It also required asking the cafeteria staff to heat up my meal without me ordering anything. (Most cafeterias, like hotels, provide mediocre food with above market prices, as they rely on their convenience and you not having any alternative.) Doing these kinds of unconventional things often doesn't feel right. There is something that prevents us from acting out of order, from not fitting in. That feeling is conformism. It's the same feeling why you may be hesitant to eat a full carton of eggs because it's "just too much" and why you may be reluctant to videotape yourself in the gym to evaluate your exercise technique because "what will others think?" Conformism is the feeling that prevents us from deviating from social norms, from being different, even if we have good reason to be different. It is the social glue that turns groups of individuals into a herd.

Do you know that feeling?

Screw that feeling.

Diet tip 14: How to stop food cravings

A successful flexible dieting mindset is not the same as thinking you can eat whatever you want in moderation. To understand why, we have to delve into the psychology of cravings. A food craving is formally defined as "an intense desire to consume a particular food (or type of food) that is difficult to resist" [140]. You just *need* to have those pancakes. Everyone is familiar with cravings and few people doubt the existence of cravings for specific foods.

Why you get food cravings is much more controversial. A common theory is that you crave certain foods because your body registers you need their nutrients. When you're hungry, this theory may sound like a solid argument to give in to your urge to eat that chocolate, but how good is our intuition really at selecting the foods we need?

Sodium deficiency indeed tends to increase our cravings for salty food because salt contains a lot of sodium [141]. However, sodium is an exceptionally tightly controlled micronutrient in the human body and even so, salt cravings are not necessarily indicative of sodium deficiency. For example, men experience more cravings for salty food than women, yet they don't have higher rates of sodium deficiency [142]. In fact, a preference for salty food also commonly results from habitual salt consumption, often leading to not just sufficient but excessive sodium consumption [143]. Sodium deficiency is rare, much more rare than excessive sodium intake in modern societies. So if you experience a craving for French fries, it's quite unlikely that's because your body knows it will thrive on its nutritional value.

Many other micronutrient deficiencies don't affect our appetite at all. In fact, trace mineral deficiencies, such as zinc deficiency, often cause a *loss* of appetite, not an increase [144, 145].

More extreme pathologies also don't support the idea that our cravings are functional. Consider pica, a disorder characterized by cravings for non-food substances such as earth, dirt and ice. While it may seem plausible that these individuals crave these because they contain minerals the individuals are deficient in, the cravings are often for non-nutritive substances that don't contain the micronutrients they're deficient in. For example, iron deficiency can cause ice pica and iron supplementation can help cure this disorder [146]. However, ice doesn't contain appreciable amounts of iron, so the disorder causes a craving for the completely wrong substance. Pica is also commonly associated with mental retardation [147]. So strong cravings for ice – we're talking bricks of frozen water here, not Ben & Jerry's – are probably better thought of as a psychiatric symptom of iron deficiency than an evolutionary adaptive, functional behavior [148]. How about earth pica: is this a more functional craving? Earth contains some minerals after all. Nope. Earth pica is not cured by mineral supplementation [149].

So no, our cravings are generally not caused by some inner sense in our body that knows we nutritionally need these foods. This idea is often nothing more than a rationalization to justify to ourselves why we're allowed to indulge.

Our bodies have not evolved miraculous nutrient sensors attuned to our nutritional status. Our bodies have mostly just evolved to eat whatever's available. We are not very selective. Actually, that's not true. We are selective but in the completely opposite direction of nutritious food: we are wired to prefer high-calorie foods, which in modern times tend to be very low in nutrients. We evolved on whole-food diets that were naturally nutritious. Throughout evolution, there has been little need to crave nutritious foods, because all foods available to us were nutritious. Rather, any evolution that has taken place has generally been in the direction of our body accommodating our environment's food availability, such as the development of lactose, alcohol and wheat tolerance, not our body trying to change our diet. We did not evolve a sophisticated appetite regulation system that allowed us to select foods rich in zinc or molybdenum when needed. We evolved to eat enough of whatever was available to prevent death by starvation.

To see which type of foods we do crave, researchers have developed the Food-Craving Inventory (FCI) [140]. The FCI has uncovered 3 key dimensions of food that make it crave-worthy: a high fat content, a high carbohydrate content and a sweet taste. Cognitive neurosciences confirm that high-carbohydrate, high-fat foods result in the greatest activation of our brain's reward pathways [150]. If you think about it, these findings are obvious. We almost invariably crave crappy foods. When is the last time you heard someone say: "God, I'm just dying for some asparagus right now"?

No, we don't crave nutritious foods. Food manufacturers understand very well what makes our taste receptors tick: lots of fat, lots of carbs, preferably both. Micronutrients don't enter into it.

My father perfectly illustrated this to me when I was a kid. He said it's easy to make tasty food. The true art of good cooking lies in making **low-calorie** food tasty. He then instructed me to mix chocolate flakes with a chunk of butter and cover it in sugar. Voila, that's all the cooking you need to make tasty food.

Put simply, we crave tasty food. That's why everyone craves the same foods. It's always highly palatable and energy-dense food that is rich in carbs or fat, usually both, and the food is almost always sweet or salty; rarely sour, bitter or umami. You simply like certain foods better than others and you want to eat what you like. No mystery, no magical fix.

In line with this sobering idea of food cravings, science refutes the idea that we can become addicted to particular foods. You can become addicted to the behavior of eating itself, but you cannot become addicted to a particular type of food or even macronutrient [62, 151]. Classical drug addiction syndrome is a pharmacological effect characterized by 3 aspects [152]:

1. Compulsion to seek and take the drug.
2. Loss of control in limiting intake.
3. Emergence of a negative emotional state (dysphoria, anxiety, irritability, etc.) reflecting motivational withdrawal syndrome when access to the drug is prevented.

These effects occur because the drug in question, such as cocaine, sensitizes dopamine pathways in the brain (amongst other effects). Dopamine is the neurotransmitter responsible for the feeling of 'wanting'. The result of this change in brain chemistry is that you develop a strong desire to take the drug and you feel poorly without it. Food doesn't have this effect, or at least any similar effect is trivial compared to that of addictive drugs.

And yes, this includes chocolate. Chocolate addiction is a myth. In scientific experiments, researchers have cleverly manipulated pieces of dark and white chocolate, cacao capsules and placebos to ascertain whether it's the actual chemicals in chocolate, like polyphenols, or just the taste of chocolate that we crave. Cacao capsules or enriching white chocolate with all the pharmacologically active compounds in chocolate had no effect on the sensation of chocolate craving [153]. Only chocolate that looked and tasted like dark chocolate could satisfy people's chocolate cravings. This demonstrates there are no inherently addictive compounds in chocolate. People just like eating chocolate.

And yes, even chocolate cravings during pregnancy seem to be an entirely psychological effect. Research has found no support for a role of hormonal changes or nutritional deficiencies during pregnancy on food cravings [154]. The severity and frequency of food cravings does not correlate with estradiol or progesterone concentrations. Moreover, the foods that women crave are generally not at all rich in the nutrients whose requirements increase during pregnancy. For example, protein requirements increase significantly during pregnancy, yet high protein foods like meat are among the most common food aversions during pregnancy. Most pregnant women just crave the same junk foods we all like.

Similarly, peri-menstrual chocolate cravings are not hormonally driven [155]. They're a cultural phenomenon that exists almost exclusively in North America, not in many other countries like Spain [156]. If you'd tell someone from Spain that your menstrual cycle gives you chocolate cravings, they'd probably look at you like you're loco loco, chica.

Rather, scientists have concluded that pregnancy seems to function as a good excuse to indulge in tasty and highly-caloric foods, because weight gain during pregnancy is deemed socially acceptable, even suggestive of being a good mother sometimes. The specific foods that are craved are largely culturally determined. In the US, pregnant women typically crave sweets and chocolate, yet in Egypt chocolate cravings are almost unheard of. In Japan, pregnant women typically crave rice, whereas Indo-Ceylon women commonly develop an aversion to rice during pregnancy, because it supposedly reminds them of housework. Nigerian mothers-in-the-making tend to crave fruit, vegetables and cereals, because they believe this is good for them. Interestingly, pregnant Tanzanian women most commonly crave meat, fish, vegetables, fruit and grains. The World Health Organization would be proud of them. Unsurprisingly based on these cultural differences in cravings, American women gain much more weight during pregnancy than women in most other cultures [154].

The whole idea of food cravings and addiction are very much a North American construct: 83% of languages do not even have a word for 'craving' and many do not have a word for 'addiction' either outside of the narrow referral to pharmaceutical drugs [157].

The reason many languages don't need words for 'craving' or 'addiction' is that there is no objective underlying physiological process that takes place during the experience of food cravings or supposed food addiction. They are self-created concepts in the brain, triggered by sociocultural cues from the environment. Specifically, the idea of a craving tends to start with actual hunger, causing a desire for food. This general desire for food then takes the form of specific foods when certain food representations in the brain are triggered [158]. This food's representation in the brain can be triggered directly by sensory input of the food – you see or smell the food – but it can also be triggered more indirectly by an advertisement, talking about the food or even just thinking about the food.

You've probably experienced this yourself. As you're walking through a street, the smell of bread gets your attention. You look to see where the smell comes from and the pastries and cakes in the window look incredible. Suddenly you're hungry and you have 'a craving'. This craving may haunt you for some time afterwards as it stays active in your memory.

The knowledge that food cravings are entirely in our mind means we should investigate our psychology, not physiology, to rid ourselves of food cravings. Common wisdom says that you get rid of a craving by satisfying it. Common wisdom is wrong. If you want to get rid of a craving, you don't satisfy it. You kill it. Specifically, you starve it. Let me explain.

A craving is born when 2 forces meet to conceive it. Hunger is the craving's mother, the egg waiting to be fertilized. The craving's father is a passer-by, some food cue that fertilizes the hunger and gives it form and direction. To prevent cravings, we need to address both forces that give rise to it: the hunger and the food cues.

Hunger during dieting is strongly associated with cravings, unsurprisingly, as it is the fundamental cause of all desire for food. Cravings increase when you're hungry and decrease when you're full [159]. So successfully starving a craving requires consuming a diet that is sufficiently satiating. For example, late night snacking and binge eating can be countered successfully by consuming a satiating meal at night [160]. Even bariatric surgery to reduce your stomach size reduces food cravings, because it reduces your appetite [161].

While appetite management is very effective to reduce food cravings, it alone does not always help get rid of cravings completely, because cravings are driven not just by physical hunger but also by a psychological desire for pleasure. This brings us to the second cause of cravings: food cues.

After a certain food representation has been activated in your brain because you started thinking about it, it's effectively a memory. You can't crave food you don't remember. As a digital nomad, I've lived in over 50 countries and my diet varies greatly in each location as different foods are available. For example, in South American countries, I experience food cravings for many plantain and cassava dishes, but in many North European and Asian countries, these foods are a rare sight. As a result, I often forget they exist and I never crave them. I'm no exception. Food cravings are highly correlated with exposure to the food. While most modern cultures mainly crave junk foods, different cultures vary strongly in which specific foods they crave based on which foods they're most exposed to [142].

As such, getting rid of a food craving is similar to getting rid of a memory. This poses a problem. Let's say you have a craving for pizza. Actively thinking about having pizza will only strengthen the memory, yet 'not thinking about pizza' isn't going to work. Think of the classic example of trying to not think about a pink elephant. Of course, you now immediately thought about a pink elephant. Our brains are incapable of conscious ignorance. So what do you do? Research has found 2 cognitive therapies or 'brain tricks' that you can employ.

Diet tip 14.1: Mindfulness training

The first successful method of coping with a craving is mindfulness training [162, 163, 164, 165]. Mindfulness comes down to acceptance of the food craving without acting on it. Whenever you get a major food craving, take a moment to reflect and realize that you have the craving. Then accept the craving for what it is, a tasty food you want to eat that has been triggered in your memory. Then move on with your day. The craving is just a feeling. You don't need to act on it.

Mindfulness effectively mobilizes our rational rider, our brain's system 2. Being in a mindset of objective observation reduces the influence of system 1, our inner impulsive elephant.

Diet tip 14.2: Episodic future thinking

Dr. Dan Gilbert proposed that one of the defining features of humanity is our ability to simulate the future. Imagining different scenarios helps us make better long-term choices. We can also use this ability to cope with acute food cravings. In cognitive behavioral therapy, this strategy is called episodic future thinking (EFT) [166]. EFT is thinking about the future in a very specific manner: you visualize yourself in a hypothetical future scenario and experience what it's like. You 'sample' the future. By virtually experiencing the future, you make it more visceral and you engage system 1, which otherwise has no concept of hypothetical future events. If system 1 'enjoys' the simulation, it takes less effort to override its desire for immediate gratification. Loading your visual memory reduces food cravings and EFT helps people make smarter long-term food choices with fewer calories [57, 167, 168].

Concretely, in the case of a food craving, you should actively and intensely visualize eating a meal other than what you're craving that will satisfy your hunger. It generally works well to think of the next planned meal that you really like or a close substitute of the craved food that can displace the craving.

For example, let's say you're at work in the office and somebody brought a chocolate birthday cake. To implement episodic future thinking, you can visualize eating the lean Tex-Mex bowl of awesomeness on my website that you planned to eat tonight [57]. Think of how you're going to enjoy this meal and how much better it is for your physique and health than the chocolate junk.

The best meal to visualize is what economists call a dominant option. A dominant option is an option that is superior to another choice in all regards. For food you rarely have a truly dominant option that is also lower in calories as well as more nutritious, but many options can come close. Here are some options of foods that have good lean alternatives.

- Cheesecake: for a single slice of typical cheesecake calorie bomb, you can eat a whole lot of the low-calorie, high-protein cheesecake on my website [169].
- Ice cream: you can make frozen yogurt or protein ice cream recipes that are really good while having a fraction of the calories.
- Pasta and noodles: glucomannan 'miracle' noodles and zoodles (spiralized zucchini) give a similar texture for literally less than a tenth of the calories.
- Pizza: you can make great egg white or cauliflower crust pizzas yourself with tastier and lower-calorie cheeses and sauces. This can easily remove two thirds of the calories.
- In general, lower-fat versions of products are often an easy way to save calories. In research, when people eat a full-fat vs. a low-fat lunch without knowing which, they can't tell the difference [170]. While you can probably taste the difference between full-fat and zero fat options, you can easily save a lot of calories by going for low-fat options.

Crucially, all scientifically successful therapies to deal with cravings share the common trait that they do not involve giving in to your cravings. They do not feed the craving. They starve it.

The forbidden fruit effect

You may wonder: won't restricting the craved foods result in a 'forbidden fruit effect' where you only end up craving the foods even more? A study from the University of Vermont sought to address this question [171]. They compared a relatively moderate 1100-Calorie diet which allowed all foods in moderation to an aggressive 400-Calorie protein-sparing modified fast with practically nothing but lean protein foods in the diet. Common wisdom would predict the aggressive diet group would go mad with cravings due to the enormous restriction of their diet. In reality, cravings greatly decreased during both diets with a trend for *better* craving management in the aggressive diet group, especially for high-protein and high-carbohydrate foods. "There was no evidence to support the belief that restricting intake of certain foods leads to increased craving for these foods or that the magnitude of weight loss is related to food cravings."

A different study on the effect of a 1200-Calorie diet vs. an 800-Calorie liquid diet confirmed these findings [172]. Throughout the entire course of the 3-month diet, the 800-Calorie group experienced consistently greater decreases in cravings. Moreover, this study included a 5-week refeeding period to check for how lasting the effects were. The lower cravings in the aggressive diet group persisted without any rebound effect when they resumed solid food consumption.

Other research confirms that consuming craved foods less frequently decreases your cravings for these foods and restricted dieting can be a very effective method to reduce cravings [173, 174]. Crucially, only the frequency of consumption, not the amount of consumption, influences cravings. It doesn't matter if you give in to your cravings a little bit or a lot. The event reinforces the presence of the craved food in your memory all the same. So portion control does not reduce cravings. You have to stop consuming the foods you crave or at least reduce their frequency of consumption. In support of this, research that compares successful and unsuccessful dieters finds that a key characteristic of successful weight loss is not giving in to your cravings [159].

The theory that giving in to a craving will satisfy it and get rid of it has never been more than wishful thinking. It's like when you're really hungover and you proclaim you'll never have alcohol again. Those resolutions only last as long as your feelings, and feelings are fleeting. After you've eaten a double Happy Meal, you may feel like you have profoundly satisfied your craving for McDonald's, but this feeling lasts about as long as your fullness. The next day, or maybe even a couple hours later already, when your hunger returns, so does the craving.

Instead, several scientific studies have found that successful weight loss diets reduce cravings by "reduction to exposure to the palatable foods that evoke craving", including a 95-participant 6-month study performed at 4 different locations [175, 176].

However, the forbidden fruit effect is not a myth. Viewing foods as 'forbidden' can increase cravings for them and result in binge eating [177]. For example, needlessly restricting chocolate consumption *without a corresponding diet* can increase chocolate cravings [178]. Prohibiting bread from weight loss diets has also been found to make diet adherence more difficult and to result in study drop-outs [132].

The essence of the forbidden fruit effect lies in its name: forbidding a food. If you feel like you can't eat a certain food against your will, you'll probably only want it more. However, if you *decide* that a certain food is not worth it for you, over time you'll lose your cravings for it. You should always keep in mind that food restriction is a form of control that serves a purpose. The mindset of thinking of "Chocolate is bad. I can never eat chocolate again" is excessively rigid and will probably backfire. You should instead think: "It's not worth it for me to fit high-calorie chocolate into my limited calorie budget during this period." As long as you keep in mind that not eating the food is a conscious choice on your end, you won't create any forbidden fruits. The food is not forbidden. It's just not worth it.

Diet tip 14.3: How to teach yourself to like healthy, low-calorie foods

In terms of evolutionary psychology, it makes perfect sense that we stop craving foods we rarely eat. Our sense of taste adapts to the food available in our environment. Let's pretend you're a hunter-gatherer from our evolutionary past. You live in an area where the only available meat is rabbit. Then you better learn to like rabbit. You're not exactly in a position to go: "No, thanks, I'm more of a steak person." Yet when you now do get access to steak, rabbit quickly becomes less palatable.

Concretely, your liking for salty and sweet foods is influenced by how much you eat them [179, 180], though one study found that only the intensity but not the pleasantness of sugar was affected by how much sugar people consumed [181].

This isn't just a case of people with a genetic disposition for a sweet tooth eating more sugar. Your preference for sweet foods can grow over time with increased sugar consumption and your preference is not always correlated with your ability to taste sweetness [180, 182]. Also, former weight loss dieters have been found to have a reduced sweet tooth compared to non-dieting individuals [179]. Think of coffee: if you learn to drink it black, you may be disgusted by coffee with sugar. Yet if you normally drink it sweetened, black coffee becomes 'ugh, bitter'. Same for chocolate and tea. That's exactly why we say some things have an acquired taste: most people do not naturally like them. You only learn to appreciate them if you consume them frequently enough. This particularly goes for alcohol, but in fact, familiarity significantly increases our liking for just about anything, including objects and people. This phenomenon has been called the mere exposure effect: we generally like things more after we've been exposed to them a few times [183].

For food, psychophysics has come very close in predicting exactly how we perceive taste. Our sense of taste and thereby how pleasant we find food follows a range-frequency model [184, 185]. Range-frequency theory (RTF) explains how we perceive magnitude, such as how large a person appears, how painful a set of squats is or how much money $5 is. Without going into the mathematics, which are needlessly complicated (but profoundly awesome if you're interested in psychophysics), RFT shows that we rate magnitudes as their rank order in a comparable reference set from our memory. The key point is we don't perceive magnitude directly but rather we see it relative to our mental comparison set. We have no scale in our head that measures sweetness: we just know when something tastes sweeter or less sweet than other things we've tasted in our memory. Since human memory is fallible and finite, we don't remember everything we've ever tasted, mostly just the recent foods we've eaten (the recency effect) [186]. Thus, how we perceive a food's taste is strongly affected by what we ate before it, and which other foods are in our diet. Your habitual diet changes your perception of taste: it becomes the reference by which you perceive any new taste.

Your regular diet's effect on your sense of taste goes deep. It's not just the experience of taste or even the pleasantness of the food but also how rewarding your brain perceives the food to be. Low-calorie diets have been found to increase the activation of the brain's reward circuitry in response to low-calorie food consumption; at the same time, the sensation of reward from high-calorie foods decreases [187, 188]. Correspondingly, diets with a low energy density also decrease your liking and wanting for energy dense foods [189]. In other words, the more you eat healthy and low-calorie foods, the more you'll get to like them and the less you'll miss higher-calorie alternatives. You can learn to like vegetables and become disgusted with McDonald's.

You may have experienced the effect of your habitual diet on your sense of taste yourself. Most of my clients live a healthy lifestyle and are used to eating minimally-processed whole foods. Almost all of them love the high-protein cheesecake recipe on my website [169]. However, individuals with a more conventional modern Western diet (read: people that eat like crap and therefore tend to become overweight) have found the cheesecake a bit lackluster. Their frame of reference is real cheesecake with 3 times the calorics, not Greek yogurt. The same goes for almost all light or healthier versions of commonly liked high-calorie dishes. You can learn to love them and not feel deprived of the real thing at all. Unless you're still eating the real thing.

As a personal example, in the Netherlands we have the world's best peanut butter: Calvé crunchy peanut butter. People that say taste is subjective and there's no objectively best peanut butter yada yada have simply not tried Calvé. *Note to self: get an affiliate deal for Calvé crunchy peanut butter before I publish this book.*

In any case, Calvé peanut butter isn't the healthiest unfortunately. It has added sugars and fats, even the notorious artificial trans-fat, or at least it used to when I still ate it. Therefore, I decided I should switch to 100% natural peanut butter with no ingredients other than peanuts and salt. I didn't like it much at first, especially not the texture with the semi-separated oil, but I grew to love it. Several months later I stayed at my parents' house for a while and they only had Calvé peanut butter. I wasn't going to buy a whole new jar, so I used the Calvé. At first it tasted off, very 'unnatural'. But once I had eaten it a few times, I loved it again. When I went home and tried 100% natural peanut butter, I didn't like it anymore and it took a week to appreciate the more 'natural' taste again.

More generally, if you always eat a certain selection of healthy, low-calorie foods, your liking for these foods increases [189, 190]. You grow to like the type of food you regularly eat [191]. Moreover, the activation of brain reward pathways in response to seeing high-calorie foods decreases during a weight loss diet without these foods and your cravings for food you never eat disappear [189, 192, 193]. In general, when you stop consuming a particular kind of food, you stop liking its taste, you find the food less pleasant to eat and even your brain's reward activation decreases when you do eat it. Eventually, the food disappears from your active memory, your mind's internal menu, just like words disappear from your active vocabulary when you stop using them. And so the craving disappears. Starving your cravings is thus not only a very effective way to get rid of them, it can also *increase* your overall diet enjoyment.

As an illustration of how your taste and cravings are affected by your diet, a 2-year study compared the effects of a high- vs. a low-carbohydrate diet [191]. Importantly, people were randomly assigned to one diet: they could not choose themselves. The high-fat, low-carbohydrate group developed a preference for higher-fat foods and experienced fewer cravings for high-carbohydrate foods. The high-carbohydrate, low-fat group experienced exactly the opposite: they developed a preference for high-carbohydrate foods and experienced fewer cravings for high-fat foods.

These findings may explain why we see such a polarization of low- vs. high-carbohydrate diets. When people try either diet approach, they come to like it and no longer see the appeal of the other approach. As a result, people form into camps, pro-carb vs. anti-carb, and both groups' experiences confirm their own beliefs.

In short, we like what we eat and we crave what we like, so we crave what we eat. If you have an undesirable food craving, be mindful that the craving is just a form of hunger given the shape of food by some trigger in your brain (mindfulness and acceptance training). Look for a better option to satisfy your hunger and visualize yourself eating it (episodic future thinking). Once you've coped with a few cravings without acting on them, things get much easier. By starving your cravings and eating healthier, lower-calorie foods that you can sustainably eat as much as you want of, your whole sense of taste and food enjoyment will change. You will develop a liking for whole foods, perhaps even start craving them, and you will no longer miss the higher-calorie foods you once craved. Starve your cravings; nourish your body.

Diet tip 15: How to cheat your diet

Cheat meals are commonly thought to keep cravings in check, but based on the psychology of food cravings, you should now understand that the opposite is often true. Cheat meals are often the very trigger that cause your cravings. By overeating on high-calorie foods that you don't normally consume in your diet – let's define this as a cheat meal for now – you activate its representation in your memory, you develop a further liking for its taste and your brain's reward activation from eating it increases. The next time you get hungry, this can manifest as a craving for the foods you had with your cheat meal. For example, indulging in your chocolate cravings has been shown to increase subsequent chocolate cravings [194]. Feeding a craving makes it stronger.

Think about which foods you sometimes crave. We already established there is a huge cultural component to this. How did you develop the craving for this food? By eating it. You don't crave foods you've never eaten. Indeed, there is a significant correlation between how often people consume a particular food and how often they crave it; moreover, changing how frequently you consume a certain food changes how often you crave it [173, 195]. Every time you have French fries, you activate its representation in your memory, making French fries more salient in your memory. The next time you get hungry and you think about food, French fries are more likely to pop up in your mind. And so a craving is born.

Crucially, there isn't much of a correlation between the *amount* of food eaten and the strength of your cravings for it [173]. Going to Burger King more often will probably make you crave burgers more often, but it doesn't matter if you had the small or the extra-large burger. When you eat a meal, the food's representation in your mind is activated, regardless of its serving size.

Knowing that portion size control doesn't help reduce cravings has a profound implication for successful dieting. 'Everything in moderation' may not be such a good idea. Indeed, we saw this in 2 of the studies mentioned earlier. The study by Harvey et al. (1993) compared a "balanced low-calorie diet" in which everything was allowed in moderation with a more aggressive and restricted diet consisting of almost nothing but protein. The more restricted diet group lost weight faster while the more moderate diet group suffered more from cravings [171]. Martin et al. (2006) compared a regular, balanced low-calorie diet with an "extremely restrictive" diet consisting of nothing but meal-replacement shakes and bars. Again, the more restricted diet group lost weight faster and experienced a greater reduction in cravings [172].

Inducing cravings and worsening your food preferences aren't the only problems with having a cheat meal. Using food as a reward teaches you to consume that food when you experience emotional stress [196]. Normally, stress does not make you eat more, because stress suppresses your appetite [197]. Self-medicating your sorrows away with comfort foods is not a biological reaction to negative mood states. It's a learned behavior, a bad relationship with food. Unfortunately, the common practice of parents trying to cheer their children up with candy when the children feel sad is probably setting the children up for an unhealthy relationship with food. Cheat foods become comfort foods. Guess what happens when the dieting gets hard? You turn to the comfort food. This is fundamentally toxic to lifestyle change and it is probably why people self-report that processed foods are more addictive than whole foods: they have become comfort foods [198]. Changing your lifestyle can be hard. It requires self-control, which can induce mental depletion and negative feelings. These negative feelings can lead you to consume comfort foods, which then trigger cravings, which make dieting even harder, and so you can enter a negative spiral ending in obesity and unhappiness.

In sum, cheat meals come with several psychological problems.

- Cheat meals can change your taste perception, making other foods in your diet less tasty.
- Cheat meals can induce a forbidden fruit effect and cravings for the consumed foods.
- Cheat meals can turn into comfort foods that you're prone to self-medicate on when you feel poorly.

Certain people, often those that become obese, are particularly prone to the dangers of cheat meals. A subset of the population experiences an increase in neural sensitization and behavioral reinforcement when consuming cheat meals (snacks), which is essentially a light version of what happens in the brain when you take cocaine or other addictive drugs [199].

Unsurprisingly based on the above problems, people with cheat days in their diet are less successful at losing weight and, more importantly, keeping it off than those who focus on consistent lifestyle change. Diet consistency is strongly predictive of successful weight loss maintenance [200, 201, 202]. On average, people with a consistent diet across the week are 1.5 times more likely to maintain their weight loss than people who eat differently in the weekends, even if they compensate by dieting more strictly during the midweek.

Furthermore, most people who have successfully lost weight and kept it off have learned to avoid certain foods in their diet, as opposed to learning how to fit them into their macros [203].

At this point, you may be wondering: "Hey! I thought you were going to teach me how to have unlimited cake? I want to get ripped eating ice cream and chocolate! Can't I have cheat meals?" Many people will be happy to sell you what you *want* to hear, but I will tell you what you *need* to hear. Going without any cheat meals is certainly not a bad idea. In fact, it may very well be in your best interest, even if you don't want to hear it. That said, fortunately, getting and staying lean doesn't require living like a monk. Here are concrete tips to have your cake and eat it too.

Diet tip 15.1: IIFYM

"If it fits your macros" (IIFYM) has become a go-to response on bodybuilding message boards in response to the question: "Can I eat food X?" Due to the 'clean eating' mentality in traditional bodybuilding circles, it was common for bodybuilders to ask which foods they could eat: which foods are 'clean' (read: good for fat loss). However, research over the past decades has conclusively demonstrated that getting lean is primarily a matter of energy balance, not food choices. As we discussed before, physics dictates that expending more energy than you consume requires the body to lose energy. It doesn't matter if your diet consists of Twinkies and burgers or broccoli and chicken breast: as long as you're in an energy deficit, you'll lose energy. Normally, your body will primarily burn off fat rather than lean body mass to make up the energy deficit. It's theoretically possible to only lose muscle and no fat, but this in practice only occurs during muscle wasting diseases. In any case, which tissue your body burns for energy is largely determined by your activity level, not the composition of your cheat meals.

One other nuance I'll ignore here is that different food choices can differentially affect your energy expenditure and energy intake. Not all energy is absorbed. Dietary fiber in particular is often only partly absorbed into the body and can largely pass through the body undigested. Moreover, different foods have a different thermic effect in the body. Certain foods, like fish and coconut oil, require more energy to absorb, digest, burn or store than others, like butter. However, in the practical context of 2 diets with the same macronutrient composition that both implement all the advice from this book, it's safe to assume that any difference in energy balance will be no more than a few percent.

With the above caveats in mind, we can say that the composition of a cheat meal is largely irrelevant for its effect on your fat loss and only its energy content really matters. As such, if you fit a meal into your diet's calorie budget, whether it's ice cream, McDonald's or nasi goreng, it's not really a cheat meal. It may not be ideal for your health, but it won't acutely hinder fat loss. For example, in a study on diabetics, allowing up to 10% room for sugary sweets to be fit in their calories did not harm diet adherence or health markers [204].

So if you really want to have a certain 'cheat meal', fit it into your macros and you can enjoy it guilt-free. Just keep in mind the potential psychological side-effects.

Diet tip 15.2: Think about food like an economist

I often tell my clients to think of their planned energy intake as a 'calorie budget' that they can spend on foods. This is not only a useful analogy for the IIFYM-principle, it also gets them in the mindset of an economist. An economist makes any decision based on a cost-benefit analysis. This requires mindfulness and deliberation, which we have previously seen can help you cope with food cravings. Later in this book I'll discuss many more benefits of mindfulness, but for now, it's good to realize that from a purely rational perspective, a certain food is either worth it or it's not. Either its benefits outweigh its costs or they don't. You analyze its macros, health benefits, satiety index, etc. and thereby determine its value (utility, as economists call it). If the value is high compared to other foods, you fit it into your macros. If not, you don't.

Importantly, in this cost-benefit analysis you should consider not just the physical qualities of the food but also the psychological costs of consuming foods that aren't part of your habitual diet, such as inducing cravings and comfort food and changing your taste perception.

So at any time, a rational person should eat only a certain selection of worth-it-foods and never eat other not-worth-it-foods. While the perfectly rational 'homo economicus' is a myth, in this case economics and psychology converge in the conclusion that you should carefully consider which foods you make a part of your diet.

Thinking like an economist may seem to conflict with the idea of IIFYM and having a flexible dieting mindset. There are important nuances here. IIFYM only considers physics, not psychology. While having a scoop of Ben & Jerry's ice cream every day can absolutely be fit into your macros without physically impairing your fat loss, in practice it may not be in your best interest to have a tub of Ben & Jerry's waiting for you in the freezer all the time. There is likely to come a time when 1 scoop doesn't satisfy you, or maybe you come home exhausted after work and your self-control is inadequate to make the decision to eat something else. An imminent ice cream binge will obviously hinder fat loss. While the mechanism by which binging on ice cream will impair your fat loss is 'simply energy intake', the fact is that you may have been better off not having made Ben & Jerry's a part of your diet. In theory, as long as you keep total energy intake in check, cheat meals won't harm fat loss, but in practice, for every ripped YouTuber you see eating ice cream, there are a thousand fat people wondering why they've never been able to see their abs.

IIFYM is a theoretical principle to illustrate the paramount importance of energy intake in the grand scheme of dieting. For a successful diet, you should not just think about this day's energy intake but rather your energy intake in your overall lifestyle. For that reason, I don't like to use the

IIFYM acronym. Rather than think 'if it fits my macros', I recommend you think: 'if it fits my lifestyle'. This emphasizes the importance of long-term sustainability. It also makes the principle applicable to *ad libitum* diets that don't have set macronutrient or calorie targets.

So while it's all fine and dandy that you can fit some candy into your macros without it impairing your results and there is strictly speaking no such thing as 'unhealthy food', you should think about which foods you deem worth fitting into your calorie budget. Such a mindset with restricted food choice permissions is associated with lower energy intake and healthier diets [134].

Remember it's a choice. Not being *allowed* to eat a certain food can increase cravings and feelings of deprivation, so you should remember that you're not eating certain high-calorie foods because you don't *want* to [205]. You *can* eat the not-worth-it foods, but it's in your own best interest not to, so you should *decide* not to eat them.

Not only does this mindset foster self-efficacy, from a psychological perspective it can be helpful to associate good things with low calorie food and bad things with high calorie foods [206, 207]. The power of association is harnessed by many diets, such as the paleo diet ('paleo =

good, non-paleo = bad'), the Atkins diet ('high carb = bad, rest = good') and clean eating in bodybuilding. These diets can be very effective in the short term. The problem is that all too often these diets ignore the reality of energy balance and people focus excessively on the rules of the diet rather than energy intake. It doesn't matter if you have no carbs in your diet: eat enough bacon and you will get fat. It doesn't matter if that cookie is 100% paleo: it's still 400 Calories. By maintaining a flexible control mindset and focusing on what primarily matters in the diet – energy intake over time – you can have a useful frame of reference for which foods to eat without becoming dogmatic. Thinking in terms of 'good' and 'bad' food can easily result in obsession and missing the forest for the trees, but building a reference of foods that are 'worth it' and 'not worth it' can help you be consistent and build food choice habits that are healthy in every sense of the word.

Diet tip 15.3: Learn to prepare low-calorie comfort foods

Recall that cheat meals don't just induce cravings. They also risk becoming comfort foods that you turn to when you feel stressed or depressed. Fortunately, comfort food doesn't have to be fattening. With a little creativity, you can make delicious foods that are very low in calories.

Remember the low-calorie snacks from the productivity chapter, for example. On my website's recipe section, you'll find more tasty, fat loss-friendly comfort foods such as the following cheesecake.

www.MennoHenselmans.com/Category/Recipes

Learning to cook is a skill that will immensely benefit you for the rest of your life.

Diet tip 15.4: How to fit indulgent cheat meals into your lifestyle

Some cheat meals just cannot be fit into your macros or daily calorie budget. Social events with a lot of alcohol, all-you-can-eat buffets and massive birthday cakes often have more calories by themselves than your entire daily energy expenditure. You may still be able to fit these kinds of cheat meals into your lifestyle, but it requires some deliberation.

Let's consider the scenario in which you consume more calories than planned by eating more of the food than you planned to eat. Is this ok? The essence of a flexible mindset is that overeating is entirely up to your discretion. Overeating will inherently reduce your fat loss progress. Your diet should be at a certain energy intake that corresponds with a certain energy balance that results in the desired rate of fat loss. Eating more than this planned energy intake will thus necessarily reduce how much energy you lose from your body. This is fundamental physics, thermodynamics: the energy balance principle. But it is up to you personally to decide whether this is worth it: the choice is up to you, not the diet.

To make the decision on whether it's worth it, you must weigh the number of calories you overeat by (the cost) against the pleasure of the cheat meal (the benefit). If you think this pizza is worth going over your calorie budget for by 1000 Calories, eat the pizza. Just keep in mind that if you want to reach a certain level of leanness, those 1000

Calories will have to come off again at some point. (In fact, due to the greater metabolic downregulation in negative energy balance than the upregulation in positive energy surplus, you'll have to undereat by a bit more than what you overate by to achieve the same net energy balance, so you'll have to reduce energy intake by more than 1000 Calories in the coming period to achieve the same net energy deficit.)

If you've made the mindful decision to fit a cheat meal into your week that cannot be fit into your daily macros, you can compensate for this by reducing energy intake in the surrounding day(s). This way, even though you may have overeaten one day, over the course of the week you can still achieve your desired state of energy balance.

However, many people intuitively compensate for such cheat meals in a very counterproductive manner. Say you've got a big family holiday dinner coming up with multiple courses of highly-caloric dishes. For most people, such a meal will result in consuming over a thousand Calories, and many strength trainees will double or triple that [208]. Many people try to compensate for such a dinner by eating nothing or very little, such as just protein shakes, beforehand. This is a mistake. You'll arrive at dinner starving with low willpower, so you effectively set yourself up for a 'screw it, it's just one meal' binge.

So what should you do? Consider the following meal plan for a fit guy.

Breakfast: omelet with 2 apples.

Lunch: steak with 500 g potatoes.

If you opt to take out the apples and the potatoes to save up calories for later, you'll save about $5 \times 80 + 2 \times 100 = 600$ Calories. However, you also removed more than half of your total food volume, so you'll probably be starving by dinnertime. Most caloric dishes have 300+ kcal per 100 grams, so if you end up eating more than 200 g extra food, a paltry portion for any fit man, you'll end up with a higher instead of lower total daily energy intake. It's more likely you'll eat 500+ grams more, which would mean you end up eating over 900 Calories more despite having starved much of the day.

Here's a better approach. Don't starve yourself beforehand. Instead, make sure you arrive at the dinner extremely well satiated. Keep your calorie intake beforehand as low as possible without compromising on satiety. The key here is to eat very filling, low-calorie foods. For example, if you eat your normal breakfast and replace the potatoes at lunch with zucchini soup, you can eat a whopping full kilo of zucchini and still save over 200 Calories. Then you end up at the dinner fully satiated with no need to gorge. You'll almost certainly eat less than you normally would, as you were already full, and you have an additional 200 Calories buffer.

There's a very good chance you'll still overeat on the day of the family dinner, but in my experience, it works far better to compensate for it afterwards than to compensate even more before. Significantly overeating for a day produces a ~40% increase in leptin, the 'appetite control hormone' I mentioned earlier [209]. You'll probably also be extra motivated to lose fat after a day of indulging yourself. So the day after overeating, restricting energy intake is easier than before that day. In contrast, going extra low in calories the day before the dinner means you decrease leptin secretion, so you'll be extra hungry at the dinner.

Diet tip 15.5: Eat out

The most acute psychological problem of a cheat meal is the creation of a craving or comfort food, but this may not be such a problem if you have no more access to the meal in question. As such, eating out at a restaurant can be psychologically better for your diet than having a cheat meal at home. Plus, it'll probably be a more memorable experience.

As a personal example, my favorite 'cheat meal' is sushi. I often get sushi cravings, but I've developed a taste for the better stuff, so I rarely ever eat supermarket sushi or take-away. I'm also far too lazy, not to mention inexperienced, to make good sushi myself at home. Plus, I dislike eating out at a restaurant by myself, so the only way to indulge in my sushi craving is to find a restaurant where they serve good sushi and find someone to accompany me. This requires planning and deliberation, which sets up a nice barrier to prevent mindless eating.

In contrast, if your favorite cheat meal is Ben & Jerry's ice cream, and this is right there in your freezer, it's far more difficult to resist the temptation. Preparing a wholesome dish is more work than just grabbing the ice cream out of the freezer, so there is now a barrier to stick to your diet. Hunger and mental depletion can make you incapable of surmounting this barrier, which may end up as a Ben & Jerry's binge in front of the TV. Not exactly a memorable experience for such a massive calorie intake.

As a general rule, I recommend not to purchase more than 1 serving size of any food that is not part of your regular diet.

If you really want that Ben & Jerry's ice cream, you'll have to go to the supermarket to get it. Then you buy 1 serving of it, not a huge tub, and you fit it into your macros.

Diet tip 15.6: Take a lesson from Japanese sushi etiquette

Speaking of sushi, traditional Japanese sushi etiquette says you should eat sushi in a specific order. You start with the least flavorful types of fish, including most white fishes, and then you work your way up to tuna and then the more flavorful and fatty types of fish, like salmon. Then you finish with the tamago sweet egg sushi. This order improves the taste experience. Remember that your taste perception is significantly affected by what you ate previously. By eating foods in order of their palatability, you ensure you will like every dish you eat instead of only the tastiest ones.

Moreover, this Japanese order of consuming your food can help you avoid inducing a craving during a cheat meal. Recall that food cravings begin when hunger takes the shape of a certain trigger food. In other words, cravings can be "a conditioned expression of hunger that is acquired by repeated experience of eating the craved food in a hungry state" [175]. This means you induce your own cravings by giving in to them when you're hungry, because you create an association between the experience of hunger and the cheat food as a means of satisfying that hunger.

You can avoid this detrimental conditioning effect by having your cheat foods when you are no longer hungry. For example, a study on chocolate cravings found that chocolate cravings increased when the participants consumed chocolate when they were hungry; however, when the participants only consumed the chocolate when they were already full, their cravings decreased [194].

So you should consume filling food before you indulge in cheat foods. This not only prevents you from inducing a craving for the cheat food, it also makes it much easier to exercise self-control and avoid binging on the cheat food. Furthermore, I personally find it very liberating to know I've already gotten in my essential nutrients, especially protein, before I indulge in my cheat foods. This ensures you never have to force-feed yourself after the cheat meal because you still have to get your protein in for the day. The reverse order is again also much less palatable. You may enjoy a hearty soup to start your meal when you're hungry, but if you've already started eating pizza and ice cream, you're probably not going to enjoy soup anymore after that.

If we go back to the example of wanting to fit Ben & Jerry's ice cream into your lifestyle, after you've bought your 1 serving size of it, you should not consume this right away. Instead, consume it after a filling, low-calorie meal. In other words, we could say the tradition of having dessert, just like the Japanese sushi sequencing, is scientifically approved.

Diet tip 16: Do this before every meal

The foundation of any rational decision lies in a cost-benefit analysis. To make such a rational decision, our brain needs the reflective abilities of system 2. Our brain's more primitive system 1 is too short-sighted: when it sees food, it wants to eat it right away, without any consideration for long-term costs, such as getting fat or unhealthy. As such, when we are mentally depleted and unable to engage system 2, our primitive brain makes our food choices for us by selecting simply the most pleasurable and convenient foods. System 1 likes nothing better than fast food. If McDonald's had a subscription discount for frequent customers, our inner elephants would be first in line. Then again, that would require foresight, which system 1 does not have…

Fortunately, in addition to all the other tips in this book, there's an extremely simple yet highly effective method to make more rational decisions on what to eat. Before eating anything, ask yourself: how many calories per 100 g does this food have?

Thinking of the caloric density demands the attention of our brain's rational rider, because our inner emotional elephants are no good with numbers. This enables you to make a rational decision about whether the food's cost, in particular its number of calories, is worth it compared to its benefits, and not just its taste. A series of experiments by Trudel & Murray have established that paying attention to the cost of eating foods significantly increases our self-control [210]. So you can consciously decide whether it's worth eating those 2 slices of pizza with ~800 Calories or if it's more prudent to wait a few more minutes until you're home so that you can enjoy a larger, more satiating meal for half the calories and successfully lose fat.

Like any habit, it will take some time to firmly entrench it in your head, so grab your calendar or set a daily alert in your phone with the note: "How many calories per 100 g does this food have?" You'll find this simple question will help you enormously to prevent mindless eating.

If you don't know the caloric density, look it up. The USDA's FoodData Central is the most reliable reference for the US and countries that don't have their own national database: https://fdc.nal.usda.gov/

You can usually directly find an entry via Google, for example: "USDA food data salmon". If you can't find the food's energy density, you'll have to estimate it. In this case, I recommend adding a 20% safety margin to account for hidden calories and wishful thinking. Especially in restaurants, there is often oil, butter or sugar in your meals that racks up calories extremely fast without being visible. Most oils add about a 100 Calories per tablespoon. Unsurprisingly, most people consistently and substantially underestimate their energy intake by around 20% and often much more. Even trained dieticians routinely underestimate their energy intake by over 10% [211].

Thinking primarily of the food's calories will also protect you from halo effects. Certain food labels cause us to significantly underestimate a food's calorie content. For example, most people significantly underestimate the number of calories in organic food [212]. We see 'organic' and we intuitively think 'good for us', but organic food isn't inherently lower in calories. While it may be healthier, although only marginally based on most research, organic food certainly isn't inherently good for fat loss [213]. You can easily get fat eating foods most people think of as healthy. For example, nuts, granola, fatty fish, coconut bars and fruit juices are all highly caloric and you can easily overeat on them. Plus, many of these labels are not strictly legally regulated. 'Free roaming' could mean the animal theoretically had access to an outdoor area of sorts, possibly unbeknownst to the animal in question.

Similarly, labels like low-fat, low-carb, gluten-free and 'no added sugar' may sound nice, but you should focus on the total number of calories. Low-fat food variants often have lots of carbs. 'No added sugar' can mean there's still a lot of sugar inherently in the food. 'No artificial sugar' may only mean they added agave syrup instead of table sugar. Don't be fooled by labels or marketing gimmicks. Stick to the facts and always consider the total number of calories in the meal or food.

Diet tip 17: Do this after every meal

If you successfully employed the previous tip to pay attention to the caloric density of whatever you ate, it was a deliberate decision to eat it. However, that doesn't mean it was the right decision. A rational cost-benefit analysis is always based on the *expected* costs and benefits.

The costs of consuming any food are relatively easy to objectify. As per the previous tip, you can quantify the cost primarily in calories. So your expected costs are ideally the same as the objective costs, barring estimation errors.

The benefits of consuming food are more difficult to quantify. You could argue you can evaluate the nutritional density and some marker of 'healthiness', but the pleasure of eating itself, arguably the most important reason of all to eat, will always remain subjective. Pleasure is especially difficult to predict in advance because of our aforementioned affective forecasting bias.

As such, deciding what to eat falls under the umbrella of judgement and decision-making skills. Keyword being skill. Deciding whether it's worth to eat something or not is a skill. If there's one thing that stands out in the research on how to develop a skill, it's that you need feedback on whether your chosen decision was successful [214]. We can apply this to food choices by asking ourselves after every meal: "Was it worth it?" This simple question induces reflection and feedback. It also allows us to finetune our list of worth-it and not-worth-it foods. If the meal was worth its calorie content, great, it stays on the worth-it list. If you feel afterwards you would have been almost as satisfied with a meal far lower in calories, it goes on the not-worth-it list so that you don't make the same mistake again.

For example, let's say you normally eat 5% fat beef in your pasta, but today you tried full-fat beef with 30% fat. After the meal, you ask yourself if it was worth it. It helps to do a quick cost-benefit analysis. Say you had 250 g of beef in the meal. With a roughly 140 kcal difference per 100 g, that's a 350-kcal difference in energy intake between the 5% and full-fat versions. In my experience, many people don't find that worth it when trying to lose fat. It's a lot of calories for relatively little difference in taste. (Remember the study showing most people can't actually taste the difference when blinded!) For comparison, you could have spent those 350 kcal on a big slice of cheesecake for dessert. Alternatively, if the 5% meal was 800 kcal in total, you could have eaten almost 50% more food instead of going with fattier beef.

Diet tip 18: How to manage your appetite

Mother Nature gifted us with a supreme ruler that tells us when to eat and how much to eat: the sensation of hunger. Like other feelings, hunger gives us purpose and direction. Hunger motivates us to eat something like fear motivates us to avoid something.

Hunger is a primary stimulus of system 1, so the hungrier you are, the more difficult it is for system 2 to stay in control. Of the many predictors of diet attrition in research, hunger is the primary reason diets fail [175, 215]. Even a seemingly psychological problem like binge eating is predicted well simply by hunger [216]. In research, comparisons of unsuccessful with successful weight losers (the only time it's great to be a loser) show that successful dieters were less hungry during the diet [217]. Meal satisfaction is also strongly related to fullness, especially for men [218]. Without hunger, dieting would essentially be as easy as just consciously deciding to eat less and there would be no need for self-control in the first place.

Fortunately, there are many ways you can control your brain's appetite signals. A comprehensive review of appetite management would merit a book on its own (I've written over 70 pages on it in the online Henselmans PT

Course), but below I will discuss the 3 most fundamental appetite management strategies.

Diet tip 18.1: Eat more, not less

The traditional advice for fat loss is: "Move more, eat less." Indeed, most people need to reduce their energy intake to lose fat. As I explained earlier, obesity is in physiological terms a problem of energy balance. If you're fatter than you'd like to be, you're consuming too many calories. So eating less may seem like the most straightforward solution and you've probably heard the advice to 'eat like a Frenchman', meaning eating small portions (a saying that I predict will soon be changed to 'eat like a Frenchperson').

Intuitive as it may seem, scientific research does not support eating like a Frenchman. In the very comprehensive Portion-Control Strategies Trial, researchers compared the effectiveness of 3 diets in 186 overweight women for a whole year [219].

1. The Standard Advice Group was instructed to reduce their portion sizes and eat healthier.

2. The Portion Selection Group was educated on what proper serving sizes were. They should eat more low-energy-density foods and fewer high-energy-density foods.

3. The Pre-portioned Foods Group was instructed to eat pre-made foods with relatively small portion sizes, some of which were provided for them.

Over the first few months of the study, the group consuming pre-made meals lost significantly more weight than the other groups while spending the least time on their diet. This is further testament to the effectiveness of following a meal plan. However, their meal plan wasn't ideal and the participants felt deprived. As a result, after 6 months when the counseling and number of pre-made meals were reduced, they quickly regained much of their weight and after a year they did almost as poorly as the other 2 groups. The other 2 groups performed equally poorly with some success over the first 6 months but more weight regain than further loss over the next 6 months. In sum, eating less isn't very effective, regardless of how you do it. Following a pre-set diet can be effective in the short term, but if it leaves you feeling deprived, it's not going to get you abs for life.

After the year of training to eat less with numerous counseling sessions, the researchers tested how well the women could now reduce their portion sizes compared to similar individuals untrained in the skill of eating like a Frenchman [220]. The women were given 4 different portion sizes of food on 4 different occasions. The result: the extensively trained women ate just as much food as untrained women and were just as susceptible to the serving size: when more food was served, they ate more.

However, the trained women still managed to decrease their average energy intake. Not by eating less, but by choosing lower-energy-density foods. This was the successful part of their training that likely led to their initial success: learning to make better food choices.

But eating lower-calorie foods without changing how much you eat will only get you so far. You have to eat **more**. The problem with eating less food is that it requires constant self-control by eating less than your appetite signals you to. By not eating less but choosing lower-calorie foods, you can get leaner without suffering hunger. Moreover, as you get leaner, your appetite increases, so you should eat progressively more and more food as you get leaner. Your appetite is kept under control by leptin. Leptin is produced in adipose tissue – fat cells. The less fat you have, the less leptin you produce and the less suppression of your appetite there is. In other words, the leaner you become, the greater your appetite becomes and the more food you need to stay satiated [221].

Eating less of what you're currently eating triggers a negative spiral of increased hunger, having to eat even less, even more hunger and ultimately self-control failure. This is a primary reason people end up yoyo dieting. If you were already coping with hunger and self-control problems when you were fatter, it's completely unsustainable to try to get leaner without changing your diet's food selection. I've worked with many bodybuilders who cared much more about how they looked than how they felt, but even in this population I've never seen someone successfully maintain a sixpack for years while chronically hungry.

"I've been starving for the last whole decade, but look at these abs, bro, totally worth it!"
- Nobody

The solution? Eat more, not less. A lot more. When you start basing your diet around healthy, low-calorie foods, you need to rethink your portion sizes. For example, when I was in the condition of my following photo, I was eating about 9 pounds (~4 kg) of food every day. (I purposefully chose a home-made photo without professional editing.) In fact, it's rare that I don't eat at least 4.5 pounds (2 kg) of food on any given day. The key is to base your diet around vegetables, fruits and lean protein sources like white fish, shellfish, poultry, lean meats and low-fat dairy.

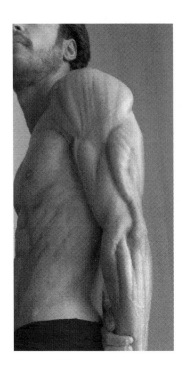

Increasing your food volume is incredibly effective to increase satiety, because your gut has gastric stretch receptors that signal satiation in response to pressure. These sensors quite literally measure how full your stomach is. So more food volume, even if it's just water or air as in carbonated beverages or a beaten protein shake, is more satiating than less food [222, 223, 224]. Researchers developed a great fat loss hack based on this information: blowing up a balloon inside someone's stomach decreases the experience of hunger [225]. The balloon trick works in obese and lean individuals alike [226]. Ok, so maybe blowing up a balloon inside your stomach isn't the best idea, but the take-home message is that satiety is more strongly influenced by food volume than food energy content [227]. Since food volume on a calorie-equated basis is the inverse of caloric density, food volume is strongly related to how few calories a food has per 100 g. The fewer calories per 100 grams a food has, the more satiating it is. This knowledge gives you enormous control over how satiating your meal plan is.

Diet tip 18.2: More protein, but not too much

An abundance of research shows high-protein diets are more satiating than low-protein diets. This has led many people to conclude 'protein is more satiating than carbohydrates and fats'. However, this is a simplification that is often flat-out incorrect.

The theory of protein's extra satiating properties is based on hormonal effects [228]. In the gut, amino acids stimulate the release of several hormones that activate satiety centers in the brain, namely glucose-dependent insulinotropic polypeptide (GIP) and glucagon-like peptide-1 (GLP-1). There is also mixed evidence for hunger suppression by cholecystokinin (CCK) stimulation and for suppression of ghrelin release, 'the hunger hormone'. This looks like a simple and convincing theory: more protein → more appetite-suppressing hormones → less appetite. However, the theory breaks down on all 3 levels in multiple studies.

First, high-protein meals do not always stimulate more appetite-mediating hormone release or suppression than high-carb or high-fat meals [229]. Moreover, different meals with the **same** macros can result in major differences in gut hormone production [230]. Unsurprisingly then, higher protein intakes also do not always result in greater appetite-suppressing hormone levels nor lower hunger hormone levels than lower-protein meals, even when the high-protein meals have a higher total energy content [230, 231, 232]. The response of gut hormone levels to protein also seems to depend on whether someone is lean or overweight [233].

Furthermore, the relation between supposedly appetite suppressing hormones and actual appetite is inconsistent and, as Lemmens et al. (2011) concluded: "too small to use hormone and glucose concentrations as appropriate biomarkers for appetite, at least at the individual level and probably at the group level." [234]

Other researchers propose that large neutral amino acids (LNAAs) that can cross the blood-brain barrier directly alter brain activation and neurotransmitter levels with appetite suppressing effects. However, Koren et al. (2007) found that A) the amount of protein in the diet doesn't affect the level or ratio of LNAAs in the blood and B) unrestricted energy intake changed over time without changes in blood amino acid levels [235]. So it's unlikely blood amino acid levels directly influence satiety.

A much more plausible theory to explain why high-protein diets are more satiating than low-protein diets is protein leverage theory. Put simply, protein leverage theory states that the body monitors protein consumption to ensure we consume enough of it [236]. Since the body doesn't have an efficient storage mechanism for amino acids like it does for carbohydrate (glycogen) and fat (adipose tissue), it makes sense from an evolutionary perspective that the body has adapted mechanisms to ensure we consume enough of this vital macronutrient. Specifically, we stay hungry until protein requirements have been met. We have a 'Protein-Stat'. In other words, protein leverage theory says protein is more satiating than carbs or fats *until we've consumed enough protein for our bodily needs.*

The exact mechanisms of protein leverage are still being uncovered, but research indicates a link between satiety signaling in the brain and amino acid utilization in our body [237]. Activation of anabolic signaling pathways (mTOR) and suppression of catabolic signaling pathways (AMPK) reduce food intake by acting on the hypothalamus. A key modulator in the brain may be GCN2 (general control nonderepressible 2), which quite directly monitors amino acid balance and thereby basically the protein quality of our diet. We also have receptors in our mouth that detect amino acids. It's thus plausible the brain can monitor our protein intake, compare it with our requirements and adjust our appetite accordingly [238].

In rodents and several other animals, including pigs, protein leverage theory has strong supporting evidence. Rats will quite reliably overeat on low-protein diets until they've consumed enough protein (= leveraging protein). After protein deprivation, when given the choice between high- and low-protein food, they tend to prefer the higher-protein food. Rats can even self-select foods with complementary amino acid profiles [239]. This preference for higher-protein foods to meet bodily demands occurs independently of energy balance.

Protein seeking correlates surprisingly well with protein needs even during periods of growth in animals. Birds intuitively self-select diets to reach a protein intake that's close to their estimated optimum [240]. They'll increase this protein intake in periods of growth and when injected with growth hormone. Birds bred to have more muscle also select higher-protein diets and male birds eat more protein than female birds.

This protein seeking can be compared to our innate so-called 'specific appetite' for sodium and water, which we also cannot effectively store or survive without.

It should be noted our ability to leverage protein is far from perfect and quite some research finds protein intake has no effect on energy intake at all, including a 2020 meta-analysis on older adults [241, 242].

Protein leverage in humans is more difficult to study because it's unethical to starve people of protein and difficult to restrict their food choices to a narrow selection for a long time. However, the research we have is promising. After low-protein diets, people's preference for higher-protein foods increases compared to after high-protein diets [243]. We also have a low drive to eat protein sources with an incomplete amino acid profile lacking in essential amino acids, as we cannot meet protein requirements with those foods [244]. These phenomena are impossible to explain with the simple model that protein is inherently more satiating than carbs or fats because it directly stimulates satiety hormones.

Another phenomenon that's impossible to explain with the traditional 'protein is the most satiating macro' theory is habituation. The satiating effect of high-protein meals decreases after high-protein diets and comes back after low protein intakes [245]. In other words, if you consume a diet higher in protein than you need, protein will lose some of its satiating effect. The body can sense excess protein intake in the form of increased protein oxidation rates. Habituation to protein's satiation again makes evolutionary sense. If we only have access to low-protein foods, we should keep eating until we've consumed enough protein so we can survive. But if we only have access to high-protein foods, we should not stop eating before we've consumed enough other nutrients. Otherwise, high-protein environments would cause us to starve ourselves. When protein is abundant, high-protein foods are just an energy source like carbs or fats, so the body should treat them as such in terms of how much we need of them.

With protein leverage in mind, "How satiating is protein?" is the wrong question to ask. We should instead ask: how much protein do we need? The short answer to that based on the scientific literature is that non-exercising individuals should consume at least 1.2 grams of protein per kilogram of total bodyweight per day (1.2 g/kg/d, or 0.54 g/lb/d) [246]. Going up to 1.6 g/kg/d may offer some further benefits for satiety and health. Strength trainees in particular should consume at least 1.6 grams per kilogram total bodyweight of protein per day (0.64 g/lb/d) for maximal gains in strength and muscle size [247]. This number is supported by a randomized controlled cross-over trial and a meta-analysis I co-authored with several of the world's leading fitness researchers [248, 249]. The following graph shows our key finding.

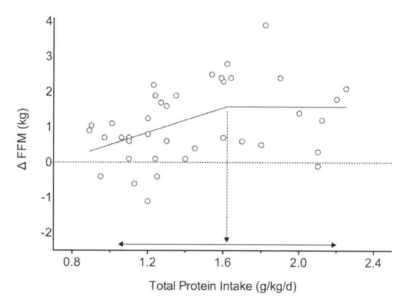

Our meta-analysis found that the benefits of consuming more protein for increases in fat-free mass (including muscle) reached a ceiling at 1.6 g/kg/d of total bodyweight. In other words, studies found that higher protein intakes than this did not improve the participants' gains.

Protein leverage theory would thus predict 1.6 g/kg/d is the optimal protein intake for satiety as well with no further benefits of going higher in protein. In sedentary individuals, the optimal protein intake for satiety should be lower in accordance with their lower bodily protein requirement. This is exactly in line with the scientific literature [250]. Studies comparing insufficient protein intakes (< 1.2 g/kg/d) with sufficient protein intakes (> 1.6 g/kg/d) reasonably consistently find appetite suppressive effects of the higher-protein diets. However, studies comparing sufficient protein intakes with excessive protein intakes find no beneficial effects. This includes a randomized cross-over trial in strength trainees I co-authored [251].

Thus, it appears there's a ceiling effect after which protein loses its extra satiating effect. This ceiling is evident in studies comparing 3 different protein intakes. For example, Li et al. (2016) performed a long-term cross-over trial of diets with 10%, 20% or 30% protein [252]. The 10% protein group slightly underperformed on satiety, but there were no differences on any appetite measure between the 20% and 30% protein intakes. The researchers overall concluded that a diet's protein intake has "minimal effects on appetite control". It appears the brain directs us to consume at least ~15% of energy intake as protein, as hunger increases below this point but satiety does not increase above it [253, 254, 255]. The average optimum protein intake for satiety may be a bit higher for some people though, as several studies find benefits of going higher than 15% in protein for satiety [256, 257, 258, 259]. 15% of energy intake corresponded to only 64-75 g protein per day in these studies and it was often insufficient to optimize body recomposition, so it's not surprising the average sweet spot for hunger control was higher than that in these studies. A review of 38 studies concluded protein is more satiating than carbs and fats in the 10-20% of energy intake range but not above that, indicating the average satiety sweet spot is a protein intake of 20% of energy intake, corresponding to about 1.2 g/kg/d for non-strength training individuals [260]. The effect was far stronger for self-reported satiety than actual eating behavior: ad libitum energy intake didn't reliably decrease even at lower protein intakes. The optimum protein intake for satiety was closely in line with the optimal protein intake for body recomposition and health (1.2 – 1.6 g/kg/d).

The literature is thus in line with protein leverage theory: up to the bodily protein requirement, protein is generally more satiating than carbs or fats per gram, but after protein needs have been met, the superior appetite suppressing effect of protein disappears.

Prospective and cross-sectional research in the general population also doesn't support a 'more is better' relation between protein intake and satiety [250]. Depending on which study you look at, protein has either no relation with body fat level, an inconsistent negative one or even a positive one. The latter would suggest higher protein intakes are associated with an increased risk of becoming overweight. Several researchers indeed believe this, stating: "consuming an amount of protein above the protein intake recommended [...] may experience a higher risk of becoming overweight or obese during adult life... Compared to diets with no more than 14% of energy from protein, diets with more than 22% of energy from protein were associated with a 23–24% higher risk of becoming overweight or obese." [261]

So is it completely the other way around: are high protein intakes fattening? No, it depends on your food choices. In practice, it's silly to even think of 'protein vs. fats/carbs'. The practical question is as follows. When your protein intake is already sufficient for body recomposition purposes but you're suffering from hunger, should you increase your protein intake further?

Probably not and here's why. Let's take every bodybuilder's favorite high-protein food: chicken breast. How difficult is it to eat 200 g of chicken breast? Unless you have the appetite of a sarcopenic grandma, the answer is: very easy indeed. After you cook it, the food volume is tiny. Even 500 g of chicken breast is no more than a snack for most big guys when it has a nice sauce. (Tip: you can make awesome zero-calorie sauce with Coca Cola Light.) 200 g of chicken breast generally has over 250 Calories. For those calories, you could eat about 3 **pounds** of zucchini, as zucchini has only 17 kcal per 100 grams. Which is going to be more filling and appetite suppressing: the baby's handful of tender chicken or the mountain of fibrous zucchini?

In general, vegetables are far more satiating than high-protein foods. For example, a given volume of mushrooms in a lunch meal is just as satiating as that volume of meat, even though the meat contains far more protein and total calories [262]. The mushroom eaters in the above study ended up with a lower energy intake over the next 4 days. When you equate for protein content, mushrooms are significantly more satiating than meat [263]. Eating mushrooms instead of meat also decreased energy intake and consequently improved weight loss in a year-long study [264]. Even bean- and pea-based meals are as satiating per calorie as higher-protein veal- and pork-based meals [265]. The combined effects of energy density and fiber on satiety can easily overshadow the satiating effect of protein.

It's thus a big generalization to talk about 'protein' and 'carbs'. Many fitness enthusiasts become so obsessed with macronutrients they forget there's more to food than its macros. When it comes to our appetite, focusing solely on macros is fundamentally misguided. Many aspects of food change how it affects our appetite: food volume, texture, palatability, fiber content, viscosity, etc. Not to mention the wide array of psychological factors that influence our appetite, such as the Delboeuf illusion, which makes us eat more food when it is served on larger plates because our brain underestimates the portion size [266].

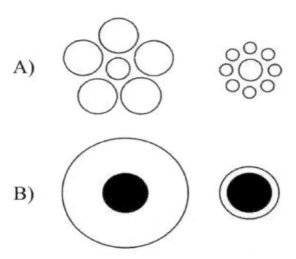

The Ebbinghaus (A) and Delboeuf (B) illusions: our brain perceives something as smaller when it's surrounded by a larger circle or circles. As a result, the brain registers less food and produces weaker satiety when you eat from large plates [267].

Meals with the same macronutrient composition can have very different effects on our appetite [230]. For example, a breakfast with the same macros of goat dairy is more satiating than that breakfast with cow dairy [268]. You can easily experience this yourself as well. Just think of a tasty whey shake compared to beaten casein fluff 'milkshake' that has swollen up to three times its volume. Same macros, but the fluffed-up casein is far more satiating than the watery whey.

When we compare different foods with different macros, the differences become extreme. Sugar and vegetables are both 'carbs' and butter and avocado are both 'fats', but is there anyone in their right mind who thinks they're equally satiating? Forget macros. Think food.

In conclusion, make sure you consume enough protein to support your activity level but don't worry about having to consume more than that. Factors like energy density and fiber are far more important than protein intake for satiety after you reached this threshold. Protein is not inherently more satiating than carbs or fats, so if you don't like high-protein foods all that much, you can be equally satiated with other foods you like more. Good alternatives for satiety, not to mention your wallet, include beans, vegetables, most fruits and potatoes (ideally oven-baked or boiled to maintain food volume).

Diet tip 18.3: How much fiber you need

Dietary fiber is paramount for satiety. It adds bulk to your food, attracts water and slows down the digestive process, all of which contribute to the sensation of fullness. On average in research, every 14 grams of fiber reduce ad libitum energy intake by 10%, though the effect is smaller for leaner individuals [269]. That's a major effect. If you're generally ending up at maintenance energy intake with your diet, all you may need to end up in a significant deficit is to consume more fiber.

Soluble fiber in particular has many benefits, as it's fermented in the gut to produce short-chain fatty acids. These fatty acids are used by the brain and directly trigger the sensation of fullness, among many other health benefits [270]. Many fruits, vegetables, beans and sweet potatoes are good sources of soluble fiber.

Importantly, supplements generally aren't an effective fiber source. Fiber supplements cannot (yet) rival whole foods in terms of satiety or health, since the health effects of fiber are influenced by the plant's cell walls and many of its other nutrients and phytochemicals during digestion [271, 272]. Some supplements are better than others, but in practice people that rely on supplements to consume enough fiber have great difficulty becoming lean, let alone staying lean for decades.

That said, a person is better off consuming enough fiber in the form of a supplement than not consuming enough in the first place. Soluble fiber supplements in particular can help improve fat loss by reducing your appetite and thereby making you consume fewer calories [273]. Just keep in mind these supplements should function like a band-aid until you get your diet in order.

Many research organizations recommend a dietary fiber intake around 25 grams per day for adult women and 38 grams for adult men. These recommendations are for non-strength training individuals. Strength trainees should see this as an absolute minimum for optimal health and appetite control, assuming no digestive pathologies are present, such as IBS.

If this seems like a lot of fiber, consider that many ancient human cultures habitually consumed fiber intakes upwards of 100 grams with estimates of average daily fiber intakes of 46 g and 86 g [274, 275]. This is in line with estimates of

40-80 g/d fiber in Australian Aboriginals and a whopping 150-225 g/d fiber in a hunter-forager group in the northern Chihuahuan Desert [276, 277]. "Analysis of vegetable foods consumed by foragers in this century and evaluation of archaic native American coproliths suggest that ancestral human fiber intake exceeded 100 g/d (Eaton 1990). Rural Chinese consume up to 77 g/d (Campbell and Chen 1994), rural Africans up to 120 g/d (Burkitt 1983)." [275] So most current fiber intake recommendations are objectively low by evolutionary standards.

Most people's difficulty with consuming enough fiber is almost entirely a matter of food choices. Whole foods, particularly plants, are typically much better sources of fiber than modern processed foods. Many authorities recommend grains such as bread as good sources of fiber, but these recommendations are often based on fiber content per 100 grams of food. That's not a relevant metric. Since the purpose of dietary fiber for fat loss is primarily to reduce energy intake, what we want is foods that are rich in fiber relative to their energy content. The following table lists the highest fiber foods per 100 Calories of the food based on the United States Department of Agriculture (USDA) database. As you can see, most starches commonly recommended as top fiber sources are objectively mediocre sources of fiber. Vegetables and fruits, especially berries, are far richer in fiber. Sweet potatoes and beans can be considered tier 2 in the best fiber hierarchy.

Food	Fiber per 100 kcal (g)
Endive	18.2
Raspberries	12.5
Blackberries	12.3
Eggplant	12
Kale	11.7
Celery	11.4
Asparagus	10.5
Cabbage	10
Spinach	9.6
Brussels sprouts	8.9
Lettuce	8.7
Green beans	8.7
Red bell peppers	8.1
Cauliflower	8
Broccoli	7.7
Green peas	7
Carrots	6.9
Beets	6.5
Oat bran	6.3
Strawberries	6.2
Zucchini, with skin	5.9
Mushrooms, portabella	5.9
Pear	5.4
Oranges	5.1
Flaxseed	5.1
Kiwifruit	4.9
Apples, with skin	4.6
Mushrooms, white	4.5
Black beans	4.5
Onions	4.2
Avocado	4.2
Blueberries	4.2

Peach	3.9
Sweet potato	3.7
Cucumber, with peel	3.4
Grapefruit	3.4
Tangerine/mandarin orange	3.4
Whole grain pasta	3.3
Lentils	3
Whole grain wheat cereal	3
Banana	2.9
Soybeans, green	2.9
Pineapple	2.8
Mango	2.7
Steel cut oats	2.7
Potato, with skin	2.7
Melons, cantaloupe	2.6
Corn, sweet, yellow	2.3
Whole grain bread	2
Quinoa, uncooked	1.9
Garlic	1.4
Grapes, red or green	1.3
Brown rice	0.7

Diet tip 18.4: Eat mindfully

So far we've covered 3 important physical factors that influence your hunger level: food volume, protein intake and fiber intake. However, your appetite is not a purely physical experience. Hunger is very much a psychological phenomenon. Our brains do not have a 'calorie sensor'. Rather, our brains use various cues to determine if we've eaten enough. This means your perception of what you've eaten can be more important than what you've actually eaten. For example, your perception of how many calories are in a food affects how satiating you feel it is: people are more full after a meal when they believe it contained more calories, even if that wasn't actually the case [33]. This nocebo effect even influences the behavior of the hunger hormone ghrelin, illustrating how our mind and body are intricately linked.

Because our brains are effectively 'deciding' rather than 'registering' when to stop eating, we tend to eat more when we're distracted [278]. When your attention is not on your food, the brain is busy with other things than registering your food intake. As a result, it sends a weaker 'stop eating' signal. This explains in part why people eat more during social events and when eating in front of the TV or when using their smartphone [279, 280]. So your parents were right to teach you not to talk with your mouth full. Not only does this make it difficult to understand you, it also disrupts your brain's satiety signaling, making you prone to overeat.

So focus on your food when you're eating. You can talk with others, but do so in between bites. Try to savor every bite. Besides, what's the point of eating if you're not enjoying it?

Diet tip 19: Minimize decision fatigue

'Eat less, move more' is the traditional fat loss advice. We've already covered why eating less isn't a good idea. You probably need to consume fewer calories, but you should eat *more* food with a lower energy density, otherwise you'll end up in a negative spiral of perpetually greater hunger and deprivation. 'Move more' on its own doesn't fare much better than eating less for fat loss.

Let's take the common advice to take the stairs instead of the elevator. Or park your car further away from work or your house to walk a bit. The benefit for fat loss is self-evident, right? More energy expenditure means greater energy deficit means greater fat loss. Unfortunately, the energy expenditure from these kinds of activities is very low.

- You burn 19.7 calories when climbing 11 floors of stairs [281]. That means if you climb 29 floors of stairs every day, you burn off 1 small apple worth of energy. The energy expenditure of descending stairs is less than half of that.
- If you park your car a mile away from work (1.6 km), you burn 80 calories to walk to work [282]. Less than in a banana.

These little bumps in energy expenditure may add up over the long run, but if you're not strategic about them, they come with a hidden cost: decision fatigue. Every time you have to decide whether you take the stairs or the elevator, your rational rider has to suppress your inner lazy elephant's instinct to take the elevator. This creates a moment of cognitive conflict, which causes the sensation of mental fatigue and weakens the influence of your brain's rational system 2.

At work we mostly perform have-to activities, so we accumulate a lot of mental fatigue. In studies we can see that when mentally fatigued dieters see food, they experience more brain activity in their reward centers and reduced connectivity with the top-down control centers of system 2, compared to non-fatigued dieters [283]. Basically, when you're fatigued, food looks extra appealing and it's harder to resist. This is why so many people have trouble sticking to their diet after a long day at work. When you get home after a long day at work, your brain is screaming for instant gratification. The last thing you want is to cook up an extensive meal, so you scavenge the kitchen cupboards looking for something tasty you can eat right then and there. So instead of your spicy turkey chili, you eat a few handfuls of nuts, a banana and you down a whey shake to get your protein in. But afterwards, you're still hungry and you also end up eating a chocolate protein bar and the rest of the bag of nuts. 2000 Calories later, you realize you undid most of the week's fat loss with some crap you didn't even enjoy that much.

The accumulation of decision fatigue is why many people flunk on their diets later at night. Binging at night is associated with obesity and it mostly happens during stressful periods in life [284].

A single episode of overeating, even if it's seemingly harmless snacking or deviating from the planned diet 'a little bit', can easily offset a week's worth of taking the stairs instead of the elevator. Not to mention full-blown binge eating. So trivial increases in energy expenditure are often not worth suffering decision fatigue for.

Over the course of the diet, the cost-benefit of these 'move more' decisions becomes even worse due to adaptive thermogenesis. As you lose weight, your nervous system becomes more conservative with energy and you become lazier [285]. The decisions become more effortful and your energy expenditure from movement decreases to boot.

So should we just stay sedentary to lose fat? Absolutely not. People with a higher physical activity level are generally leaner than sedentary people and physically active people are typically more successful on fat loss diets [286, 287]. Plus, being sedentary is terrible for your posture and health. The solution to reap these benefits without accumulating decision fatigue is to harness the power of habits.

Diet tip 20: How to build activity habits

Technology was the cornerstone of The Industrial Revolution. Technology led to the rise of factories. Then factory workers were replaced with machines. And now machine operators are being replaced with computers. The key to all of this is automation: optimize the process and then let it run without any further decision making. Instead of needing a team of craftsmen to build a cart and wagon, we now have car factories producing a car every 40 seconds [288]. Automation is a powerful thing.

You can make the power of automation work for your own body as well. Your brain functions much like a computer and it too can automate tasks. We call these automated behaviors habits. Habits enable you to spend the limited attention of system 2 on more intellectual tasks while system 1 controls routine activities. Habits are why you can think about what you're going to have for breakfast while you're brushing your teeth. How exhausting would it be if you had to consciously control every brush?

And how amazing would it be if your diet ran on auto-pilot? Fat loss would merely be a matter of time. Indeed, research finds good habits are more effective than high self-control to resist temptations and stick to your diet [289]. In general, most diet and exercise behaviors are habitual and only weakly predicted by our intentions, especially when self-control or motivation are low [332].

The good news is, by building good diet and activity habits, we can make diets feel like the original meaning of the word. The original Greek word *diaeta* meant 'way of life', not 'short-term period of suffering to get abs for my beach holiday'.

The bad news is, building habits is difficult and takes time. To build a habit, we have to make system 1, particularly our basal ganglia, take over the directions that first came from system 2, specifically the prefrontal cortex. Your conscious brain basically teaches your automated brain to perform routine tasks. Teaching system 1 something is a lot like teaching your dog something. It learns mostly by association and doesn't understand *why* you want a habit. A habit loop is formed when your brain has ingrained an association between a cue and a behavior, so that the cue automatically triggers the behavior. As an example of an undesirable habit, you may have learned to bite your nails (the behavior) when you experience anxiety (the cue).

It's much easier to form habits when the habit loop ends with a reinforcer, like a reward. Going back to our example of brushing our teeth, the success of toothpaste is often attributed to Pepsodent. They put mint in their toothpaste to give you that tingling 'sparkly clean' sensation. It's the same reason shampoo has foam. It serves no chemical function. It just makes you feel like the shampoo achieves something. The reward reinforces the behavior loop, making it easier to form the habit to brush your teeth and shampoo your hair. Exercise is also a relatively easy habit to get into, as you experience direct rewards from exercising, even aside from its long-term benefits: the body's endorphins produced during exercise serve as natural drugs that make you feel slightly high. In the gym, getting a pump in your muscles also makes them look bigger: they are in fact bigger due to cellular swelling. Arnold 'The Governator' Schwarzenegger famously said the pump is better than cumming. I don't know about that, but it certainly illustrates the power of a reinforcer to form habit loops.

Some researchers even claim a reward is essential for the formation of a habit, but this is not the case. For example, habits can also stay for a long time when the behavior no longer results in any reward, like a rat pressing a lever that used to deliver food in its cage [290]. Athletes often have rituals before competitions that are effectively purposeless habits, like having to listen to their 'lucky song' even when they perform badly. It's very fortunate we can form habits without rewards for the behavior, because many healthy habits have no direct reward, including most ways to increase energy expenditure. There is no direct reward for taking the stairs or walking to work. Fatigue and sweat may even act as a negative reinforcer.

So how do we form a habit without a reward? For all the scientific knowledge we have, the solution to form unrewarded habits is quite a blunt force approach: sheer repetition. It generally takes 18 to 254 days, on average about 2 months, to automate a behavior and form a habit [291]. This is too long to rely on self-control. If you want to build a habit of taking the bicycle to work, this will not work if you decide every day if you're going to take the bicycle or the car. Instead, you should think in terms of lifestyle decisions. Forget about day-to-day decisions. Instead, make rules for yourself that you decide for once and for all and then follow them blindly. Rain or no rain, take the bicycle to work. Do not break the pattern until the habit has formed, otherwise it will take forever.

Going back to parking your car further away from work, only do this if you have a reliable parking spot. You don't want to spend any brainpower looking for a parking spot. If you have a regular spot, great, always take that spot. If it's not available, take whatever's most convenient and don't waste brainpower making a conscious decision.

If there are specific staircases at work with a manageable number of flights, always walk them. Or make a rule to always climb stairs of 3 or fewer flights. Don't bother with any staircases that don't fit your rule.

More generally, don't bother trying to increase your energy expenditure with trivial activities. Instead, focus on building sustainable activity habits.

Diet tip 21: Use action triggers

While true habits can only be formed with lots of repetition, there is a shortcut we can use to mimic the power of habits: implementation intentions [292]. Implementation intentions are action triggers, rules you create for yourself in the format of: if situation X arises, I will perform action Y. For example, "Straight after I leave the office, I'll go to the gym." Astute readers will notice this structure is similar to habits: a cue triggers a behavior. Implementation intentions are indeed comparable to an implanted habit and their strength is similar in nature. The benefit of forming an association between the trigger situation and the behavior is that your brain's associative system 1 can help store the information. You're then no longer reliant on conscious thought to execute the behavior. When the situation arises, it triggers the association with the behavior, reminding you of your intention. Moreover, your intention is now the default option in your mind, meaning that without further deliberation, you'll do it without requiring self-control.

Implementation intention is not a very catchy term, pretty much doomed never to become popular despite its effectiveness, but there is useful wisdom in the name. It comes from a contrast with goal intentions.

A goal intention is what most people would just call a goal or an intention: expressing you want to do something. A lot of motivation advice centers on goals. The problem with goals is that they're empty. Everybody wants everything. I want a pet dragon, a harem with 10 Victoria's Secret models and an office in the White House. Maybe you're a proponent of never giving up on your dreams, but I can say I've definitely given up on these dreams, because dreams are exactly what they are. The problem with goals is that they don't have to be realistic. Even if they are realistic, they are just the expression of desire. In economic terms, they are a wanted benefit, but they are missing the second component of any rational choice: the cost. Even if the goal is a result of a deliberate cost-benefit analysis, they are often not actionable. If something is not actionable, it doesn't change your behavior. For fat loss too, a comprehensive meta-analysis of 11 studies showed that there is no relation between people's weight loss goals and how much weight they actually manage to lose [293]. Unrealistic goals can even backfire: in a few studies, the more ambitious someone's weight loss goals, the *less* likely the participants were to stick with the diet [294]. This is probably because many people have extremely unrealistic expectations of how much fat they can lose in a short time [295, 296, 297].

To achieve change, we don't just need goals or intentions. We need action, implementation. Hence the term implementation intention. Implementation intentions are action plans. Their strength lies in being 100% actionable. They are specific and they are concrete. Implementation intentions are significantly more effective than goal intentions to achieve a wide range of goals, including dieting, exercising and being productive without procrastination [298, 299]. Implementation intentions are also far more effective than the traditional approach to focus on motivation. For example, according to one study, having people make implementation intentions to exercise is almost 3 times as effective as instructing people of the benefits of exercise [300].

However, you shouldn't ignore the 'why'. Traditionally, implementation intentions centered only on the when, where and how of a behavior. Modern research has found that for complex behavior change, including changing your diet, it's important to not only have an action plan but also know the reason for it [301]. If you're a typical woman in the general population, you may shun strength training or give it a halfhearted effort only because you have some vague idea you should be doing it. You want to be more flexible and reduce your injury risk, so you do yoga. You want to lose fat, so you jog on the treadmill. You want to get toned, so you go to BodyPump classes. However, the reality is strength training achieves all of those goals better at once than any of these other forms of exercise [302, 303]. Full range of motion strength training with free-weight exercises achieves all of the following.

- It reduces your injury risk more than stretching.
- It increases your muscle (fascicle) lengths more than stretching.
- It helps you lose more fat than the same time spent on cardio by increasing your energy expenditure both acutely as well as chronically and by suppressing your appetite more effectively.
- It helps you get toned more effectively than lower-intensity exercise, because being toned is simply the result of lowering your body fat percentage and increasing lean body mass: in essence, toning is the same as bodybuilding, so you need to do heavy exercises that build muscle mass.

Understanding why strength training is probably the ticket to your dream physique has fueled the 'strong, not skinny' revolution of the past years. Similarly, calorie awareness is highly helpful to decide which foods are worth it for you.

So whenever you have a goal (intention), turn it into an implementation intention. Specify the when, where, how and why. Take, for example, the following goal: "I'm going to take better care of myself." That's a great idea, but in that form it's still a rather useless goal intention. You'll still have to rely on your willpower to make the decisions that will make you better off. Instead, you should use implementation intentions that specify your action plan in detail. For example, if you're prone to miss breakfast at home and end up getting calorie-bomb sandwiches and 400-Calorie Starbucks coffees on the go, here's an implementation intention to improve your breakfast. "When my alarm goes at 06:00 h, I will take my morning shower. After I get dressed, I'll mix a pack of Greek yogurt with half a pack of mixed berries with sucralose sweetener to have for breakfast."

Let's say your exercise adherence could also use a boost. You sometimes have to work late and then you have to rush home for dinner with the family without any time left to get to the gym. In that case, you could add the following implementation intention: "I will set an alarm for Sunday, Tuesday and Thursday evening, telling me to pack my gym bag, so that on Monday, Wednesday and Friday morning after breakfast, I can go straight to the gym in time before work."

Earlier in the book, I explained why meal planning is so successful at promoting diet adherence. Now you can understand why even better: a meal plan is essentially an extensive list of implementation intentions. A meal plan specifies exactly the what (the food ingredients), when and where (the day and time), how (the recipe) and why (it fits your macros or diet principles) of your diet. Many of the tips in this book are essentially implementation intentions. Using implementation intentions while dieting has been found to double weight loss compared to group counseling; they've also been found to increase fruit and vegetable consumption by over 50% [304, 305].

For best effect, combine implementation intentions with visualization: visualize yourself going through the action plan. In the above breakfast example, picture yourself waking up and having breakfast in vivid detail, like a movie. In which cupboard is the bowl? What's the brand of Greek yogurt you buy? Things you forget to prepare will show up as missing details. For example, you may realize during the visualization you normally only turn on the dishwasher when you go to work, so there won't be a clean bowl unless you also get into the habit of activating the dishwasher at night before you go to bed. Personally, I use extensive door-to-door visualization to plan all my trips, especially flights. I travel to a new country around once a month, or at least I used to before the COVID-19 pandemic. Visualizing myself walking through customs reminds me to bring my passport and check my visa status. Visualizing myself arriving reminds me I need to check if Uber works at my destination and if I can buy a SIM card at the airport. The vivid details from visualization help you nail down the specificity you need in your action plans to achieve your goals.

Diet tip 22: How to change bad eating habits

Just as important for our diet as building good habits is breaking bad habits. Unlike building a good habit, breaking a bad habit is not as simple as sheer repetition. It's very difficult to completely get rid of a habit. Once a strong association has formed in our head between a cue and a behavior, we are not much different from lab rats that keep pressing on a lever even though it has long ceased to provide food into their cage. Every smoker, comfort eater and procrastinator can attest that "Just stop it" doesn't help much. Negative implementation intentions don't help either and can even backfire [306]. Take the following implementation intention: "When I feel stressed, I will not snack on nuts." System 1 works purely associatively. It's not very smart when it comes to negatives. All that happens is an association forms between stress and nuts. When you feel stressed, you then think of nuts. Even if you can resist the urge to eat them, you'll probably only develop a craving.

So how do we break an undesirable eating habit? Researchers have identified 3 methods to get rid of a bad habit: substitution, discontinuation and inhibition [333]. Habit inhibition is the most straightforward method we all have experience with. Inhibition means suppressing the urge to perform the habitual behavior. For example, when you feel the urge to snack, you just don't give in to that urge. The problem of this strategy is twofold. First, it doesn't get rid of the habit. It only suppresses it temporarily, so you'll have to keep dealing with it indefinitely. Second, inhibition relies on willpower, so it's only effective when you have good self-control and it's more difficult when you're tired or stressed. Since many people tend to snack more precisely when they're tired or stressed, trying to rely on sheer willpower to suppress a bad snacking habit is generally doomed to fail.

Habit discontinuation is a much more viable long-term method to get rid of a bad eating habit. Discontinuation refers to prevention of the cue that triggers the habitual behavior. I've already discussed several strategies that are essentially habit discontinuation methods, such as not having high-calorie foods visible in your kitchen or on your desk. Those foods serve as blatant cues to snack. Remember: don't bind bacon to the cat's back.

Sometimes the cues that trigger your bad eating habits are not so evident. Research has found that 'cue monitoring' is effective to reduce snacking behavior [334]. Whenever you've deviated from your diet, take a moment to reflect why this happened and consider the following:

- What did you eat?
- What time was it?
- Where was it?
- What were you doing before you deviated from your diet?
- Whom were you with?

These questions help you identify the cues that trigger your bad habits so that you can avoid them. You'll find that the cue for snacking is often stress or displeasure: you self-medicate on comfort foods to make you feel better. The advice from the productivity chapter to take frequent breaks is highly applicable here to improve your diet as well. Breaks not only prevent your working memory from being overfilled, they also prevent mental fatigue and the associated discomfort. As long as you're content, you're not at risk for comfort eating. As the saying goes, an ounce of prevention is worth a pound of cure.

However, while often very effective in practice to stop a habitual behavior, habit discontinuation doesn't really 'break' a bad habit. It doesn't address your brain's association between a cue and the undesirable behavior. If you have the habit of smoking when you're stressed, stress management is great, but you obviously can't always prevent yourself from being stressed.

The most effective solution to truly break a bad habit is habit substitution [333]. Substitution means you replace the undesirable habitual behavior with a desirable behavior. It's much easier to change a cue-behavior association in our mind than to eradicate it. Instead of trying to stop the behavior impulse, it's easier to change the reward. Nicotine gum and other smoking substitutes are successful examples of overriding bad habits. If you have the bad habit of smoking when you feel stressed, you can override this with the implementation intention to chew on nicotine gum when you feel stressed. Strong habits may not immediately be replaced, as the situation triggers not only your intended but also your habitual behavior. You then still have to make the effortful decision to get your nicotine gum instead of your cigarette [307]. Visualization and a very concrete, specific implementation intention are key to make it successful. When you make the implementation intention to chew nicotine gum when you feel stressed, think of which pocket the gum is in, what it feels like to grab it, the sound the package makes when you pop the gum out and the sensation when you chew on the gum.

In some cases, you can also change the reward to a negative reinforcer. Not all reinforcers are rewards. For example, a highly effective way to stop biting your nails is to wear an invisible but disgusting nail polish. Every time you bite your nails, you get a nasty taste in your mouth, which conditions a negative association with the behavior.

Changing the reward of bad habits is also more effective to improve your diet than changing your eating behaviors themselves. It will always require self-control to prevent yourself from eating when you want to, but it's relatively easy to change *what* you eat. As you learned, there's no such thing as an addictive food. You can be addicted to eating in general but not to specific foods. If you have the bad habit of comfort eating and you tend to snack on nuts when you're feeling down or stressed, a good solution is to switch to the very low-calorie snacks I gave in the 'zero rewards' chapter on productivity. They provide the sensation of pleasure without the calories most snacks have.

Even better, your new reward doesn't have to be food. It's the general sensation of pleasure that your brain is yearning, not a specific food or even food in general. Psychological hunger can be satiated with other sources of pleasure than food. Think back on the many break options from the productivity chapter. Watching an episode of your favorite TV series, getting a massage or playing a videogame can all replace comfort foods.

Diet tip 23: Get a standing desk

Humans have not adapted to living their life seated. The human body is an organism that requires activity to stay alive. The analogy with bodies of water is particularly fitting here, since our bodies consist of ~60% water [308]. What happens to a body of water when there's no flow? It rapidly turns into a nasty cesspool. Even when you exercise regularly, the time you spend seated is still an independent predictor of dozens of postural and health complications [309].

Now, if you understood why 'move more' is a recipe for failure, you also understand that just standing up and walking around at random times of the day is not very effective. Instead, get a standing desk, preferably even a treadmill desk. I know they have a reputation for being weird and geeky, but if you think about it rationally, they are amazing. Studies show that a standing desk is a uniquely effective way to increase your activity level without requiring any effort.

- In one study, an afternoon of standing office work burned 174 kcal extra compared to staying seated in a population of 80% women [310]. Indirect calorimetry research shows an 11.5% increase in energy expenditure when performing deskwork standing instead of seated and a 7.8% increase when alternating sitting and standing [311].

- A treadmill desk can increase energy expenditure much further still, with estimates up to 100-150 extra kcal per hour, even for women [312, 313]. A year-long prospective trial found a 33% increase in activity level after office workers implemented a treadmill desk, which was associated with significant weight loss without any dieting efforts [312].

Male strength trainees can increase their energy expenditure by several hundreds of Calories a day by working while walking or standing instead of sitting.

Treadmill desks can be expensive, but they're a legitimate business investment. If you have an employer, see if you can get one from the company. If you're self-employed, you can declare its cost as a business expense to save tax money.

When you first start standing more, your legs will fatigue. That's fine. Just sit down for a period and go back to standing. This is where implementation intentions come in handy again: "I always start working standing. When my legs fatigue, I sit down. Whenever I have to get up for any reason, I go back to my standing desk." Ergonomic alarms can be helpful too, though I find more natural cues tend to be more sustainable as implementation intentions.

Diet tip 24: Use availability effects

Remember the tip on avoiding sin by avoiding temptation? It referred to availability effects. Food has strong availability effects: we eat what's readily available to us, especially what's within sight and within grabbing range. When system 1 registers food, its intuition is generally to eat it. Not doing so requires inhibition from system 2. People in households in which junk food is visible on the kitchen counter have been found to be over 30 pounds heavier than people in households with a clean kitchen counter [89]. We eat on average 92% of the food we serve, regardless of how much we serve [314]. This finding is called 'the clean-plate effect'.

We've discussed how in many instances, not having caloric foods readily available is a big step towards a leaner you. There's also a flip-side of the availability coin: you want to have low-calorie foods easily available. And the most low-calorie food there is, is water. So put a big bottle of water on your desk when you're working or studying. First, it keeps you hydrated. Second, high volumes of water can suppress your appetite and thereby improve fat loss [315]. Third, water automatically prevents prolonged sedentary posture because of the acts of drinking and going to the bathroom more frequently. If you don't naturally drink much, it can help to have a rule, such as that the bottle must be empty before lunch and before you leave the office.

It's also crucial to have your kitchen filled with foods that are conducive to your diet goals instead of junk. There's perhaps no more important diet rule than this: if you know you shouldn't eat it, don't buy it. To put this into practice, we have to upgrade a vital yet commonly overlooked skill: grocery shopping.

Diet tip 25: The most useful skill that nobody regards as a skill

Dieting is essentially an economical dilemma. You can spend your calories on 2 kinds of food: consumption and investment foods.

1. Consumption foods are convenient and tasty but highly caloric or otherwise unconducive to your fitness goals (inflammatory, high in toxic trans fats, etc.).
2. Investment foods are lower in calories or otherwise better for your goals (higher in protein, satiety, micronutrients, etc.).

Eating consumption foods provides instant gratification, but they have few long-term benefits and possibly even damaging effects.

Eating investment goods provides significant long-term benefits, but they typically require a bit more preparation if you want them to be as tasty as consumption foods.

Your brain's intuitive system 1, primal in nature as it is, has no foresight: it can't think of the long run. It therefore almost always prefers consumption foods that provide instant pleasure. It sees little value in foods that require more preparation or provide their benefits only later. It's thus up to your rational system 2 to do what's in your best long-term interest. To enforce its will, it has to suppress system 1: you have to exert self-control. Cognitive conflict between systems 1 and 2 stimulates the anterior cingulate cortex (ACC) to shift your attention away from what you're doing to preserve wellbeing. When a certain amount of inner conflict is reached, your self-control fails: you succumb to the primal instincts of system 1 and eat the consumption foods instead of the investment foods.

We've covered many tips on how to prevent this self-control failure at home, in restaurants and at work, but perhaps no place is more important than the supermarket. If you don't buy it, it can't ruin your diet. So if you know you shouldn't eat a certain food, don't buy it! Moreover, if you have foods in your house that you don't want to eat, throw them away (assuming they're yours, of course). It may intuitively seem like a waste, but rationally speaking, these foods have negative value. If you keep the food, you're either going to eat it, which you don't want it, or you'll just end up throwing it away later. To ensure you only buy foods that have your system 2's approval, you should never go shopping when you're hungry.

Diet tip 25.1: Shop satiated

Hunger is your nemesis not just at home but also in the supermarket. When you're hungry, you'll be much more likely to buy all sorts of crap your system 2 did not approve of. You want food now and your plan to make chicken and broccoli doesn't look so appealing anymore when you're having a stare-down with an extra-large pizza in the supermarket.

"I may try this sometime." You're probably going to eat the whole pack.

"Oh I'll just try a bite of this." You're definitely going to eat the whole pack.

"I'll eat this next Saturday with my friends." Yep, you're going to eat the whole pack, and probably before Saturday.

To fill your house with diet-proof foods, a particular piece of paper is paramount.

Diet tip 25.2: Your grocery list is sacrosanct

Modern supermarkets overwhelm you with choices. Choice may seem like a good thing: rationally, the more choice you have, the better: more options can never make you worse off. In reality, our brains are ill-equipped to deal with an abundance of choice. Excess choice leads to a phenomenon known as choice paralysis [316, 317, 318]. In a classic series of experiments, students were offered to write an essay on one of 6 or 24+ possible topics. The students reported greater satisfaction with their choice and achieved better grades when they only had 6 options than when they had 24+ options. Similarly, when shoppers in a mall were offered to buy jams, having the option of 6 flavors led to greater satisfaction than 24+ options.

How can fewer choices make us better off? Making a deliberate choice is inherently a system 2 activity. Unfortunately, system 2 has very limited resources compared to system 1 and the use of system 2 is effortful. Just try calculating $(15 + 19) \times 8$ and you'll feel your brain grind. A large amount of choice rapidly accumulates decision fatigue, especially when the choices differ on several aspects: price, packaging, macronutrients, brand, etc. [317]. If the choice is overwhelming, the cognitive discomfort sometimes makes people not make any choice at all [316]. When system 2 is overwhelmed, system 1 is free to rule and you make poor choices guided mostly by convenience and taste instead of what's best for your diet.

Successful supermarkets know you suffer from decision fatigue and will take advantage of this by strategically placing certain items in salient positions. These are typically consumption foods you didn't plan to buy but will immediately trigger system 1's interest with a tasty appearance. This is why there's often a section with ready-to-eat junk foods and candy at the cashier, even though there's another section for that elsewhere in the supermarket. By the end of your shopping, you've accumulated maximum decision fatigue and you're most prone to make bad choices. Something tasty, visible and ready-to-eat within arm's reach will be hardest to refuse at that point.

How can you protect yourself from such psychological trickery? Arguably your most effective weapon against choice paralysis is the humble but mighty grocery shopping list. For successful and efficient shopping, your grocery list is sacrosanct. It should be complete, it should be specific and it should be followed to the letter. Any choice between different brands or competing products should be made only once and written down. If there are 5 kinds of Greek yogurt in the supermarket, compare the prices and macros once and pick the best one. Alternatively, if the taste differs significantly and is important, pick all viable options and decide at home which one you like best. From then on, you buy that one. This way, you never have to waste system 2's effort on the decision again.

When you've pre-decided every food in your diet, grocery shopping should be an efficient affair. You go in, you buy exactly what's on your list, and you *insert Ahnald's voice* ~~get to the choppa~~ get out. No choices means no room for bad decisions and no decision fatigue. You'll also save a lot of time.

Diet tip 25.3: Stay in the safe zones

Supermarkets are a bit like a concentric version of Dante's Inferno for dieters. In supermarkets in seemingly the entire world, the outer isles are filled with lean and healthy foods. Good diet foods are mostly fresh whole foods and many require freezing, so it's most convenient to have those on the outer borders of the supermarket. But beware ye traveller of venturing deeper into the inner isles, for they are packed with sinful gluttonies. You'll reach a Diet Inferno with row after row of never-expiring processed junk foods. Stay safe, stay healthy, stay in the outer isles.

Diet tip 25.4: How to organize your grocery list

When you're familiar with your supermarket, as you probably should be, you can arrange the items in your grocery list in the order you'll find the foods in your supermarket. If you first walk into the vegetable section, write down the vegetables you need at the top. This way, you only have to walk through the supermarket once without going back-and-forth all the time. The less time you spend surrounded by food, the better.

An online Google Doc is a convenient format for your grocery list. Since it's a digital document, you can easily reorder it with cut-and-paste. You can create it on your computer or phone when you're meal planning. You can then easily access it in the supermarket on your smartphone. If you don't have internet on your mobile, you can download an offline copy before you go shopping. Tip: enable 'anyone with the link can edit' so you can access the document from all devices.

Diet tip 25.5: Order online

More and more supermarkets are offering online shopping with at-home delivery. This is a great development, as it not only saves time, it also allows you to search whatever foods you're looking for just by entering their name instead of having to wade through the Diet Inferno.

Diet tip 26: Umami preloads

Remember the tongue map you were taught at school that says your sweet taste receptors are at the tip of your tongue, while bitter taste receptors are at the back? I never understood how this was supposed to work, as I can readily taste salt with the tip of my tongue and sugar on the back. Indeed, the tongue map is at best a gross oversimplification based on old research [319]. Two main aspects are incorrect about the tongue map.

First, all taste receptors occur pretty much everywhere on the tongue. Some may just have a slightly higher concentration at certain regions.

Second, the 4 classic tastes – sweet, sour, salty and bitter – are not all we can taste. There is a 5th taste: umami. It's much more common in Japanese cuisine than Western cuisine, so it's no surprise the taste was discovered in Japan. It's more surprising that this discovery took place over a 100 years ago and many people in the West are still unaware of it. Umami is a savory flavor found in foods such as cheese, meat, fish and soy products. Its key determinant is free-form glutamate and it didn't take long for scientists to extract this from food to imbue the delicious umami flavor in other dishes.

The umami flavor extract is available in the form of mono-sodium l-glutamate, better known as MSG. The fate of MSG is similar to that of all synthetic food additives that seem too good to be true, like artificial sweeteners. It became immensely popular and then feared for being unhealthy to the point that some regions banned its use. Fortunately, sometimes we can have our savory cake and eat it too. The fear of MSG rests on it being synthetic, but not everything that is 'synthetic' is bad for you. Toothpaste, shampoo, deodorant and tons of processed foods are filled with synthetic ingredients that have been extensively tested for their safety. And not everything that is natural is good for you. Gasoline is natural, but I think we agree you shouldn't put that in your protein shake.

While chemically created, MSG is just sodium and glutamate mixed in water. Glutamate is a naturally occurring amino acid found in almost all foods, with particularly high concentrations in high-protein foods, peas and corn. Decades of scientific research have led to a widespread consensus from nutritional authorities that MSG is safe for human consumption in any remotely reasonable quantities [320]. Some people persist in claiming they have MSG hypersensitivity, but when these people are put in double-blinded placebo-controlled studies, their symptoms miraculously disappear, or their symptoms are just as bad in the placebo-condition. As such, MSG intolerance is generally a nocebo effect: it's in your head, not an actual physical side-effect of consuming MSG.

The safety of MSG is good news not just for our taste buds but also for our self-control. Curiously, drinking a soup flavored with MSG before a meal seems to improve our self-control, as measured by greater activation in the part of the brain that governs self-control during dietary decisions (the dorsolateral prefrontal cortex), greater response inhibition ('more control') and reduced eye fixation switching ('more focus') [321]. Two other studies also found reduced energy intake after drinking MSG-flavored soups [322, 323]. Soups without added MSG did not have these effects.

It's probably the glutamate in MSG that improves our self-control. Glutamate acts as a neurotransmitter, among many other functions, and it can already affect us before we've consumed it. We have mGluR receptors in our mouth and digestive tract that detect glutamate. Via the vagus-nerve, they can affect brain activation. The glutamate may need to be in its free form, not bound like it is in many high-protein foods, to affect our self-control, because only the free form affects our taste receptors.

Regardless of the precise mechanism of action, greater self-control is always welcome, so try high-glutamate starters before large meals. A simple and proven way would be to consume a broth with added MSG, but several natural foods are rich in free glutamate. My favorites are tomatoes and mushrooms. You can make very healthy, satiating, low-calorie and yet very tasty soups with these foods. Try out the 3-minute tomato soup on my website, for example [324]. Exercising can increase our preference for the umami taste, so there's a good chance you'll like umami too [325]. A glutamate-rich diet may not just make dieting easier but also improve self-control throughout the day.

Diet tip 27: Learn how often to weigh yourself

Harbinger of bad news, the bathroom scale is feared by many. Weighing yourself can be an unpleasant experience, so much so that many people recommend not weighing yourself. However, the scale also provides useful data to see how your diet is progressing. Should you weigh yourself and if so, how often?

Let me ask you a counter-question. Do you think it's wise for an ostrich to bury its head in the sand when it's in danger? Of course not, and neither does the ostrich, in contrast to a popular myth. Ostriches only stick their head in the sand to inspect their eggs. When in danger, they run away or fight. Not weighing yourself because you're afraid of what the scale may say is no different than burying your head in the sand so you don't see the lion coming at you. The lion's there and your weight is what it is. Not seeing it doesn't change its physical reality.

Weighing yourself provides objective feedback on how your diet is progressing. If your weight is trending in the desired direction, it's good to see the positive reinforcement. If it's going in the opposite direction, you may not like to see that, but you do need to, because it means you need to work on your diet. As such, weighing yourself is a win-win scenario. In contrast to the pop wisdom that weighing yourself is obsessive, scientific research overwhelmingly supports the benefits of weighing yourself. Frequent weigh-ins are significantly correlated with weight loss compliance and weight loss success, as well as weight loss maintenance [135, 219, 326, 327, 328, 329]. Weighing yourself consistently also helps prevent holiday weight gain and diets that involve self-weighing are more effective to lose weight than diets that don't require weight monitoring [330, 331].

Weighing yourself is not a burden. It's a form of control. So weigh yourself daily in the morning after having gone to the bathroom and before you've eaten. It's a simple habit that requires only a trivial amount of time and it enables you to log your weekly average weight trend, which is incredibly useful data about your diet progress.

That said, weighing yourself at any other time of day than fasted in the morning is generally futile, as your weight will be majorly confounded by multiple factors. Your weight goes down after you go to the bathroom. When you eat or drink, it goes up. So if you're 500 g heavier in the afternoon compared to another morning, all this may mean is that you drank an extra glass of water that you haven't excreted yet.

So always weigh yourself fasted in the morning and only then.

More generally, daily weight fluctuations mean practically nothing. Several factors impact your day-to-day weight that say nothing about your physique.

- Mass in your digestive tract. You could be a pound heavier than yesterday simply because today you haven't gone to the bathroom yet, whereas yesterday you did.

- Water retention. Chemically speaking, your body consists mostly of water. Your total water weight can and does vary on a daily basis as a result of many factors, including your consumption of water and minerals, sodium in particular, as well as your diet composition.

- Glycogen storage. Changes in carbohydrate intake and other dietary factors can impact your total body's glycogen storage level. Each gram of intramuscular glycogen attracts ~3 g of water into the muscle, which can add up to a weight change of several hundred grams.

These are not reasons to avoid weighing yourself. On the contrary, these are reasons to weigh yourself every single day so you can take the weekly average and use that as a more reliable reference point. Don't worry about changes in your day-to-day weight. Focus on the long-term trend of the weekly average.

CHAPTER 5: HOW TO MAKE EXERCISE LESS EFFORTFUL

As our species conquered nature, our evolutionary instincts became detached from our wellbeing. While being active is good for us, we are fundamentally lazy animals, because being averse to effort used to amount to being economical with energy expenditure. Hunter-gatherers were forced to be active to hunt, trek, forage and fight. In our more civilized times, all the trekking and foraging we need to do to obtain food is to walk to the fridge or a supermarket. Yet our instinct to move and use our bodies is still there, so now we exercise on machines and we fight in rings with referees.

This more deliberate form of exercise allows us to maximize the physical and health benefits of being active, yet its deliberate nature also requires from us a new level of self-control. Increases in physical strength, endurance or muscle size are adaptations that only occur to a significant extent when you subject your body to high levels of stress. Imposing this stress on ourselves requires us to push through our comfort zone. Unlike fighting for our lives, training in the gym is primarily a system 2 activity, a rational choice. Our inner rational rider chooses to invest effort and time to develop ourselves in the long run. To squeeze out those last reps or run that last mile, we must suppress system 1's inclination to avoid pain. Our anterior cingulate cortex registers not just cognitive dissonance but also physical pain, so we develop not just physical but also mental fatigue.

When we experience too much mental fatigue, we lose the focus and motivation to continue training. As a result, being mentally fatigued prior to strength training can reduce our total repetition performance in the gym [1, 33]. Performing fewer reps means less training stimulation and generally less muscle growth, energy expenditure and strength development.

Fortunately, there are several strategies we can employ to make our workouts less effortful. Even if you belong to the hardcore crowd that would rather drive 30 minutes and buy a day pass at a new gym than miss a workout on Christmas eve', there's no reason to make exercise harder than it needs to be, unless you're a masochist. Let's start with a tip to get yourself to the gym in the first place.

Workout tip 1: Use caffeine (more) strategically

Remember Dan Ariely's experiment showing we're unaware of how being aroused by porn affects our sexual preferences? It demonstrated affective forecasting bias, specifically projection bias: when we think of how we'll feel in the future, we extrapolate our current feelings to that time. We intuitively assume how we feel now is how we'll feel later as well.

We also face projection bias when we have to predict how we'll feel about working out. We feel tired now, so we don't go to the gym because we think we'll still feel tired in the gym and cannot imagine sinking down into a deep squat with heavy iron on your back. Yet if you've gone to the gym anyway in these situations, you'll know that the fatigue was entirely psychological and there is nothing wrong with your neuromuscular system. After warming up, the mental fatigue normally disappears completely.

The solution? Instead of trying to fight your feelings, change your feelings. Force your body into an energetic state. The two best ways to achieve this in my experience are cold showers and caffeine. The problem with cold showers is that when you feel exhausted, a cold shower sounds about as enticing as watching The Jerry Springer Show while Justin Bieber is playing in the background (read: an audio-visual catastrophe). That leaves caffeine. And it works wonders. Here's how to use it properly.

1. Schedule your exact weekly workout times in your agenda. Example: every Monday, Wednesday and Friday you leave work at 17:00 h to go to the gym.

2. Thirty minutes before you plan to go to the gym, consume a serving of caffeine. In the above example, that would be 16:30 h.

By the time you've planned to go to the gym, the caffeine should have kicked in and you should be roaring to go.

To make best use of caffeine, you should be strategic with its use. You cannot effectively use high doses of caffeine chronically, as caffeine induces tolerance to its own effects and subsequent withdrawal symptoms when you stop using it [2]. Many people assume legal drugs are perfectly safe and only associate withdrawal with illegal drugs, but objectively there is little relation between the toxicity and addictiveness of many recreational drugs and their legal status [3]. Tolerance to caffeine builds up quickly and at low dosages. Using just 1.5-3 mg/kg/d, which is below the threshold required to physiologically increase strength training performance, induces complete tolerance to a dosage of 3/mg/kg within 4 weeks [4].

To avoid tolerance, you may think: why not just use progressively more of it? Other than that it's not sustainable, you're in for a nasty withdrawal period afterwards. At about 750 mg per day your tolerance to caffeine can become complete, meaning you cease to get any benefit out of it [2]. You may feel like you do, but all the caffeine does is ward off withdrawal symptoms: you feel less worse rather than better, compared to if you had never used caffeine. Researchers had long overestimated the positive impacts of caffeine because they didn't exclude chronic users. The participants then had to avoid caffeine for a few days before the study, which caused them to be in withdrawal, so caffeine's 'positive' effects were merely withdrawal symptom reversal. They didn't really feel better on caffeine: they just felt worse without it.

Tolerance and withdrawal build up much sooner than most people realize: 100 mg caffeine per day is often enough to cause withdrawal when you stop using it [2]. That's about one cup of coffee. The most common withdrawal symptoms are headaches, fatigue, depression, difficulty concentrating and irritability. If your training sessions are notably poorer without stimulants, you may very well be in withdrawal. Withdrawal can also cause muscle stiffness and weakness.

So if you regularly drink 2 or more cups of coffee a day, you're probably suffering from some of the side-effects, namely decreased sleep quality, increased cortisol production and increased anxiety [5]. The 'benefit' you get may mostly be fighting your withdrawal symptoms. Many people are stuck in a negative spiral where they use progressively more caffeine and become progressively more sleep deprived and reliant on caffeine to feel normal. The only way out of the spiral is to go through withdrawal and be more rational with your caffeine dosing.

On the bright side, caffeine's withdrawal symptoms appear to be just as psychological as its ergogenic effects: objective cognitive ability isn't majorly affected during withdrawal, even though subjectively it feels like it is [6].

The severity and duration of withdrawal is dose dependent, but you should have dealt with the worst of it after 3 days and pretty much all of it after 9 days. Afterwards, you may be pleasantly surprised how good just 100 mg of caffeine can make you feel when taken on an empty stomach.

As a more sustainable dosing strategy to increase motivation in your workouts, limit your total weekly dosage to 700 mg and limit caffeine use to pre-workout. So if you train 3x per week, you can consume 700 / 3 = 233 mg caffeine before each workout.

For best results, consume caffeine powder. Pure anhydrous caffeine powder (or capsules) are more ergogenic (performance enhancing) than coffee with the same amount of total caffeine, probably due to interacting components in coffee that reduce caffeine's beneficial effects [7]. While one study found the opposite, namely that coffee was more effective than the same amount of pure caffeine, this was likely due to the greater placebo effect of noticing that they were drinking coffee [8]. A subsequent study found that supplementing caffeine along with decaffeinated coffee was more effective than both coffee and pure caffeine in the same amounts [9]. Overall, the research supports that pure caffeine supplementation is more effective than drinking the same amount of caffeine in coffee. It's also much easier to dose accurately, as the caffeine content of coffee and other caffeinated beverages can vary wildly.

While anecdotally energy drinks seem to be more effective than pure caffeine, double-blinded research consistently finds that the other ingredients in most energy drinks, including B-vitamins, taurine, glucuronolactone and carnitine, do not provide any isolated or additional benefit compared to pure caffeine consumption [10, 11]. As such, the greater effectiveness of energy drinks compared to pure caffeine supplementation to increase subjective arousal appears to be a placebo effect. At least given the same amount of caffeine consumption: independent third-party lab testing has found that many energy drinks contain ~20% more caffeine than what's on the label [12].

In conclusion, anhydrous caffeine is the supplementation form of choice for ergogenic effects. It seems to be most physically effective and you can dose it most accurately. 100 mg pills are generally most convenient, but you can pull plastic capsules open to consume only a part of the pill's contents if needed.

To track your total caffeine consumption, you can use the following chart. Product labels are preferable, but it may be wise to add a 20% error margin to energy drinks. Note that the caffeine content of tea and coffee strongly depends on how strong you make them.

Product	Serving size (fl. oz)	Caffeine in one serving (mg)
Coffee		
Regular drip or percolated	8	95–330
Brewed or percolated, decaffeinated	8	3–12
Instant, prepared from powder	8	30–70
Espresso	1	50–150
Tea		
Black, regular, brewed or tea bag	8	40–74
Black, decaffeinated	8	2–5
Green, brewed or tea bag	8	25–50
Oolong, brewed or tea bag	8	21–64
White, brewed or tea bag	8	15
Instant, prepared from powder	6	33–64
Yerba mate, brewed or tea bag	8	65–130
Iced tea	12	27–42
Beverages		
Carbonated beverages with caffeine added	12	22–69
Alcoholic beverages with caffeine added	1	3–9
Energy drinks with caffeine added	8.2–23.5	33–400
Caffeinated waters	16.9–20.0	42–125
Foods		
Chocolates	8 oz	0–6
Sweets	Various	1–122
Snacks, from US Department of Agriculture database	1 oz or 1 bar	3–41
Snacks, gums, and mints	Various	20–400
Fast foods	Various	1–49

Adapted from the 2012 USFDA report on caffeinated food and CBs [Somogyi, L.P. (2012) *Caffeine Intake in the U.S. Population* (http://www.fda.gov/downloads/AboutFDA/CentersOffices/OfficeofFoods/CFSAN/CFSANFOIAElectronicReadingRoom/UCM333191.pdf)].

To remain maximally caffeine-sensitive for your pre-workouts, it's best to simply avoid all caffeinated beverages. If you enjoy coffee, you can keep drinking as much decaffeinated coffee and tea, or herbal tea, as you want, as the caffeine content should be below the threshold of psychoactivity.

If you protest you don't like the taste of decaf coffee, realize this may very well be a nocebo effect. In double-blind research, the psychological effects of caffeinated and decaffeinated coffee are very similar with major expectation (placebo) effects [13, 14]. People that consumed decaf coffee under the illusion they were drinking caffeinated coffee responded the same way on cognitive and psychological tests as people drinking caffeinated coffee, indicating they couldn't tell the difference. Moreover, if you've supplemented anhydrous caffeine in powder form, you'll know caffeine itself is absolutely disgusting. I'm not talking acquired taste. I'm talking worse than chewing on paracetamol. Just like for regular coffee, the brand of decaf coffee also matters greatly for the taste, so it's good to experiment with a few different brands.

Workout tip 2: Listen to the right music

No counterintuitive psychology here, music can help you get energized and reduce your perceived effort in the gym [15, 16, 17]. Upbeat and energizing genres, such as rock music, are most effective on average, so if you're in for a morning workout and the personal trainers put on their 'I just got out of bed' lounge music, don't hesitate to ask for something more upbeat. The most important thing though is that *you* personally like the music, so bringing your own music is more reliable than relying on your gym's choice.

Workout tip 3: Intra-workout drinks

Remember the 'spit or swallow' experiments? They showed carbohydrate mouth rinsing can be as effective as actually consuming the sugary drink because it often isn't the physical energy you need from the drink but the psychological boost you get from the pleasurable sensation of sweetness in your mouth. We can use this knowledge to our advantage in the gym.

Most people bring either water or a caloric sports drink, like Gatorade or a protein shake, to the gym. The sports drink should be effective to reduce mental fatigue, but water has the advantage of not having calories. To get the best of both worlds – higher vigor without the calories – you could do an actual mouth rinse, but many people find it distasteful to constantly rinse your mouth with a drink and then spit it out. It's also impractical, as there's often nowhere to spit it out (though the face of 'that guy' curling in the squat rack comes to mind). Instead, try an artificially sweetened drink without (m)any calories. The pleasurable sensation of sweetness can help ward off mental fatigue without the need for calories. There are so many zero-calorie sodas and beverages these days, you should be able to find one you like. If not, make your own with zero-calorie flavor drops, such as MyProtein's FlavDrops (no affiliate). For maximum enjoyment, bring your drink in a thermal flask and put in ice cubes so you can feel good drinking your ice-cold sweetness while others are sipping on lukewarm water.

In case you're worried about the safety of artificial sweeteners, don't be. At least for the best ones, sucralose and aspartame combined with acesulfame-K, extensive scientific research indicates they are safe for human consumption up to pretty preposterous amounts [18, 19]. You can read a comprehensive review on the safety of aspartame on my site: www.MennoHenselmans.com/Is-Aspartame-Safe

insert advertisement from the Coca Cola company

Workout tip 4: Optimize your training frequency

It may seem counterintuitive, but training a muscle more frequently can reduce perceived exertion in the gym [20]. If you think about it, it makes perfect sense for fatigue management to split your sets for a muscle group across the week instead of doing them all in the same workout, as traditional bro bodybuilding workouts have you do. Many people new to high-frequency training are concerned about training a muscle even when you trained it the day before, yet they don't consider the muscle surely recovered more in 24 hours than in 2 minutes. If you do 18 sets of chest work on Monday (known as national bench press day for a reason), you spend 17 of those sets in a significantly fatigued state. Now if you split those 18 sets across Monday, Wednesday and Friday, your chest is on average much less fatigued during its training.

Just like the physical fatigue, mental fatigue has fewer negative effects when you train often. Research clearly finds that mental fatigue primarily impairs repetition performance in the later parts of a workout, not so much the start [1]. Most people can push themselves hard for at least some time, but the grind of a long workout eventually gets to you. In line with this fatigue, we also see that most people start resting longer and longer during their workouts [21]. If you keep your workouts shorter, you can prevent excess fatigue – both physically and mentally – from developing.

Distributing the sets you do for a muscle group across more training days can also reduce delayed onset muscle soreness (DOMS) [22]. On top of being nice to experience less pain, this may suggest there's less muscle damage, which could mean your body recovers more easily. In support of this, training muscles with higher frequencies increases testosterone production and improves the T:C ratio, a measure of overtraining [23, 24, 25].

Since there are likely no downsides to training a muscle more often, given the same number of sets for that muscle, and potential benefits, higher frequency training is often a win-win programming method [26]. If you're struggling to put in maximal effort for a muscle with several exercises or sets, consider dividing them across your workouts. And if you find yourself running out of gas near the end of your workouts, consider doing more, shorter workouts across the week. Programming more full-body style training also allows you to alternate between exercises involving different musculature with supersets and circuit training, which can easily cut your workout length in half without reducing your results.

Workout tip 5: Optimize your training intensity

It's again very counterintuitive, but heavy weight training is less effortful than going lighter and doing more reps. Given the same proximity to failure, lower-intensity work results in greater loss of muscle force production and higher perceived exertion-discomfort [27, 28]. So if you want good results for minimum effort, you should do high-intensity training with a large relative load.

If you think about it, it's logical that lower intensities are considerably more fatiguing than higher intensities. Let's take a set to failure at an intensity of 95% vs. 30% of your 1 repetition maximum (RM). At 95%, most people can only complete 2 reps. So the level of fatigue is such that they cannot lift their 2RM anymore. That doesn't say much. On a bad day, someone may not be able to lift their 2RM even though they haven't experienced any muscular fatigue yet. In contrast, after a set at 30% of 1RM, which is about a 30RM, you're so fatigued that you can't even lift your 30RM anymore, let alone your 2RM.

Moreover, the lower the intensity, the greater the total tonnage you lift in the set. If we assume a 100 kg 1RM, total tonnage after the 2RM is only 95 kg x 2 = 190 kg.

After the 30RM, it's 30 kg x 30 = 900 kg. So your muscles did over 4 times more physical work.

If you've tried lifting for high reps seriously for a while, you should already have felt how fatiguing high-rep work is. 20-rep squat workouts are known as 'widow makers' for a reason. It feels like you're doing cardio and strength training at the same time, because, well, you are. The 20th rep is effectively a 1RM attempt right after having ran a 400m sprint. You can in fact see based on kinematics, particularly the barbell velocity, that the last rep of a high-rep set looks very much like a 1RM [29]. Both are how the movement looks when your force production just barely exceeds the resistance.

To get the most bang for your exertion buck you're generally best of training in the 4-10 rep range. Just beware heavy lifting also poses greater stress on your connective tissues, notably your joints and tendons. So while lifting heavy makes your workouts less fatiguing, it also increases injury risk. There are also other potential benefits to going higher in reps, such as stimulating different growth pathways, but that's beyond the scope of this book. In terms of effort, going heavy is the way to go.

Workout tip 6: Use free weights

Machines may seem like the most convenient way to train, but they're generally not the best choice to optimize your efforts in the gym. People generally find training with free weights more pleasurable and enjoyable than training with machines [30]. There's something primitively fulfilling about being able to lift heavy metal that machines can't seem to mimic. Free weights also allow natural movement patterns, in contrast to the typically fixed motion trajectories of machines. Restricted movement increases the risk of pattern overload and makes the movement less 'functional' in the sense that it reduces performance carry-over to other movements. A study by Spennewyn (2008) illustrates the downsides of restricted movement well: performing a training program in a free-movement machine compared to a fixed-movement machine resulted in significantly greater strength development, better improvements in balance and less pain during exercise [31].

Since our self-control ability is intricately linked to our sense of wellbeing, it makes sense that research finds that free weight strength training enhances cognitive self-control to a greater extent than machine-based training [32].

CHAPTER 6: HOW TO MOTIVATE YOURSELF

At this point you should be several steps closer to having an indomitable will, top productivity, consistent diet adherence and easier workouts. The final step to excel in life is to learn how to motivate yourself and foster a winning mindset. Self-control failure only occurs during have-to tasks that don't provide enough instant gratification for the more primitive parts of our brain, system 1. If you can change your perception of the task as have-to work into want-to passion, you won't need self-control anymore to stay focused. This will benefit not only your work, your studies, your diet and your workouts but also everything else you do in life. So let's look into the psychology of human motivation.

What is motivation and how do we get it?

As we briefly touched on in the productivity chapter, there are 2 types of motivation: intrinsic and extrinsic motivation [1].

- Intrinsic motivation comes from within. You have a drive, a passion, to do something and you probably don't even know why exactly.
- Extrinsic motivation comes from outside yourself. It's instrumental. You do something to get paid, to avoid being arrested or you buy flowers for your date to score.

Extrinsic motivation generally comes from system 2, the rational part of our brain. You do something to achieve a specific purpose. Even if system 1 also likes to achieve that purpose, it will not support your efforts to get it, as it has no foresight. Filling in forms to get coupons to buy cheaper food, for example, is purely a system 2 activity. System 1 likes food, but it only likes eating it. It does not like filling in forms to eat later. It just wants to eat pronto. That's why you get bored so fast during tasks like filling in forms: system 2 has to work overtime to stay in charge and suppress system 1's screams to do something more enjoyable. Intrinsic motivation, on the other hand, comes from system 1, so it's not effortful to stay focused. You're naturally drawn to it.

Take, for example, exercise. Intrinsic motivation is significantly associated with long-term exercise adherence, whereas extrinsic motivation is often short-lived for your workouts [2]. Exercise is effortful and it takes a lot of work to achieve significant results. If you hate exercising, its cost-benefit is terrible.

- You can eat a bit more, but that energy bar you eat on the way home from the gym may already negate the energy deficit you created.

- You improve your health, but you don't notice this until at best weeks later.

- You gain muscle and strength, but the effort this takes is huge compared to the results. If you purely look at putting in the work to get the results, slaving away at the gym, suffering pain several hours a week for months on end, that's not an easy sell for our primitive system 1. If system 1 is not on board, our rational rider will often lose the reins.

No, nobody achieves a fitness model physique purely for instrumental reasons. Extrinsic motivation to exercise does not predict how often people go to the gym, whereas intrinsic motivation does [3]. Dieting is even worse, as hunger signals from our brain's inner elephants constantly try to take the reins out of our rational riders'... neurons. People that perceive their workouts as purely instrumental 'chores' are also more likely to reward themselves with snacks afterwards and tend to eat more than people that perceive their workouts as fun [4]. I'd argue heavy strength

training isn't really 'fun' in the traditional sense –
'fulfilling' is arguably a more appropriate term – but it's
clear that intrinsically motivated training is more
sustainable. The people that try to get fit on extrinsic
motivation are the people that sign up for a yearly
membership on January 1st, never to be seen again after
June. To successfully improve your physique and fitness,
you need the drive and consistency of intrinsic motivation.
The same applies to setting up a successful business or truly
excelling at anything in life. When lots of people are doing
something, only the intrinsically motivated ones will
persevere to the top.

So how do we develop intrinsic motivation? Intrinsic
motivation has been studied extensively in the field of self-
determination theory. It has 3 key components:
competence, autonomy and relatedness [5, 6, 7, 8]. Let's
start with competence.

Motivation tip 1: Cultivate competence

Do you know the type of person that just loves playing the guitar yet just outright sucks at it: the type that slaves away at practice for years on end fueled by their own fiery passion, not caring about the fact every time they play, the audience cringes? Me neither.

People are naturally motivated for things they're good at. Competence is self-reinforcing, both internally and externally. For yourself, competence stimulates confidence and self-efficacy. To others, competence gives social status. So if you want to like something and foster intrinsic motivation, you should aim to get good at it.

Paradoxically, a sense of competence can in some cases be even more intrinsically motivating than enjoying the activity itself. Competence is reinforcing and research has found that the reinforcing value of many activities, including exercise, drug use, overeating and gambling, predicts engaging in the activity more strongly than liking the activity [9]. You don't need to like something to do it. You just need to want it. Liking is not the same as wanting: they are distinct processes in our brains. In very simplified terms, the sensation of liking something is produced by the neurotransmitter serotonin, whereas the sensation of wanting something is produced by the neurotransmitter dopamine. In the gym, you may not like an exercise because you can't do it well. Your first step here should not be to immediately switch to a different exercise but to try to get better at the exercise. Learn proper technique and master the movement. When dieting, you may not like certain foods that are healthy and low in calories. Don't immediately stop eating them. Try different recipes. The reinforcing value of becoming good at something and achieving results can be stronger motivators than liking what you're doing.

In general, exercise doesn't have to be 'fun'. There's nothing 'fun' about grinding through the last 3 reps of a 12-rep max set of squats. Rather, exercise should be fulfilling. And nothing is as fulfilling as mastering something. Other than simply doing your activity of choice a lot, below are several more concrete tips to develop competence in anything.

Motivation tip 1.1: Research

Don't just do your workouts or your job. Research them. Stay up-to-date with the latest science. Talk to other experts. For example, I know many mid-level managers who feel their jobs are unfulfilling, because they feel what they do doesn't matter, but you can still take pride in doing a good job. Consider management courses with roleplay practice and read up on management sciences. If you can learn how to motivate others and make them more productive, as you're doing right now by reading this book, this competence should in turn motivate you.

For your fitness, competence is particularly important for intrinsic motivation. If you don't get results from your diet and training, it's very hard to stay motivated. Getting fit is difficult for many people, so it often pays off to learn about applied nutrition and exercise science. If you're a serious strength trainee and you're not subscribed to my email newsletter yet, I offer a free email course with 14 fitness lessons at www.MennoHenselmans.com/Subscribe

Motivation tip 1.2: Tracking

Tracking your progression also helps highlight your results. I've had many impatient clients that felt like 'nothing was happening', yet when they looked at their body fat measurements and strength progression, it was evident that they were making good progress and this helped them stay on track. At a minimum, I recommend that everyone into fitness tracks the following.

- The performance progression in your workouts. For strength trainees, this should normally include the weight x reps for each exercise, or at least your benchmark exercises. Endurance trainees like runners should probably track their distances, running times and ideally their heart rate.
- Your weight: remember the diet adherence chapter on how daily weigh-ins are strong predictors of diet adherence.
- Some measure of your body composition, even if it's just a basic waist circumference tape measure.

Companies should employ so-called Key Performance Indicators, such as sales, profit, churn, conversion rates and client satisfaction. If you can directly quantify productivity, such as in sales for a salesman or trading profit for a trader, that's ideal, but often you can still have very useful indicators with a bit of creativity. For example, email customer service representatives can insert an automated signature into their emails that lets customers rate their satisfaction with the help they received.

Objective results help you have faith in the process, as competence reinforces intrinsic motivation. However, your mindset to acquire this competence is perhaps even more important. Targeting a specific level of competence as your explicit goal can backfire.

Motivation tip 2: How to set goals

In college my roommate and I often played Super Smash Bros. on the Nintendo GameCube, a fighting game. We were very evenly matched when we started playing. We were both very competitive and we hated losing. Yet our mindsets differed enormously and over time this completely changed how we developed. He played every match to win it and saw losing as a sign he was bad. He knew my weaknesses, so he would exploit those. He knew there were certain attacks I would not use, so he didn't prepare for those. When there was an attack sequence that would consistently hit me, even if he knew it could be countered, he would keep using it over and over for as long as it hit me. I had a very different mindset: I played to get better and saw losing as a lesson for improvement, albeit a painful one. If I knew there was a strategy that had a clear counter, I would not use it, even if I knew my opponent didn't know the counter yet. I would prepare for every strategy, even if I knew my opponent wasn't the type to use it. Essentially, I always pretended my opponent was perfect. When my opponent used the same attack sequence over and over, I would not avoid it but practice the counter-move. I would lose 10 games to that attack sequence but by then had mastered the counter and it would never work against me again. Over time, I started winning almost all our games and he lost the motivation to play. In this story of 2 college kids playing a Nintendo fighting game is a profound life lesson of how to set goals for yourself.

Common wisdom says goals help you stay focused and increase motivation. Winning a game, benching 300 pounds, looking like Michelle Lewin, being 10% body fat, many people have concrete goals. Psychologists call these types of goals performance goals or goal intentions: you have the intention to achieve something. As we touched on in the chapter on dieting, the problem with these goals is that's all they are: desire. They're empty. Who wouldn't want to be a billionaire or look like a supermodel? Just a desire without a plan or being prepared to do what it will take to achieve the goal is meaningless. We covered a better way to set goals: implementation intentions AKA action triggers: if-then rules for yourself that concretely tell you what to do. However, implementation intentions will also not foster intrinsic motivation, as they don't give you long-term direction. They are largely instrumental, like extrinsic motivation.

To cultivate intrinsic motivation, you need to take your mind off all the things outside of your body that you want. When you're focused on the future goal, you lose presence in the now and you enjoy the activity less, which over time reduces motivation [10]. Think of running a marathon while you're constantly thinking of the distance to the finish line. Or staring at a clock in the waiting room for your dentist appointment: it seems to make time go by slower, not faster. I once asked a decorated marathon runner what he thinks about during those long marathons. He said he only thinks one thing: "One more step."

Your focus should be on improving yourself. Psychologists call this a growth mindset: you devote yourself to personal growth, not some arbitrary endpoint that you may or may not end up at. You devote yourself to the journey, not the destination. A popular version of the growth mindset in sports is coach John Wooden's success rule: "Do your best to become the best you are capable of becoming." [11] A wide range of studies in academics, sports and the corporate world show that people with a growth mindset outperform people with performance goals [12, 13, 14, 15]. In the gym the difference between mindsets is night and day. Performance chasers often end up ego lifting, training their ego more effectively than their body. They try to squat with as much weight on the bar as possible, which means they do partial reps and never develop good exercise technique. Those with a growth mindset don't care about what they squat, only that they squat more next time than they do now. They consequently develop good form with full range of motion and make far better progress in the long run.

Whatever you do in life that's important to you, do it to get better. Don't set any arbitrary performance goals. Your goal should always simply be to get better. Don't play a chess match to beat your opponent. Play to become a better chess player. Don't diet to become X kilograms. Develop sustainable habits to lower your body fat percentage until you're happy with what you see in the mirror. Don't go to the gym to bench 300 pounds. Train to get stronger. One more step.

Motivation tip 3: How to become more autonomous

At high school I had to read the book *Lord of the Flies* for my literature class. Like I did with most books on the reading list, I didn't actually read the book. I skimmed it a bit and read the CliffsNotes summary online. I couldn't care less what happened to some British lads on an imaginary island. Ironically, however, years later I read the book on my own accord and I loved it. Only halfway through did I realize I had written a book report about it at school once.

Nothing's fun anymore when you *have to* do it. Our current species evolved largely as hunter-gatherers. We evolved to explore, to be free, and that's what most people enjoy. In terms of self-determination theory, autonomy is the second key component of intrinsic motivation [5, 6, 7, 8].

Being autonomous is largely a matter of your mindset. I observed this incredibly clearly both as a business consultant and at University College Utrecht (UCU). UCU is the international honor's college of Utrecht University, which itself already ranks top 100 in the world on most university rankings. It's often ranked as Holland's best university. What separated UCU's top of the top students from other students? It wasn't intelligence. UCU students may be a little smarter and indeed they averaged higher grades than other students, but it wasn't so obvious that you could pick a UCU student out of a crowd of other students purely based on their IQ. The most striking difference by far was that when you asked a UCU student anything they didn't know, they never responded: "I don't know." Instead, they'd say something like: "Let me look that up." A small minority of UCU folks would brag about how UCU was the elite of the elite, and I often joked to them the only difference between UCU students and the rest of the world was that UCU students knew how to Google. As it turns out though, having the mindset of figuring stuff out on your own is in fact a monumental driver of success. An autonomous mindset stimulates self-efficacy and intrinsic motivation. There is little more powerful than a person driven to get the job done. As an employer, I can confidently say I value autonomy much higher than intelligence in the people I work with.

As a business consultant too, one of the most important aspects of success was being autonomous. My firm of course advertised our consultants to clients as being highly competent, but often we honestly had very little idea of what exactly we should be doing at the client in the first place. We were essentially 'dumped' there with the mandate: 'make this place better'. But that actually worked, because we were all people that would figure it out. The first thing I always did was catalogue where I could get information: what were the key databases and contact persons. After that, essentially everything would just be a matter of searching and asking.

So strike the phrase "I don't know" from your head and replace it with: "I'll figure it out."

Motivation tip 4: Connect

Why do we wear the clothes we wear, drive the cars we drive and use the language we use? Most of it isn't strictly functional. According to acclaimed French sociologist Pierre Bourdieu, our taste in cultural matters is largely a method of social distinction. In his renowned book *Distinction*, he presents scientific support for how our taste in things is primarily an expression of our sociocultural group. Let's take buying a car. Would you rather get a second-hand silver Honda or a red Ferrari? Strictly functionally, both will get you from A to B without much of an objective difference. In fact, the Ferrari is impractically low to the ground to drive in many places and is typically less economical in fuel usage, so the Honda is generally the more functional choice. However, the Ferrari's economical disadvantage is also its greatest advantage: it's incredibly expensive. A Ferrari says: "I'm rich." In fact, a Ferrari, especially a red one, arguably says: "I'm rich, bitch."

Economists call this conspicuous consumption. Bourdieu calls it social distinction. If you call it vulgar, Bourdieu's research would predict you're highly educated and cultured. Rather than the Ferrari, you may prefer a Tesla. A Tesla says: "I care about the environment, and this car coincidentally also shows I'm rich, but that's not the reason I bought it."

Don't worry. We all do it. In fact, you can't escape social distinction, because even if you were to 'not play this game' and you choose not to have Instagram, to buy only unbranded clothing and to drive a second-hand Honda, those choices would still speak volumes about your cultural values. Humans are social animals and we naturally cluster together into groups of like-minded individuals to form communities. Gothics, skaters, business men, society is full of related groups of people that we can often even identify with a label. It's no surprise then that the third key component of what intrinsically motivates us is relatedness [5, 6, 7, 8]. To do something without requiring self-control, you need to feel some sort of socio-cultural connection to it.

We associate with people we like in part to 'bask in their reflected glory' [16]. For example, research in sports fans shows that when their team is winning, fans wear the team's shirt more and they identify more strongly with their team, yet when their team is losing, it's: "Oh yeah I'm not that much of a fan really. I just watch them occasionally when I'm bored."

In fitness, we also have tribes: keto, bodybuilders, paleo, the bros, the functional trainers, etc. One of the most successful tribes is arguably CrossFit. They have perfected the development of relatedness. Their workouts are not individual training sessions but social activities. A CrossFit gym isn't even called a gym. It's a 'box'. All boxes look alike and have the same equipment. Everyone does the same Workout of the Day. Their workouts have their own names, often those of mid-upper-class Caucasian women, in line with their target audience's socio-economic status. They're vocal about not being superficial and not training for aesthetics: they do 'functional training'. Their diet is as primal as their workouts: CrossFit and paleo are a match made in heaven. These factors create intrinsic motivation to CrossFit by fostering relatedness. CrossFit's communal spirit also explains why it imploded so badly after its former CEO Greg Glassman belittled George Floyd's death: people suddenly didn't want to be related to CrossFit anymore.

Evidence-based fitness is also a tribe, but it's an empty one compared to CrossFit. Relatedness is very much an emotional attachment. Anything that promotes rationality will lack in relatedness, as by definition it stimulates us to shut off the more primal part of our brain that forms associations, system 1. That's why, for example, religions have historically been far more powerful than atheism in bringing people together. Relatedness is a far stronger motivation for behavior than information, generally speaking [17]. I can't effectively motivate my fitness clients by saying: "Follow the program, Bob! Your program is exactly in line with the scientific literature. You're a man of science, Bob!"

Similarly, our attitudes towards foods are easier to change with associations with the food than factual information [18]. For example, you'd probably have more success convincing someone of becoming a vegan by showing them a video of animal abuse than by listing related statistics. That's also why it can actually be beneficial to have bad associations with unhealthy or caloric foods, as long as you keep in mind you're restricting foods by choice.

To foster willpower-free motivation via relatedness, I have 2 final tips for you in this book.

Motivation tip 4.1: Find a community

One of the most direct ways to develop relatedness is to find others like you that do the same thing you do. This can be your colleagues or people in your gym, but it doesn't have to be. If you're a serious strength trainee training in a standard commercial gym, you probably don't connect with the general population gym goers that are just cluelessly messing about. You may be annoyed by commercial gym rules that actively interfere with your goals, such as not being able to train barefoot, not being able to use chalk or not being allowed to deadlift. Not to mention the behavior of the other gym members, such as the guy doing biceps curls in the only squat rack, or if you're a strong woman, the incessant comments 'not to get too big' or 'not to lift too heavy'. You'll probably find more like-minded communities on social media and internet forums. Sociocultural connections don't have to be physical anymore in our digital, globalized age.

The same goes for your job. Say you're an IT professional and you don't connect with the other programmers at the office. You may get along better with the community at StackOverflow.com or Reddit.

My father is currently a freelance interim CEO in the psychological healthcare industry. As the CEO, especially one that by design doesn't stick around for many years, there's a limit to how familiar he can get with others at work: you can be collegial, but you also have to remain the executive. He has still developed a network of peers consisting of other CEOs and managers during all the conferences and courses he's done. Similarly, as a self-employed digital nomad, most of my social network is spread across the world. Don't limit your network to your acute surroundings.

Motivation tip 4.2: How purpose motivates us, even when it's nonsense

Have you ever requested something from a colleague and gotten the response: "That's not my job"? That mindset is very demotivating. If you think of yourself as a job description, a list of tasks with no ulterior motive than to complete the tasks in exchange for your salary, you have no purpose. Without purpose, you are missing out on a large piece of motivation.

The power of purpose was illustrated well by a study by Langer et al. [19]. The researchers gave one of their agents a top secret mission... to cut forward in line in a print shop. The operative was tasked to perform this mission using 3 different strategies. The first strategy was simply politely asking if they could cut in line. This didn't cut it, no pun intended. While 60% of people let someone go first for the small request of 5 copies, when it concerned 20 copies only 24% of people agreed to wait. The second strategy was again asking to go first but adding "because I'm in a rush".

This majorly increased compliance to 94% for the small request and 42% for the large request, illustrating the power of 'why'. The results of the third strategy were even more enlightening. The third strategy was the same request to cut in line but adding "because I have to make copies". You may think: well, duh? Everybody's in line to make copies. That's obvious and uninformative, yet a completely nonsensical 'why' also increased compliance to 93% for the small request. It didn't increase compliance for the large request though: if you want people to do you a large favor, your reason actually has to make some sense.

To be intrinsically motivated for anything, you must know why you're doing it. A big reason to do anything is to help people. Helping people is inherently rewarding, as we discussed in the chapter on productivity. So you're not 'the person that processes customer complaints'. You're the person that makes unhappy customers happy. If you don't create anything or help anyone directly with your job, it can help to think of the greater purpose of the company. What is its vision, its purpose? A little basking in reflected glory also never hurt anyone.

So my final tip in this book for you is: always have a clear purpose in mind and let others know what your purpose is. It'll help motivate yourself and others alike.

AFTERWORD

My goal of this book was to help guide you on a journey to superhuman self-control. While I don't expect you to put on a cape and fly, I hope your brain's rational rider has gotten some useful tips to control your inner emotional elephant. You should now understand exactly what self-control is, how it works in your brain, and how to cultivate an indomitable will. Your self-control is not physically finite, so there is no need to train it, only to learn how to pull the reins on the elephant. Your personal growth journey will be beset on all sides by terrible nocebos, temptations, decision fatigue, projection bias, cravings and many more terrors of the human psyche, but you know how to navigate these obstacles now. You know how to structure your day and take advantage of your biorhythm, different stimulus modalities and immersive breaks. You're armed with the Zeigarnik effect, implementation intentions, an optimized to-do list, the Yerkes-Dodson law and many more weapons of mass productivity. You know what to do before and after every meal, how to program your workouts, how to manage your appetite, how to change your habits, how to set goals and how to track your progression. Your mindset is flexible and set on growth, connections and success. Go grow. Go connect. Go conquer.

P.S. I'd greatly appreciate it if you would leave an honest review on Amazon to help others find this book.

REFERENCES

Chapter 1: 2-system theory

1. Dutton, D. G. & Aron, A. P. (1974). Some evidence for heightened sexual attraction under conditions of high anxiety. *Journal of personality and social psychology, 30*(4), 510–517.
2. White, G. L., Fishbein, S., & Rutsein, J. (1981). Passionate love and the misattribution of arousal. *Journal of Personality and Social Psychology, 41*(1), 56–62.
3. Marin, M. M., Schober, R., Gingras, B., & Leder, H. (2017). Misattribution of musical arousal increases sexual attraction towards opposite-sex faces in females. *PloS one, 12*(9), e0183531.
4. Bronkhorst A. W. (2015). The cocktail-party problem revisited: early processing and selection of multitalker speech. *Attention, perception & psychophysics, 77*(5), 1465–1487.
5. Heeger, D. J., Simoncelli, E. P., & Movshon, J. A. (1996). Computational models of cortical visual processing. *Proceedings of the National Academy of Sciences of the United States of America, 93*(2), 623–627.
6. Flor, H., Elbert, T., Knecht, S., Wienbruch, C., Pantev, C., Birbaumer, N., Larbig, W., & Taub, E. (1995). Phantom-limb pain as a perceptual correlate of cortical reorganization following arm amputation. *Nature, 375*(6531), 482–484.
7. Saunders, B., Milyavskaya, M., Etz, A., Randles, D. & Inzlicht, M. (2018). Reported Self-control is not Meaningfully Associated with Inhibition-related Executive Function: A Bayesian Analysis. *Collabra: Psychology 4*(1), 39.
8. Holden, C. (1979). Paul MacLean and the triune brain. *Science, 204*(4397), 1066–1068.
9. Tosches, M. A., Yamawaki, T. M., Naumann, R. K., Jacobi, A. A., Tushev, G. & Laurent, G. (2018). Evolution of pallium, hippocampus, and cortical cell types revealed by single-cell transcriptomics in reptiles. *Science, 360*(6391), 881–888.
10. Inzlicht, M., Schmeichel, B. J., & Macrae, C. N. (2014). Why self-control seems (but may not be) limited. *Trends in cognitive sciences, 18*(3), 127–133.

Chapter 2: Thy will be done

1. Mischel, W., Ebbesen, E. B., & Raskoff Zeiss, A. (1972). Cognitive and attentional mechanisms in delay of gratification. *Journal of Personality and Social Psychology, 21*(2), 204–218.
2. Shoda, Y., Mischel, W., & Peake, P. K. (1990). Predicting adolescent cognitive and self-regulatory competencies from preschool delay of gratification: Identifying diagnostic conditions. *Developmental Psychology, 26*(6), 978–986.
3. Schlam, T. R., Wilson, N. L., Shoda, Y., Mischel, W., & Ayduk, O. (2013). Preschoolers' delay of gratification predicts their body mass 30 years later. *The Journal of pediatrics, 162*(1), 90–93.
4. Baumeister, R. F., Bratslavsky, E., Muraven, M., & Tice, D. M. (1998). Ego depletion: is the active self a limited resource? *Journal of personality and social psychology, 74*(5), 1252–1265.
5. Vohs, K. D., & Heatherton, T. F. (2000). Self-regulatory failure: a resource-depletion approach. *Psychological science, 11*(3), 249–254.
6. Dorris, D.C., Power, D.A., & Kenefick, E (2012). Investigating the effects of ego depletion on physical exercise routines of athletes. *Psychology of Sport and Exercise, 13*(2), 118–125.

7. Haynes, A., Kemps, E., & Moffitt, R. (2016). Too Depleted to Try? Testing the Process Model of Ego Depletion in the Context of Unhealthy Snack Consumption. *Applied psychology. Health and well-being*, *8*(3), 386–404.

8. Gailliot, M. T., & Baumeister, R. F. (2007). The physiology of willpower: linking blood glucose to self-control. *Personality and social psychology review : an official journal of the Society for Personality and Social Psychology, Inc*, *11*(4), 303–327.

9. Denson, T.F., von Hippel, W., Kemp, R.I., & Teo, L.S. (2010). Glucose consumption decreases impulsive aggression in response to provocation in aggressive individuals. *Journal of Experimental Social Psychology, 46*(6), 1023–1028.

10. Owen, L., Scholey, A. B., Finnegan, Y., Hu, H., & Sünram-Lea, S. I. (2012). The effect of glucose dose and fasting interval on cognitive function: a double-blind, placebo-controlled, six-way crossover study. *Psychopharmacology*, *220*(3), 577–589.

11. Kurzban R. (2010). Does the brain consume additional glucose during self-control tasks? *Evolutionary psychology : an international journal of evolutionary approaches to psychology and behavior*, *8*(2), 244–259.

12. Molden, D. C., Hui, C. M., Scholer, A. A., Meier, B. P., Noreen, E. E., D'Agostino, P. R., & Martin, V. (2012). Motivational versus metabolic effects of carbohydrates on self-control. *Psychological science*, *23*(10), 1137–1144.

13. Lange, F., Seer, C., Rapior, M., Rose, J., & Eggert, F. (2014). Turn It All You Want: Still No Effect of Sugar Consumption on Ego Depletion. *Journal of European Psychology Students, 5*(3), 1–8.

14. Cornwell, J. F., Franks, B., & Higgins, E. T. (2014). Truth, control, and value motivations: the "what," "how," and "why" of approach and avoidance. *Frontiers in systems neuroscience*, *8*, 194.

15. Saunders, B., Lin, H., Milyavskaya, M., & Inzlicht, M. (2017). The emotive nature of conflict monitoring in the medial prefrontal cortex. *International journal of psychophysiology : official journal of the International Organization of Psychophysiology*, *119*, 31–40.

16. Francis, Z. L., & Inzlicht, M. (2016). *Proximate and ultimate causes of ego depletion*. In E. R. Hirt, J. J. Clarkson, & L. Jia (Eds.), *Self-regulation and ego control* (p. 373–398). Elsevier Academic Press.

17. Randles, D., Harlow, I., & Inzlicht, M. (2017). A pre-registered naturalistic observation of within domain mental fatigue and domain-general depletion of self-control. *PloS one*, *12*(9), e0182980.

18. Hofmann, W., Vohs, K. D., & Baumeister, R. F. (2012). What people desire, feel conflicted about, and try to resist in everyday life. *Psychological science*, *23*(6), 582–588.

19. Schmeichel, B. J., Harmon-Jones, C., & Harmon-Jones, E. (2010). Exercising self-control increases approach motivation. *Journal of personality and social psychology*, *99*(1), 162–173.

20. Wagner, D. D., Altman, M., Boswell, R. G., Kelley, W. M., & Heatherton, T. F. (2013). Self-regulatory depletion enhances neural responses to rewards and impairs top-down control. *Psychological science*, *24*(11), 2262–2271.

21. Seligman, M.E.P., Ernst, R.M., Gillham, J., Reivich, K., & Linkins, M. (2009). Positive education: positive psychology and classroom interventions. *Oxford Review of Education, 35*(3), 293–311.

22. Boksem, M.A.S., Meijman, T.F., & Lorist, M.M. (2006). Mental fatigue, motivation and action monitoring. *Biological Psychology, 72*(2), 123–132.

23. Muraven, M., & Slessareva, E. (2003). Mechanisms of Self-Control Failure: Motivation and Limited Resources. *Personality and Social Psychology Bulletin, 29*(7), 894–906.

24. Giacomantonio, M., Ten Velden, F.S., & De Dreu, C.K.W. (2016). Framing effortful strategies as easy enables depleted individuals to execute complex tasks effectively. *Journal of Experimental Social Psychology, 62*, 68–74.

25. Comerford, D.A., & Ubel, P.A. (2013). Effort Aversion: Job choice and compensation decisions overweight effort. *Journal of Economic Behavior & Organization, 92*, 152–162.

26. Moller, A. C., Deci, E. L., & Ryan, R. M. (2006). Choice and ego-depletion: the moderating role of autonomy. *Personality & social psychology bulletin*, *32*(8), 1024–1036.

27. Veilleux, J.C., Skinner, K.D., Baker, D.E., & Chamberlain, K.D. (2021). Perceived willpower self-efficacy fluctuates dynamically with affect and distress intolerance. Journal of Research in Personality, 90, 104058.

28. Sanders, M. A., Shirk, S. D., Burgin, C. J., & Martin, L. L. (2012). The gargle effect: rinsing the mouth with glucose enhances self-control. *Psychological science*, *23*(12), 1470–1472.

29. Hagger, M. S., & Chatzisarantis, N. L. (2013). The sweet taste of success: the presence of glucose in the oral cavity moderates the depletion of self-control resources. *Personality & social psychology bulletin*, *39*(1), 28–42.

30. Konishi, K., Kimura, T., Yuhaku, A., Kurihara, T., Fujimoto, M., Hamaoka, T., & Sanada, K. (2017). Mouth rinsing with a carbohydrate solution attenuates exercise-induced decline in executive function. *Journal of the International Society of Sports Nutrition*, *14*, 45.

31. Murray, K. O., Paris, H. L., Fly, A. D., Chapman, R. F., & Mickleborough, T. D. (2018). Carbohydrate Mouth Rinse Improves Cycling Time-Trial Performance without Altering Plasma Insulin Concentration. *Journal of sports science & medicine*, *17*(1), 145–152.

32. Bavaresco Gambassi, B., Gomes de Santana Barros Leal, Y., Pinheiro Dos Anjos, E. R., Antonelli, B. A., Gomes Gonçalves E Silva, D. C., Hermes Pires de Mélo Montenegro, I., di Cássia de Oliveira Angelo, R., Suruagy Correia Moura, I., & Schwingel, P. A. (2019). Carbohydrate mouth rinse improves cycling performance carried out until the volitional exhaustion. *The Journal of sports medicine and physical fitness*, *59*(1), 1–5.

33. Ginieis, R., Franz, E. A., Oey, I., & Peng, M. (2018). The "sweet" effect: Comparative assessments of dietary sugars on cognitive performance. *Physiology & behavior*, *184*, 242–247.

34. MacLean, E. L., Hare, B., Nunn, C. L., Addessi, E., Amici, F., Anderson, R. C., Aureli, F., Baker, J. M., Bania, A. E., Barnard, A. M., Boogert, N. J., Brannon, E. M., Bray, E. E., Bray, J., Brent, L. J., Burkart, J. M., Call, J., Cantlon, J. F., Cheke, L. G., Clayton, N. S., ... Zhao, Y. (2014). The evolution of self-control. *Proceedings of the National Academy of Sciences of the United States of America*, *111*(20), E2140–E2148.

35. Stevens, J. R., Hallinan, E. V., & Hauser, M. D. (2005). The ecology and evolution of patience in two New World monkeys. *Biology letters*, *1*(2), 223–226.

Chapter 3: How to be more productive

1. Miles, E., Sheeran, P., Baird, H., Macdonald, I., Webb, T. L., & Harris, P. R. (2016). Does self-control improve with practice? Evidence from a six-week training program. *Journal of experimental psychology. General*, *145*(8), 1075–1091.

2. Inzlicht, M., & Berkman, E. (2015). Six Questions for the Resource Model of Control (and Some Answers). *Social and personality psychology compass*, *9*(10), 511–524.

3. Veling, H., Lawrence, N. S., Chen, Z., van Koningsbruggen, G. M., & Holland, R. W. (2017). What Is Trained During Food Go/No-Go Training? A Review Focusing on Mechanisms and a Research Agenda. *Current addiction reports*, *4*(1), 35–41.

4. Jaeggi, S. M., Buschkuehl, M., Jonides, J., & Shah, P. (2011). Short- and long-term benefits of cognitive training. *Proceedings of the National Academy of Sciences of the United States of America*, *108*(25), 10081–10086.

5. Melby-Lervåg, M., & Hulme, C. (2013). Is working memory training effective? A meta-analytic review. *Developmental psychology*, *49*(2), 270–291.

6. Berkman, E. T., Kahn, L. E., & Merchant, J. S. (2014). Training-induced changes in inhibitory control network activity. *The Journal of neuroscience : the official journal of the Society for Neuroscience*, *34*(1), 149–157.

7. Reeves, R. R., Ladner, M. E., Hart, R. H., & Burke, R. S. (2007). Nocebo effects with antidepressant clinical drug trial placebos. *General hospital psychiatry*, *29*(3), 275–277.

8. Barsky, A. J., Saintfort, R., Rogers, M. P., & Borus, J. F. (2002). Nonspecific medication side effects and the nocebo phenomenon. *JAMA, 287*(5), 622–627.

9. Benedetti, F., Pollo, A., Lopiano, L., Lanotte, M., Vighetti, S., & Rainero, I. (2003). Conscious expectation and unconscious conditioning in analgesic, motor, and hormonal placebo/nocebo responses. *The Journal of neuroscience : the official journal of the Society for Neuroscience, 23*(10), 4315–4323.

10. Hahn R. A. (1997). The nocebo phenomenon: concept, evidence, and implications for public health. *Preventive medicine, 26*(5 Pt 1), 607–611.

11. Spiegel H. (1997). Nocebo: the power of suggestibility. *Preventive medicine, 26*(5 Pt 1), 616–621.

12. Jakšić, N., Aukst-Margetić, B., & Jakovljević, M. (2013). Does personality play a relevant role in the placebo effect? *Psychiatria Danubina, 25*(1), 17–23.

13. Symon, A., Williams, B., Adelasoye, Q. A., & Cheyne, H. (2015). Nocebo and the potential harm of 'high risk' labelling: a scoping review. *Journal of advanced nursing, 71*(7), 1518–1529.

14. Ariel, G., & Saville, W. (1972). Anabolic steroids: the physiological effects of placebos. *Medicine and Science in Sports, 4*(2), 124–126.

15. Foroughi, C. K., Monfort, S. S., Paczynski, M., McKnight, P. E., & Greenwood, P. M. (2016). Placebo effects in cognitive training. *Proceedings of the National Academy of Sciences of the United States of America, 113*(27), 7470–7474.

16. MENNINGER VON LERCHENTHAL E. (1948). Death from psychic causes. *Bulletin of the Menninger Clinic, 12*(1), 31–36.

17. Job, V., Dweck, C. S., & Walton, G. M. (2010). Ego depletion--is it all in your head? implicit theories about willpower affect self-regulation. *Psychological science, 21*(11), 1686–1693.

18. Job, V., Walton, G. M., Bernecker, K., & Dweck, C. S. (2015). Implicit theories about willpower predict self-regulation and grades in everyday life. *Journal of personality and social psychology, 108*(4), 637–647.

19. Muraven, M., & Slessareva, E. (2003). Mechanisms of self-control failure: motivation and limited resources. *Personality & social psychology bulletin, 29*(7), 894–906.

20. Clarkson, J. J., Hirt, E. R., Jia, L., & Alexander, M. B. (2010). When perception is more than reality: the effects of perceived versus actual resource depletion on self-regulatory behavior. *Journal of personality and social psychology, 98*(1), 29–46.

21. Clarkson, J. J., Hirt, E. R., Jia, L., & Alexander, M. B. (2010). When perception is more than reality: the effects of perceived versus actual resource depletion on self-regulatory behavior. *Journal of personality and social psychology, 98*(1), 29–46.

22. Dormann, C., Fay, D., Zapf, D., & Frese, M. (2006). A State-Trait Analysis of Job Satisfaction: On the Effect of Core Self-Evaluations. *Applied Psychology, 55*(1), 27–51.

23. Hansemark, O.C. (1998). The effects of an entrepreneurship programme on Need for Achievement and Locus of Control of reinforcement. *International Journal of Entrepreneurial Behavior & Research, 4*(1), 28–50.

24. Cameron, K., Mora, C., Leutscher, T., & Calarco, M. (2011). Effects of Positive Practices on Organizational Effectiveness. The Journal of Applied Behavioral Science, 47(3), 266–308.

25. Giacomantonio, M., Ten Velden, F.S., & De Dreu, C.K.W. (2016). Framing effortful strategies as easy enables depleted individuals to execute complex tasks effectively. *Journal of Experimental Social Psychology, 62*, 68–74.

26. Bandura A. (1977). Self-efficacy: toward a unifying theory of behavioral change. *Psychological review, 84*(2), 191–215.

27. McGraw, K.O., & Fiala, J. (1982). Undermining the Zeigarnik effect: Another hidden cost of reward. *Journal of Personality, 50*(1), 58–66.

28. Halkjelsvik, T., & Rise, J. (2015). Persistence motives in irrational decisions to complete a boring task. *Personality & social psychology bulletin, 41*(1), 90–102.

29. James, I., & Kendell, K. (1997). Unfinished Processing in the Emotional Disorders: The Zeigarnik Effect. *Behavioural and Cognitive Psychotherapy, 25*(4), 329–337.

30. Milyavskaya, M., & Inzlicht, M. (2017). What's So Great About Self-Control? Examining the Importance of Effortful Self-Control and Temptation in Predicting Real-

Life Depletion and Goal Attainment. Social Psychological and Personality Science, 8(6), 603–611.

31. Duvivier, R. J., van Dalen, J., Muijtjens, A. M., Moulaert, V. R., van der Vleuten, C. P., & Scherpbier, A. J. (2011). The role of deliberate practice in the acquisition of clinical skills. *BMC medical education, 11*, 101.

32. Lavie, P., & Scherson, A. (1981). Ultrashort sleep-walking schedule. I. Evidence of ultradian rhythmicity in 'sleepability'. *Electroencephalography and clinical neurophysiology, 52*(2), 163–174.

33. Lavie, P., Zomer, J., & Gopher, D. (1995). Ultradian Rhythms in Prolonged Human Performance. 32.

34. Masicampo, E.J., Martin, S.R., & Anderson, R.A. (2014). Understanding and Overcoming Self-control Depletion. *Social and Personality Psychology Compass, 8*(11), 638–649.

35. vouchercloud. (n.d.). *How Many Productive Hours in a Work Day? Just 2 Hours, 23 Minutes...* https://www.vouchercloud.com/resources/office-worker-productivity

36. Reid, E. (2015). Embracing, Passing, Revealing, and the Ideal Worker Image: How People Navigate Expected and Experienced Professional Identities. *Organization Science, 26*(4), 941–1261.

37. Robinson, S. (2012, March 14). *Bring back the 40-hour work week.* Salon. https://www.salon.com/test2/2012/03/14/bring_back_the_40_hour_work_week/

38. Rogers, A. E., Hwang, W. T., Scott, L. D., Aiken, L. H., & Dinges, D. F. (2004). The working hours of hospital staff nurses and patient safety. *Health affairs (Project Hope), 23*(4), 202–212.

39. Nesthus, T., Schroeder, D., Connors, M., Rentmeister-Bryant, H., & DeRoshia, C. (2007). *Flight Attendant Fatigue* (Report No. DOT/FAA/AM-07/21). Federal Aviation Administration. https://www.faa.gov/data_research/research/med_humanfacs/oamtechreports/2000s/media/200721.pdf

40. Ericsson, K, Krampe, R. T., & Tesch-Roemer, C. (1993). The Role of Deliberate Practice in the Acquisition of Expert Performance. *Psychological Review, 100*(3), 363–406.

41. Focht, B.C., & Hausenblas, H.A. (2001). Influence of Quiet Rest and Acute Aerobic Exercise Performed in a Naturalistic Environment on Selected Psychological Responses. *Journal of Sport and Exercise Psychology, 23*(2), 108–121.

42. Szuhany, K. L., Bugatti, M., & Otto, M. W. (2015). A meta-analytic review of the effects of exercise on brain-derived neurotrophic factor. *Journal of psychiatric research, 60*, 56–64.

43. Church, D. D., Hoffman, J. R., Mangine, G. T., Jajtner, A. R., Townsend, J. R., Beyer, K. S., Wang, R., La Monica, M. B., Fukuda, D. H., & Stout, J. R. (2016). Comparison of high-intensity vs. high-volume resistance training on the BDNF response to exercise. *Journal of Applied Physiology, 121*(1), 123–128.

44. Erickson, K. I., Miller, D. L., & Roecklein, K. A. (2012). The aging hippocampus: interactions between exercise, depression, and BDNF. *The Neuroscientist : a review journal bringing neurobiology, neurology and psychiatry, 18*(1), 82–97.

45. Oppezzo, M. & Schwartz, D.L. (2014). Give Your Ideas Some Legs: The Positive Effect of Walking on Creative Thinking. *Journal of Experimental Psychology: Learning, Memory, and Cognition, 40*(4), 1142–1152.

46. Steinberg, H., Sykes, E. A., Moss, T., Lowery, S., LeBoutillier, N., & Dewey, A. (1997). Exercise enhances creativity independently of mood. *British journal of sports medicine, 31*(3), 240–245.

47. Shevchuk N. A. (2008). Adapted cold shower as a potential treatment for depression. *Medical hypotheses, 70*(5), 995–1001.

48. Mooventhan, A., & Nivethitha, L. (2014). Scientific evidence-based effects of hydrotherapy on various systems of the body. *North American journal of medical sciences, 6*(5), 199–209.

49. Derrick, J.L. (2012). Energized by Television: Familiar Fictional Worlds Restore Self-Control. *Social Psychological and Personality Science, 4*(3), 299–307.

50. Baxter, V., & Kroll-Smith, S. (2005). Normalizing the Workplace Nap: Blurring the Boundaries between Public and Private Space and Time. *Current Sociology, 53*(1), 33–55.

51. Rosekind, M. R., Smith, R. M., Miller, D. L., Co, E. L., Gregory, ., KB, Webbon, L. L., Gander, P. H., & Lebacqz, J. V. (1995). Alertness management: strategic naps in operational settings. *Journal of sleep research, 4*(S2), 62–66.

52. Mulrine, H. M., Signal, T. L., van den Berg, M. J., & Gander, P. H. (2012). Post-sleep inertia performance benefits of longer naps in simulated nightwork and extended operations. *Chronobiology international, 29*(9), 1249–1257.

53. Smith-Coggins, R., Howard, S. K., Mac, D. T., Wang, C., Kwan, S., Rosekind, M. R., Sowb, Y., Balise, R., Levis, J., & Gaba, D. M. (2006). Improving alertness and performance in emergency department physicians and nurses: the use of planned naps. *Annals of emergency medicine, 48*(5), 596–604.e6043.

54. Mednick, S. C., Nakayama, K., Cantero, J. L., Atienza, M., Levin, A. A., Pathak, N., & Stickgold, R. (2002). The restorative effect of naps on perceptual deterioration. *Nature neuroscience, 5*(7), 677–681.

55. Napping may not be such a no-no. Research is showing that the daytime snooze may have benefits and not interfere with nighttime sleep. (2009). *Harvard health letter, 35*(1), 1–2.

56. Zeidan, F., Johnson, S. K., Diamond, B. J., David, Z., & Goolkasian, P. (2010). Mindfulness meditation improves cognition: evidence of brief mental training. *Consciousness and cognition, 19*(2), 597–605.

57. Slagter, H. A., Lutz, A., Greischar, L. L., Francis, A. D., Nieuwenhuis, S., Davis, J. M., & Davidson, R. J. (2007). Mental training affects distribution of limited brain resources. *PLoS biology, 5*(6), e138.

58. Levy, David & Wobbrock, Jacob & Kaszniak, Alfred & Ostergren, Marilyn. (2012). The effects of mindfulness meditation training on multitasking in a high-stress information environment. Proceedings - Graphics Interface. 45-52.

59. Friese, M., & Wänke, M. (2014). Personal prayer buffers self-control depletion. *Journal of Experimental Social Psychology, 51*, 56–59.

60. Egan, P.M., Hirt, E.R., & Karpen, S.C. (2012). Taking a fresh perspective: Vicarious restoration as a means of recovering self-control. *Journal of Experimental Social Psychology, 48*(2), 457–465.

61. Boksem, M. A., Meijman, T. F., & Lorist, M. M. (2006). Mental fatigue, motivation and action monitoring. *Biological psychology, 72*(2), 123–132.

62. Tang, S.-H. & Hall, V.C. (1995). The overjustification effect: A meta-analysis. *Applied Cognitive Psychology, 9*(3), 365–404.

63. Frey, B.S., & Jegen, R. (2001). Motivation Crowding Theory. *Journal of Economic Surveys, 15*(5), 589–611.

64. Rosenfield, D., Folger, R., & Adelman, H. F. (1980). When rewards reflect competence: A qualification of the overjustification effect. *Journal of Personality and Social Psychology, 39*(3), 368–376.

65. Masicampo, E.J., Martin, S.R., & Anderson, R.A. (2014), Understanding and Overcoming Self-control Depletion. *Social and Personality Psychology Compass, 8*(11), 638–649.

66. Schmeichel, B. J., & Vohs, K. (2009). Self-affirmation and self-control: affirming core values counteracts ego depletion. *Journal of personality and social psychology, 96*(4), 770–782.

67. Li, Q., & Wang, Z. (2016). The modality effect of ego depletion: Auditory task modality reduces ego depletion. *Scandinavian journal of psychology, 57*(4), 292–297.

68. Tuk, M. A., Zhang, K., & Sweldens, S. (2015). The propagation of self-control: Self-control in one domain simultaneously improves self-control in other domains. *Journal of experimental psychology. General, 144*(3), 639–654.

69. Li, Q., & Wang, Z. (2016). The modality effect of ego depletion: Auditory task modality reduces ego depletion. *Scandinavian journal of psychology, 57*(4), 292–297.

70. MILLER G. A. (1956). The magical number seven plus or minus two: some limits on our capacity for processing information. *Psychological review, 63*(2), 81–97.

71. Bühner, M., König, C.J., Pick, M., & Krumm, S. (2006). Working Memory Dimensions as Differential Predictors of the Speed and Error Aspect of Multitasking Performance. *Human Performance, 19*(3), 253–275.

72. Wood, E., Zivcakova, L., Gentile, P., Archer, K., De Pasquale D., & Nosko, D. (2012). Examining the impact of off-task multi-tasking with technology on real-time classroom learning. *Computers & Education, 58*(1), 365–374.

73. Hinson, J. M., Jameson, T. L., & Whitney, P. (2003). Impulsive decision making and working memory. *Journal of experimental psychology. Learning, memory, and cognition, 29*(2), 298–306.

74. Szameitat, A. J., Hamaida, Y., Tulley, R. S., Saylik, R., & Otermans, P. C. (2015). "Women Are Better Than Men"-Public Beliefs on Gender Differences and Other Aspects in Multitasking. *PloS one, 10*(10), e0140371.

75. Mäntylä T. (2013). Gender differences in multitasking reflect spatial ability. *Psychological science, 24*(4), 514–520.

76. Stoet, G., O'Connor, D.B., Conner, M., & Laws, K.R. (2013). Are women better than men at multi-tasking? *BMC Psychology* **1**, 18.

77. Lopez, R. B., Heatherton, T. F., & Wagner, D. D. (2020). Media multitasking is associated with higher risk for obesity and increased responsiveness to rewarding food stimuli. *Brain imaging and behavior, 14*(4), 1050–1061.

78. Sanbonmatsu, D. M., Strayer, D. L., Medeiros-Ward, N., & Watson, J. M. (2013). Who multi-tasks and why? Multi-tasking ability, perceived multi-tasking ability, impulsivity, and sensation seeking. *PloS one, 8*(1), e54402.

79. Ariely, D., & Wertenbroch, K. (2002). Procrastination, deadlines, and performance: self-control by precommitment. *Psychological science, 13*(3), 219–224.

80. Asmus, S., Karl, F., Mohnen, A., & Reinhart, G. (2015). The Impact of Goal-setting on Worker Performance - Empirical Evidence from a Real-effort Production Experiment. *Procedia CIRP, 26*, 127–132.

81. Stewart, J. (2015). The persistence of Parkinson's law. *Quadrant, 59*(9), 62–65.

82. Bryan, J.F., & Locke, E.A. (1967). Parkinson's Law as a goal-setting phenomenon. *Organizational Behavior and Human Performance, 2*(3), 258–275.

83. Kamma, Damodaram & Geetha, G. & Neela, J.. (2013). Countering Parkinson's law for improving productivity. ACM International Conference Proceeding Series. 91-96.

84. Sinan Aral & Erik Brynjolfsson & Marshall Van Alstyne, 2007. "Information, Technology and Information Worker Productivity: Task Level Evidence," NBER Working Papers 13172, National Bureau of Economic Research, Inc.

85. Agrawal, N., & Wen Wan, E. (2009). Regulating Risk or Risking Regulation? Construal Levels and Depletion Effects in the Processing of Health Messages. *Journal of Consumer Research, 36*(3), 448–462.

86. Chambers, D. (2014). Overstating the Satisfaction of Lawyers. *Law & Social Inquiry, 39*(2), 313–333.

87. Legal Cheek. (2018, November 20). *Research: 50% of lawyers dislike their job.* https://www.legalcheek.com/2018/11/research-50-of-lawyers-hate-their-job/

88. Duvivier, R. J., van Dalen, J., Muijtjens, A. M., Moulaert, V. R., van der Vleuten, C. P., & Scherpbier, A. J. (2011). The role of deliberate practice in the acquisition of clinical skills. *BMC medical education, 11*, 101.

89. Blatter, K., & Cajochen, C. (2007). Circadian rhythms in cognitive performance: methodological constraints, protocols, theoretical underpinnings. *Physiology & behavior, 90*(2-3), 196–208.

90. Henselmans, M. (n.d.). *The best time to work out: there's a science to it.* MennoHenselmans.com. https://mennohenselmans.com/best-time-to-work-out/

91. Monk T. H. (2005). The post-lunch dip in performance. Clinics in sports medicine, 24(2), e15–xii.

92. Baer, D. (2014, December 2). Always Wear The Same Suit: Obama's Presidential Productivity Secrets. *Fast Company.* https://www.fastcompany.com/3026265/always-wear-the-same-suit-obamas-presidential-productivity-secrets

93. Baumeister, R. (2018). Self-Regulation and Self-Control: Selected works of Roy F. Baumeister (1st ed.). Routledge.

94. Ferrari, J.R., Roster, C.A., Crum, K.P., & Pardo, M.A. (2018). Procrastinators and Clutter: An Ecological View of Living with Excessive "Stuff". *Current Psychology, 37*, 441–444.

95. Dumas, J. E., Nissley, J., Nordstrom, A., Smith, E. P., Prinz, R. J., & Levine, D. W. (2005). Home chaos: sociodemographic, parenting, interactional, and child correlates. *Journal of clinical child and adolescent psychology : the official journal for the Society of Clinical Child and Adolescent Psychology, American Psychological Association, Division 53, 34*(1), 93–104.

96. Evans, G.W., Saltzman, H., & Cooperman, J.L. (2001). Housing Quality and Children's Socioemotional Health. *Environment and Behavior, 33*(3), 389–399.

97. Corapci, F., & Wachs, T.D. (2002). Does Parental Mood or Efficacy Mediate the Influence of Environmental Chaos Upon Parenting Behavior? *Merrill-Palmer Quarterly, 48*(2), 182-201.

98. Vartanian, L.R., Kernan, K.M., & Wansink, B. (2016). Clutter, Chaos, and Overconsumption: The Role of Mind-Set in Stressful and Chaotic Food Environments. *Environment and Behavior, 49*(2), 215–223.

99. Vohs, K. D., Redden, J. P., & Rahinel, R. (2013). Physical order produces healthy choices, generosity, and conventionality, whereas disorder produces creativity. *Psychological science, 24*(9), 1860–1867.

100. Saxbe, D. E., & Repetti, R. (2010). No place like home: home tours correlate with daily patterns of mood and cortisol. *Personality & social psychology bulletin, 36*(1), 71–81.

101. McMains, S., & Kastner, S. (2011). Interactions of top-down and bottom-up mechanisms in human visual cortex. *The Journal of neuroscience : the official journal of the Society for Neuroscience, 31*(2), 587–597.

102. Knight, C., & Haslam, S. A. (2010). The relative merits of lean, enriched, and empowered offices: an experimental examination of the impact of workspace management strategies on well-being and productivity. *Journal of experimental psychology. Applied, 16*(2), 158–172.

103. Nieuwenhuis, M., Knight, C., Postmes, T., & Haslam, S. A. (2014). The relative benefits of green versus lean office space: three field experiments. *Journal of experimental psychology. Applied, 20*(3), 199–214.

104. Anderson, K.A., Revelle, W., & Lynch, M.J. (1989). Caffeine, impulsivity, and memory scanning: A comparison of two explanations for the Yerkes-Dodson Effect. *Motivation and Emotion, 13*(1), 1–20.

105. Yerkes, R.M., & Dodson, J.D. (1908). The relation of strength of stimulus to rapidity of habit-formation. Journal of Comparative Neurology and Psychology, 18(5), 459–482.

106. Lupien, S. J., Maheu, F., Tu, M., Fiocco, A., & Schramek, T. E. (2007). The effects of stress and stress hormones on human cognition: Implications for the field of brain and cognition. *Brain and cognition, 65*(3), 209–237.

107. BROADHURST P. L. (1957). Emotionality and the Yerkes-Dodson law. *Journal of experimental psychology, 54*(5), 345–352.

108. Corbett, M. (2015). From law to folklore: work stress and the Yerkes-Dodson Law. *Journal of Managerial Psychology, 30*(6), 741–752.

109. Diamond, D. M., Campbell, A. M., Park, C. R., Halonen, J., & Zoladz, P. R. (2007). The temporal dynamics model of emotional memory processing: a synthesis on the neurobiological basis of stress-induced amnesia, flashbulb and traumatic memories, and the Yerkes-Dodson law. *Neural plasticity, 2007*, 60803.

110. Patel, K. (2019, September 18). *Nicotine.* Examine.com. https://examine.com/supplements/nicotine/

111. Diamond, D. M., Campbell, A. M., Park, C. R., Halonen, J., & Zoladz, P. R. (2007). The temporal dynamics model of emotional memory processing: a synthesis on the neurobiological basis of stress-induced amnesia, flashbulb and traumatic memories, and the Yerkes-Dodson law. *Neural plasticity, 2007*, 60803.

112. Franke, A. G., Gränsmark, P., Agricola, A., Schühle, K., Rommel, T., Sebastian, A., Balló, H. E., Gorbulev, S., Gerdes, C., Frank, B., Ruckes, C., Tüscher, O., & Lieb, K. (2017). Methylphenidate, modafinil, and caffeine for cognitive enhancement in chess: A

double-blind, randomised controlled trial. *European neuropsychopharmacology : the journal of the European College of Neuropsychopharmacology, 27*(3), 248–260.
113. Patel, K. (2021, January 7). *Theanine.* Examine.com.
https://examine.com/supplements/theanine/
114. Stevenson, R.J. (2016). The longer term effects of diet on the human brain. *Agro Food Industry Hi-Tech, 27*(2), 39–42.
115. Attuquayefio, T., & Stevenson, R. J. (2015). A systematic review of longer-term dietary interventions on human cognitive function: Emerging patterns and future directions. *Appetite, 95*, 554–570.

Chapter 4: How to stick to your diet

1. Hill J. O. (2006). Understanding and addressing the epidemic of obesity: an energy balance perspective. *Endocrine reviews, 27*(7), 750–761.
2. Zinchenko, A., & Henselmans, M. (2016). Metabolic Damage: do Negative Metabolic Adaptations During Underfeeding Persist After Refeeding in Non-Obese Populations? *Medical Research Archives, 4*(8).
3. Lieberman, H. R., Caruso, C. M., Niro, P. J., Adam, G. E., Kellogg, M. D., Nindl, B. C., & Kramer, F. M. (2008). A double-blind, placebo-controlled test of 2 d of calorie deprivation: effects on cognition, activity, sleep, and interstitial glucose concentrations. *The American journal of clinical nutrition, 88*(3), 667–676.
4. Wadden, T. A., Stunkard, A. J., Day, S. C., Gould, R. A., & Rubin, C. J. (1987). Less food, less hunger: reports of appetite and symptoms in a controlled study of a protein-sparing modified fast. *International journal of obesity, 11*(3), 239–249.
5. Karl, J. P., Thompson, L. A., Niro, P. J., Margolis, L. M., McClung, J. P., Cao, J. J., Whigham, L. D., Combs, G. F., Jr, Young, A. J., Lieberman, H. R., & Pasiakos, S. M. (2015). Transient decrements in mood during energy deficit are independent of dietary protein-to-carbohydrate ratio. *Physiology & behavior, 139*, 524–531.
6. Grigolon, R. B., Brietzke, E., Trevizol, A. P., McIntyre, R. S., & Mansur, R. B. (2020). Caloric restriction, resting metabolic rate and cognitive performance in Non-obese adults: A post-hoc analysis from CALERIE study. *Journal of psychiatric research, 128*, 16–22.
7. Leclerc, E., Trevizol, A. P., Grigolon, R. B., Subramaniapillai, M., McIntyre, R. S., Brietzke, E., & Mansur, R. B. (2020). The effect of caloric restriction on working memory in healthy non-obese adults. *CNS spectrums, 25*(1), 2–8.
8. Shukitt-Hale, B., Askew, E. W., & Lieberman, H. R. (1997). Effects of 30 days of undernutrition on reaction time, moods, and symptoms. *Physiology & behavior, 62*(4), 783–789.
9. Herzog, N., Friedrich, A., Fujita, N., Gais, S., Jauch-Chara, K., Oltmanns, K. M., & Benedict, C. (2012). Effects of daytime food intake on memory consolidation during sleep or sleep deprivation. *PloS one, 7*(6), e40298.
10. Mohd Yasin, W., Muzaffar Ali Khan Khattak, M., Mazlan Mamat, N. and Azdie Mohd Abu Bakar, W. (2013). Does religious fasting affect cognitive performance? *Nutrition & Food Science, 43*(5), 483–489.
11. Green, M. W., Elliman, N. A., & Rogers, P. J. (1995). Lack of effect of short-term fasting on cognitive function. *Journal of psychiatric research, 29*(3), 245–253.
12. Solianik, R., & Sujeta, A. (2018). Two-day fasting evokes stress, but does not affect mood, brain activity, cognitive, psychomotor, and motor performance in overweight women. *Behavioural brain research, 338*, 166–172.
13. Solianik, R., Sujeta, A., Terentjevienė, A., & Skurvydas, A. (2016). Effect of 48 h Fasting on Autonomic Function, Brain Activity, Cognition, and Mood in Amateur Weight Lifters. *BioMed research international, 2016*, 1503956.
14. Martin, C. K., Anton, S. D., Han, H., York-Crowe, E., Redman, L. M., Ravussin, E., & Williamson, D. A. (2007). Examination of cognitive function during six months of calorie restriction: results of a randomized controlled trial. *Rejuvenation research, 10*(2), 179–190.

15. Green, M. W., Elliman, N. A., & Rogers, P. J. (1997). The effects of food deprivation and incentive motivation on blood glucose levels and cognitive function. *Psychopharmacology, 134*(1), 88–94.

16. Attuquayefio, T., & Stevenson, R. J. (2015). A systematic review of longer-term dietary interventions on human cognitive function: Emerging patterns and future directions. *Appetite, 95*, 554–570.

17. Johnson, D. D., Dorr, K. E., Swenson, W. M., & Service, F. J. (1980). Reactive hypoglycemia. *JAMA, 243*(11), 1151–1155.

18. Markus, C. R., & Rogers, P. J. (2020). Effects of high and low sucrose-containing beverages on blood glucose and hypoglycemic-like symptoms. *Physiology & behavior, 222*, 112916.

19. Charles, M. A., Hofeldt, F., Shackelford, A., Waldeck, N., Dodson, L. E., Jr, Bunker, D., Coggins, J. T., & Eichner, H. (1981). Comparison of oral glucose tolerance tests and mixed meals in patients with apparent idiopathic postabsorptive hypoglycemia: absence of hypoglycemia after meals. *Diabetes, 30*(6), 465–470.

20. Palardy, J., Havrankova, J., Lepage, R., Matte, R., Bélanger, R., D'Amour, P., & Ste-Marie, L. G. (1989). Blood glucose measurements during symptomatic episodes in patients with suspected postprandial hypoglycemia. *The New England journal of medicine, 321*(21), 1421–1425.

21. Lev-Ran, A., & Anderson, R. W. (1981). The diagnosis of postprandial hypoglycemia. *Diabetes, 30*(12), 996–999.

22. Mantantzis, K., Schlaghecken, F., Sünram-Lea, S. I., & Maylor, E. A. (2019). Sugar rush or sugar crash? A meta-analysis of carbohydrate effects on mood. *Neuroscience and biobehavioral reviews, 101*, 45–67.

23. Vanitallie T. B. (2006). Sleep and energy balance: Interactive homeostatic systems. *Metabolism: clinical and experimental, 55*(10 Suppl 2), S30–S35.

24. Eicke, B. M., Seidel, E., & Krummenauer, F. (2003). Volume flow in the common carotid artery does not decrease postprandially. *Journal of neuroimaging : official journal of the American Society of Neuroimaging, 13*(4), 352–355.

25. Jensen, G., Nielsen, H. B., Ide, K., Madsen, P. L., Svendsen, L. B., Svendsen, U. G., & Secher, N. H. (2002). Cerebral oxygenation during exercise in patients with terminal lung disease. *Chest, 122*(2), 445–450.

26. Wurtman J. J. (1984). The involvement of brain serotonin in excessive carbohydrate snacking by obese carbohydrate cravers. *Journal of the American Dietetic Association, 84*(9), 1004–1007.

27. Grimmett, A., & Sillence, M. N. (2005). Calmatives for the excitable horse: a review of L-tryptophan. *Veterinary journal (London, England : 1997), 170*(1), 24–32.

28. Orr, W. C., Shadid, G., Harnish, M. J., & Elsenbruch, S. (1997). Meal composition and its effect on postprandial sleepiness. *Physiology & behavior, 62*(4), 709–712.

29. Kim, S.W., & Lee, B. (2009). Metabolic state, neurohormones, and vagal stimulation, not increased serotonin, orchestrate postprandial drowsiness. *Bioscience Hypotheses, 2*(6), 422-427.

30. Reyner, L. A., Wells, S. J., Mortlock, V., & Horne, J. A. (2012). 'Post-lunch' sleepiness during prolonged, monotonous driving - effects of meal size. *Physiology & behavior, 105*(4), 1088–1091.

31. Booth, A. O., Wang, X., Turner, A. I., Nowson, C. A., & Torres, S. J. (2018). Diet-Induced Weight Loss Has No Effect on Psychological Stress in Overweight and Obese Adults: A Meta-Analysis of Randomized Controlled Trials. *Nutrients, 10*(5), 613.

32. Devitt, A. A., & Mattes, R. D. (2004). Effects of food unit size and energy density on intake in humans. *Appetite, 42*(2), 213–220.

33. Crum, A. J., Corbin, W. R., Brownell, K. D., & Salovey, P. (2011). Mind over milkshakes: mindsets, not just nutrients, determine ghrelin response. *Health psychology : official journal of the Division of Health Psychology, American Psychological Association, 30*(4), 424–431.

34. Censin, J. C., Peters, S., Bovijn, J., Ferreira, T., Pulit, S. L., Mägi, R., Mahajan, A., Holmes, M. V., & Lindgren, C. M. (2019). Causal relationships between obesity and the leading causes of death in women and men. *PLoS genetics, 15*(10), e1008405.

35. Kopelman P. G. (2000). Obesity as a medical problem. *Nature, 404*(6778), 635–643.

36. Bok, E., Jo, M., Lee, S., Lee, B. R., Kim, J., & Kim, H. J. (2019). Dietary Restriction and Neuroinflammation: A Potential Mechanistic Link. *International journal of molecular sciences, 20*(3), 464.

37. Kuk, J. L., Christensen, R., & Wharton, S. (2019). Absolute Weight Loss, and Not Weight Loss Rate, Is Associated with Better Improvements in Metabolic Health. *Journal of obesity, 2019*, 3609642.

38. Huynh, C. (n.d.). *The truth about processed vs unprocessed foods.* MennoHenselmans.com. https://mennohenselmans.com/processed-foods/

39. Redman, L. M., & Ravussin, E. (2011). Caloric restriction in humans: impact on physiological, psychological, and behavioral outcomes. *Antioxidants & redox signaling, 14*(2), 275–287.

40. Mitchell, S. J., Bernier, M., Mattison, J. A., Aon, M. A., Kaiser, T. A., Anson, R. M., Ikeno, Y., Anderson, R. M., Ingram, D. K., & de Cabo, R. (2019). Daily Fasting Improves Health and Survival in Male Mice Independent of Diet Composition and Calories. *Cell metabolism, 29*(1), 221–228.e3.

41. Mattison, J. A., Colman, R. J., Beasley, T. M., Allison, D. B., Kemnitz, J. W., Roth, G. S., Ingram, D. K., Weindruch, R., de Cabo, R., & Anderson, R. M. (2017). Caloric restriction improves health and survival of rhesus monkeys. *Nature communications, 8*, 14063.

42. Colman, R. J., Anderson, R. M., Johnson, S. C., Kastman, E. K., Kosmatka, K. J., Beasley, T. M., Allison, D. B., Cruzen, C., Simmons, H. A., Kemnitz, J. W., & Weindruch, R. (2009). Caloric restriction delays disease onset and mortality in rhesus monkeys. *Science (New York, N.Y.), 325*(5937), 201–204.

43. Caristia, S., Vito, M., Sarro, A., Leone, A., Pecere, A., Zibetti, A., Filigheddu, N., Zeppegno, P., Prodam, F., Faggiano, F., & Marzullo, P. (2020). Is Caloric Restriction Associated with Better Healthy Aging Outcomes? A Systematic Review and Meta-Analysis of Randomized Controlled Trials. *Nutrients, 12*(8), 2290.

44. Heilbronn, L. K., & Ravussin, E. (2003). Calorie restriction and aging: review of the literature and implications for studies in humans. *The American journal of clinical nutrition, 78*(3), 361–369.

45. Heilbronn, L. K., de Jonge, L., Frisard, M. I., DeLany, J. P., Larson-Meyer, D. E., Rood, J., Nguyen, T., Martin, C. K., Volaufova, J., Most, M. M., Greenway, F. L., Smith, S. R., Deutsch, W. A., Williamson, D. A., Ravussin, E., & Pennington CALERIE Team (2006). Effect of 6-month calorie restriction on biomarkers of longevity, metabolic adaptation, and oxidative stress in overweight individuals: a randomized controlled trial. *JAMA, 295*(13), 1539–1548.

46. Ravussin, E., Redman, L. M., Rochon, J., Das, S. K., Fontana, L., Kraus, W. E., Romashkan, S., Williamson, D. A., Meydani, S. N., Villareal, D. T., Smith, S. R., Stein, R. I., Scott, T. M., Stewart, T. M., Saltzman, E., Klein, S., Bhapkar, M., Martin, C. K., Gilhooly, C. H., Holloszy, J. O., … CALERIE Study Group (2015). A 2-Year Randomized Controlled Trial of Human Caloric Restriction: Feasibility and Effects on Predictors of Health Span and Longevity. *The journals of gerontology. Series A, Biological sciences and medical sciences, 70*(9), 1097–1104.

47. de Cabo, R., Carmona-Gutierrez, D., Bernier, M., Hall, M. N., & Madeo, F. (2014). The search for antiaging interventions: from elixirs to fasting regimens. *Cell, 157*(7), 1515–1526.

48. Franceschi, C., Ostan, R., & Santoro, A. (2018). Nutrition and Inflammation: Are Centenarians Similar to Individuals on Calorie-Restricted Diets? *Annual review of nutrition, 38*, 329–356.

49. Broskey, N. T., Marlatt, K. L., Most, J., Erickson, M. L., Irving, B. A., & Redman, L. M. (2019). The Panacea of Human Aging: Calorie Restriction Versus Exercise. *Exercise and sport sciences reviews, 47*(3), 169–175.

50. Roberson, L. L., Aneni, E. C., Maziak, W., Agatston, A., Feldman, T., Rouseff, M., Tran, T., Blaha, M. J., Santos, R. D., Sposito, A., Al-Mallah, M. H., Blankstein, R., Budoff, M. J., & Nasir, K. (2014). Beyond BMI: The "Metabolically healthy obese" phenotype & its association with clinical/subclinical cardiovascular disease and all-cause mortality -- a systematic review. *BMC public health, 14*, 14.

51. Espinosa De Ycaza, A. E., Donegan, D., & Jensen, M. D. (2018). Long-term metabolic risk for the metabolically healthy overweight/obese phenotype. *International journal of obesity (2005)*, *42*(3), 302–309.

52. Farmer, R. E., Mathur, R., Schmidt, A. F., Bhaskaran, K., Fatemifar, G., Eastwood, S. V., Finan, C., Denaxas, S., Smeeth, L., & Chaturvedi, N. (2019). Associations Between Measures of Sarcopenic Obesity and Risk of Cardiovascular Disease and Mortality: A Cohort Study and Mendelian Randomization Analysis Using the UK Biobank. *Journal of the American Heart Association*, *8*(13), e011638.

53. Bell, J. A., & Hamer, M. (2016). Healthy obesity as an intermediate state of risk: a critical review. *Expert review of endocrinology & metabolism*, *11*(5), 403–413.

54. Blüher M. (2020). Metabolically Healthy Obesity. *Endocrine reviews*, *41*(3), 405–420.

55. Steel, D., Kemps, E., & Tiggemann, M. (2006). Effects of hunger and visuo-spatial interference on imagery-induced food cravings. *Appetite*, *46*(1), 36–40.

56. Morris, J., Keith Ngai, M. Y., Yeomans, M. R., & Forster, S. (2020). A high perceptual load task reduces thoughts about chocolate, even while hungry. *Appetite*, *151*, 104694.

57. Tapper, K., & Turner, A. (2018). The effect of a mindfulness-based decentering strategy on chocolate craving. *Appetite*, *130*, 157–162.

58. Baron, P., & Watters, R.G. (1982). Effects of goal-setting and of goal levels on weight loss induced by self-monitoring. *Applied Psychology, 31*(3), 369–382.

59. CDC. (n.d.). *Obesity and Overweight*. https://www.cdc.gov/nchs/fastats/obesity-overweight.htm

60. Tsai, A. G., & Wadden, T. A. (2005). Systematic review: an evaluation of major commercial weight loss programs in the United States. *Annals of internal medicine*, *142*(1), 56–66.

61. Keim, N. L., Stern, J. S., & Havel, P. J. (1998). Relation between circulating leptin concentrations and appetite during a prolonged, moderate energy deficit in women. *The American journal of clinical nutrition*, *68*(4), 794–801.

62. Hill, A. J., Weaver, C. F., & Blundell, J. E. (1991). Food craving, dietary restraint and mood. *Appetit, 17*(3), 187–197.

63. Lopez, R. B., Courtney, A. L., & Wagner, D. D. (2019). Recruitment of cognitive control regions during effortful self-control is associated with altered brain activity in control and reward systems in dieters during subsequent exposure to food commercials. *PeerJ, 7*, e6550.

64. Vohs, K. D., & Heatherton, T. F. (2000). Self-regulatory failure: a resource-depletion approach. *Psychological science*, *11*(3), 249–254.

65. Keller K. L. (2017). Brain stimulation for treatment of obesity: will stimulating the prefrontal cortex reduce overeating? *The American journal of clinical nutrition*, *106*(6), 1331–1332.

66. Dye, L., Lluch, A., & Blundell, J. E. (2000). Macronutrients and mental performance. *Nutrition (Burbank, Los Angeles County, Calif.)*, *16*(10), 1021–1034.

67. Leigh Gibson, E., & Green, M. W. (2002). Nutritional influences on cognitive function: mechanisms of susceptibility. *Nutrition research reviews*, *15*(1), 169–206.

68. Ooi, C. P., Loke, S. C., Yassin, Z., & Hamid, T. A. (2011). Carbohydrates for improving the cognitive performance of independent-living older adults with normal cognition or mild cognitive impairment. *The Cochrane database of systematic reviews*, *2011*(4), CD007220.

69. Makris, A., Darcey, V. L., Rosenbaum, D. L., Komaroff, E., Vander Veur, S. S., Collins, B. N., Klein, S., Wyatt, H. R., & Foster, G. D. (2013). Similar effects on cognitive performance during high- and low-carbohydrate obesity treatment. *Nutrition & diabetes*, *3*(9), e89.

70. Wells, A. S., Read, N. W., Laugharne, J. D., & Ahluwalia, N. S. (1998). Alterations in mood after changing to a low-fat diet. *The British journal of nutrition*, *79*(1), 23–30.

71. Yackobovitch-Gavan, M., Nagelberg, N., Demol, S., Phillip, M., & Shalitin, S. (2008). Influence of weight-loss diets with different macronutrient compositions on health-related quality of life in obese youth. *Appetite*, *51*(3), 697–703.

72. Hession, M., Rolland, C., Kulkarni, U., Wise, A., & Broom, J. (2009). Systematic review of randomized controlled trials of low-carbohydrate vs. low-fat/low-calorie diets in the management of obesity and its comorbidities. *Obesity reviews : an official journal of the International Association for the Study of Obesity, 10*(1), 36–50.

73. Nordmann, A. J., Nordmann, A., Briel, M., Keller, U., Yancy, W. S., Jr, Brehm, B. J., & Bucher, H. C. (2006). Effects of low-carbohydrate vs low-fat diets on weight loss and cardiovascular risk factors: a meta-analysis of randomized controlled trials. *Archives of internal medicine, 166*(3), 285–293.

74. Tobias, D. K., Chen, M., Manson, J. E., Ludwig, D. S., Willett, W., & Hu, F. B. (2015). Effect of low-fat diet interventions versus other diet interventions on long-term weight change in adults: a systematic review and meta-analysis. *The lancet. Diabetes & endocrinology, 3*(12), 968–979.

75. McVay, M. A., Voils, C. I., Geiselman, P. J., Smith, V. A., Coffman, C. J., Mayer, S., & Yancy, W. S., Jr (2016). Food preferences and weight change during low-fat and low-carbohydrate diets. *Appetite, 103*, 336–343.

76. Borradaile, K. E., Halpern, S. D., Wyatt, H. R., Klein, S., Hill, J. O., Bailer, B., Brill, C., Stein, R. I., Miller, B. V., 3rd, & Foster, G. D. (2012). Relationship between treatment preference and weight loss in the context of a randomized controlled trial. *Obesity (Silver Spring, Md.), 20*(6), 1218–1222.

77. Leavy, J. M., Clifton, P. M., & Keogh, J. B. (2018). The Role of Choice in Weight Loss Strategies: A Systematic Review and Meta-Analysis. *Nutrients, 10*(9), 1136.

78. Swift, J. K., & Callahan, J. L. (2009). The impact of client treatment preferences on outcome: a meta-analysis. *Journal of clinical psychology, 65*(4), 368–381.

79. Caltabiano, M. L., & Shellshear, J. (1998). Palatability versus healthiness as determinants of food preferences in young adults: a comparison of nomothetic and idiographic analytic approaches. *Australian and New Zealand journal of public health, 22*(5), 547–551.

80. Peters, J. C., Beck, J., Cardel, M., Wyatt, H. R., Foster, G. D., Pan, Z., Wojtanowski, A. C., Vander Veur, S. S., Herring, S. J., Brill, C., & Hill, J. O. (2016). The effects of water and non-nutritive sweetened beverages on weight loss and weight maintenance: A randomized clinical trial. *Obesity (Silver Spring, Md.), 24*(2), 297–304.

81. Magnuson, B. A., Burdock, G. A., Doull, J., Kroes, R. M., Marsh, G. M., Pariza, M. W., Spencer, P. S., Waddell, W. J., Walker, R., & Williams, G. M. (2007). Aspartame: a safety evaluation based on current use levels, regulations, and toxicological and epidemiological studies. *Critical reviews in toxicology, 37*(8), 629–727.

82. Grotz, V. L., & Munro, I. C. (2009). An overview of the safety of sucralose. *Regulatory toxicology and pharmacology : RTP, 55*(1), 1–5.

83. Henselmans, M. (n.d.). *Is aspartame safe?* MennoHenselmans.com. https://mennohenselmans.com/is-aspartame-safe/

84. Lange, F., Seer, C., Rapior, M., Rose, J., & Eggert, F. (2014). Turn It All You Want: Still No Effect of Sugar Consumption on Ego Depletion. *Journal of European Psychology Students, 5*(3), 1–8.

85. Molden, D. C., Hui, C. M., Scholer, A. A., Meier, B. P., Noreen, E. E., D'Agostino, P. R., & Martin, V. (2012). Motivational versus metabolic effects of carbohydrates on self-control. *Psychological science, 23*(10), 1137–1144.

86. Sanders, M. A., Shirk, S. D., Burgin, C. J., & Martin, L. L. (2012). The gargle effect: rinsing the mouth with glucose enhances self-control. *Psychological science, 23*(12), 1470–1472.

87. Hagger, M. S., & Chatzisarantis, N. L. (2013). The sweet taste of success: the presence of glucose in the oral cavity moderates the depletion of self-control resources. *Personality & social psychology bulletin, 39*(1), 28–42.

88. Wansink, B., Painter, J. E., & Lee, Y. K. (2006). The office candy dish: proximity's influence on estimated and actual consumption. *International journal of obesity (2005), 30*(5), 871–875.

89. Wansink, B., Hanks, A. S., & Kaipainen, K. (2016). Slim by Design: Kitchen Counter Correlates of Obesity. *Health education & behavior : the official publication of the Society for Public Health Education, 43*(5), 552–558.

90. Ward, A., & Mann, T. (2000). Don't mind if I do: disinhibited eating under cognitive load. *Journal of personality and social psychology*, *78*(4), 753–763.

91. Shiv, B., & Fedorikhin (1999). Heart and Mind in Conflict: the Interplay of Affect and Cognition in Consumer Decision Making. *Journal of Consumer Research, 26*(3), 278–292.

92. Mischel, W., Ebbesen, E. B., & Zeiss, A. R. (1972). Cognitive and attentional mechanisms in delay of gratification. *Journal of personality and social psychology*, *21*(2), 204–218.

93. Lee, J. (2001). Diet Programs and Compliance: Do Prepared Meal Programs Increase Adherence? *Nutrition Bytes, 7*(1).

94. Wing, R. R., Jeffery, R. W., Burton, L. R., Thorson, C., Nissinoff, K. S., & Baxter, J. E. (1996). Food provision vs structured meal plans in the behavioral treatment of obesity. *International journal of obesity and related metabolic disorders : journal of the International Association for the Study of Obesity*, *20*(1), 56–62.

95. Metz, J. A., Kris-Etherton, P. M., Morris, C. D., Mustad, V. A., Stern, J. S., Oparil, S., Chait, A., Haynes, R. B., Resnick, L. M., Clark, S., Hatton, D. C., McMahon, M., Holcomb, S., Snyder, G. W., Pi-Sunyer, F. X., & McCarron, D. A. (1997). Dietary compliance and cardiovascular risk reduction with a prepared meal plan compared with a self-selected diet. *The American journal of clinical nutrition*, *66*(2), 373–385.

96. Pi-Sunyer, F. X., Maggio, C. A., McCarron, D. A., Reusser, M. E., Stern, J. S., Haynes, R. B., Oparil, S., Kris-Etherton, P., Resnick, L. M., Chait, A., Morris, C. D., Hatton, D. C., Metz, J. A., Snyder, G. W., Clark, S., & McMahon, M. (1999). Multicenter randomized trial of a comprehensive prepared meal program in type 2 diabetes. *Diabetes care*, *22*(2), 191–197.

97. Hatton, D. C., Haynes, R. B., Oparil, S., Kris-Etherton, P., Pi-Sunyer, F. X., Resnick, L. M., Stern, J. S., Clark, S., McMahon, M., Morris, C., Metz, J., Ward, A., Holcomb, S., & McCarron, D. A. (1996). Improved quality of life in patients with generalized cardiovascular metabolic disease on a prepared diet. *The American journal of clinical nutrition*, *64*(6), 935–943.

98. McCarron, D. A., Oparil, S., Chait, A., Haynes, R. B., Kris-Etherton, P., Stern, J. S., Resnick, L. M., Clark, S., Morris, C. D., Hatton, D. C., Metz, J. A., McMahon, M., Holcomb, S., Snyder, G. W., & Pi-Sunyer, F. X. (1997). Nutritional management of cardiovascular risk factors. A randomized clinical trial. *Archives of internal medicine*, *157*(2), 169–177.

99. Metz, J. A., Stern, J. S., Kris-Etherton, P., Reusser, M. E., Morris, C. D., Hatton, D. C., Oparil, S., Haynes, R. B., Resnick, L. M., Pi-Sunyer, F. X., Clark, S., Chester, L., McMahon, M., Snyder, G. W., & McCarron, D. A. (2000). A randomized trial of improved weight loss with a prepared meal plan in overweight and obese patients: impact on cardiovascular risk reduction. *Archives of internal medicine*, *160*(14), 2150–2158.

100. Rock, C. L., Flatt, S. W., Sherwood, N. E., Karanja, N., Pakiz, B., & Thomson, C. A. (2010). Effect of a free prepared meal and incentivized weight loss program on weight loss and weight loss maintenance in obese and overweight women: a randomized controlled trial. *JAMA*, *304*(16), 1803–1810.

101. Haynes, R. B., Kris-Etherton, P., McCarron, D. A., Oparil, S., Chait, A., Resnick, L. M., Morris, C. D., Clark, S., Hatton, D. C., Metz, J. A., McMahon, M., Holcomb, S., Snyder, G. W., Pi-Sunyer, F. X., & Stern, J. S. (1999). Nutritionally complete prepared meal plan to reduce cardiovascular risk factors: a randomized clinical trial. *Journal of the American Dietetic Association*, *99*(9), 1077–1083.

102. Flechtner-Mors, M., Ditschuneit, H. H., Johnson, T. D., Suchard, M. A., & Adler, G. (2000). Metabolic and weight loss effects of long-term dietary intervention in obese patients: four-year results. *Obesity research*, *8*(5), 399–402.

103. Ducrot, P., Méjean, C., Aroumougame, V., Ibanez, G., Allès, B., Kesse-Guyot, E., Hercberg, S., & Péneau, S. (2017). Meal planning is associated with food variety, diet quality and body weight status in a large sample of French adults. *The international journal of behavioral nutrition and physical activity*, *14*(1), 12.

104. Ogden, J., Biliraki, C., Ellis, A., Lammyman, F., & May, E. (2021). The impact of active or passive food preparation versus distraction on eating behaviour: An experimental study. *Appetite, 160*, 105072.

105. Heber, D., Ashley, J. M., Wang, H. J., & Elashoff, R. M. (1994). Clinical evaluation of a minimal intervention meal replacement regimen for weight reduction. *Journal of the American College of Nutrition, 13*(6), 608–614.

106. Astbury, N. M., Piernas, C., Hartmann-Boyce, J., Lapworth, S., Aveyard, P., & Jebb, S. A. (2019). A systematic review and meta-analysis of the effectiveness of meal replacements for weight loss. *Obesity reviews : an official journal of the International Association for the Study of Obesity, 20*(4), 569–587.

107. Farshchi, H. R., Taylor, M. A., & Macdonald, I. A. (2004). Regular meal frequency creates more appropriate insulin sensitivity and lipid profiles compared with irregular meal frequency in healthy lean women. *European journal of clinical nutrition, 58*(7), 1071–1077.

108. Thomas, E. A., Higgins, J., Bessesen, D. H., McNair, B., & Cornier, M. A. (2015). Usual breakfast eating habits affect response to breakfast skipping in overweight women. *Obesity (Silver Spring, Md.), 23*(4), 750–759.

109. Alhussain, M. H., Macdonald, I. A., & Taylor, M. A. (2016). Irregular meal-pattern effects on energy expenditure, metabolism, and appetite regulation: a randomized controlled trial in healthy normal-weight women. *The American journal of clinical nutrition, 104*(1), 21–32.

110. Witbracht, M., Keim, N. L., Forester, S., Widaman, A., & Laugero, K. (2015). Female breakfast skippers display a disrupted cortisol rhythm and elevated blood pressure. *Physiology & behavior, 140*, 215–221.

111. Farshchi, H. R., Taylor, M. A., & Macdonald, I. A. (2004). Decreased thermic effect of food after an irregular compared with a regular meal pattern in healthy lean women. *International journal of obesity and related metabolic disorders : journal of the International Association for the Study of Obesity, 28*(5), 653–660.

112. Astbury, N. M., Taylor, M. A., & Macdonald, I. A. (2011). Breakfast consumption affects appetite, energy intake, and the metabolic and endocrine responses to foods consumed later in the day in male habitual breakfast eaters. *The Journal of nutrition, 141*(7), 1381–1389.

113. Taylor, M. A., & Garrow, J. S. (2001). Compared with nibbling, neither gorging nor a morning fast affect short-term energy balance in obese patients in a chamber calorimeter. *International journal of obesity and related metabolic disorders : journal of the International Association for the Study of Obesity, 25*(4), 519–528.

114. Elfhag, K., & Rössner, S. (2005). Who succeeds in maintaining weight loss? A conceptual review of factors associated with weight loss maintenance and weight regain. *Obesity reviews : an official journal of the International Association for the Study of Obesity, 6*(1), 67–85.

115. Cho, S., Dietrich, M., Brown, C. J., Clark, C. A., & Block, G. (2003). The effect of breakfast type on total daily energy intake and body mass index: results from the Third National Health and Nutrition Examination Survey (NHANES III). *Journal of the American College of Nutrition, 22*(4), 296–302.

116. Brown, A. W., Bohan Brown, M. M., & Allison, D. B. (2013). Belief beyond the evidence: using the proposed effect of breakfast on obesity to show 2 practices that distort scientific evidence. *The American journal of clinical nutrition, 98*(5), 1298–1308.

117. Dhurandhar, E. J., Dawson, J., Alcorn, A., Larsen, L. H., Thomas, E. A., Cardel, M., Bourland, A. C., Astrup, A., St-Onge, M. P., Hill, J. O., Apovian, C. M., Shikany, J. M., & Allison, D. B. (2014). The effectiveness of breakfast recommendations on weight loss: a randomized controlled trial. *The American journal of clinical nutrition, 100*(2), 507–513.

118. Lloyd, H. M., Green, M. W., & Rogers, P. J. (1994). Mood and cognitive performance effects of isocaloric lunches differing in fat and carbohydrate content. *Physiology & behavior, 56*(1), 51–57.

119. Lloyd, H. M., Rogers, P. J., Hedderley, D. I., & Walker, A. F. (1996). Acute effects on mood and cognitive performance of breakfasts differing in fat and carbohydrate content. *Appetite, 27*(2), 151–164.

120. Craig A. (1986). Acute effects of meals on perceptual and cognitive efficiency. *Nutrition reviews, 44 Suppl*, 163–171.

121. Cham, S., Koslik, H. J., & Golomb, B. A. (2016). Mood, Personality, and Behavior Changes During Treatment with Statins: A Case Series. *Drug safety - case reports*, *3*(1), 1.

122. Olson, M. B., Kelsey, S. F., Matthews, K. A., Bairey Merz, C. N., Eteiba, W., McGorray, S. P., Cornell, C. E., Vido, D. A., & Muldoon, M. F. (2008). Lipid-lowering medication use and aggression scores in women: a report from the NHLBI-sponsored WISE study. *Journal of women's health (2002)*, *17*(2), 187–194.

123. Golomb, B. A., Dimsdale, J. E., Koslik, H. J., Evans, M. A., Lu, X., Rossi, S., Mills, P. J., White, H. L., & Criqui, M. H. (2015). Statin Effects on Aggression: Results from the UCSD Statin Study, a Randomized Control Trial. *PloS one*, *10*(7), e0124451.

124. Ariely, D., & Loewenstein, G. (2006). The heat of the moment: the effect of sexual arousal on sexual decision making. *Journal of Behavioral Decision Making, 19*(2), 87–98.

125. Wilson, T.D., & Gilbert, D.T. (2003). Affective Forecasting. *Advances in Experimental Social Psychology, 35*, 345–411.

126. Sayette, M. A., Loewenstein, G., Griffin, K. M., & Black, J. J. (2008). Exploring the cold-to-hot empathy gap in smokers. *Psychological science*, *19*(9), 926–932.

127. Smith, C. F., Williamson, D. A., Bray, G. A., & Ryan, D. H. (1999). Flexible vs. Rigid dieting strategies: relationship with adverse behavioral outcomes. *Appetite, 32*(3), 295–305.

128. Stewart, T. M., Williamson, D. A., & White, M. A. (2002). Rigid vs. flexible dieting: association with eating disorder symptoms in nonobese women. *Appetite, 38*(1), 39–44.

129. Tylkaa, T.L., Calogerob, R.M., & Daníelsdóttir, S. (2015). Is intuitive eating the same as flexible dietary control? Their links to each other and well-being could provide an answer. *Appetite, 95*, 166–175.

130. Teixeira, P. J., Carraça, E. V., Marques, M. M., Rutter, H., Oppert, J. M., De Bourdeaudhuij, I., Lakerveld, J., & Brug, J. (2015). Successful behavior change in obesity interventions in adults: a systematic review of self-regulation mediators. *BMC medicine, 13*, 84.

131. Westenhoefer J. (1991). Dietary restraint and disinhibition: is restraint a homogeneous construct? *Appetite, 16*(1), 45–55.

132. Loria-Kohen, V., Gómez-Candela, C., Fernández-Fernández, C., Pérez-Torres, A., García-Puig, J., & Bermejo, L. M. (2012). Evaluation of the usefulness of a low-calorie diet with or without bread in the treatment of overweight/obesity. *Clinical nutrition (Edinburgh, Scotland)*, *31*(4), 455–461.

133. Palascha A, van Kleef E, van Trijp HC. How does thinking in Black and White terms relate to eating behavior and weight regain? J Health Psychol. 2015 May;20(5):638-48.

134. Camilleri, G. M., Méjean, C., Bellisle, F., Andreeva, V. A., Kesse-Guyot, E., Hercberg, S., & Péneau, S. (2017). Intuitive Eating Dimensions Were Differently Associated with Food Intake in the General Population-Based NutriNet-Santé Study. *The Journal of nutrition*, *147*(1), 61–69.

135. Varkevisser, R., van Stralen, M. M., Kroeze, W., Ket, J., & Steenhuis, I. (2019). Determinants of weight loss maintenance: a systematic review. *Obesity reviews : an official journal of the International Association for the Study of Obesity*, *20*(2), 171–211.

136. Kashdan, T. B., & Rottenberg, J. (2010). Psychological flexibility as a fundamental aspect of health. *Clinical psychology review*, *30*(7), 865–878.

137. Van Dyke, N., & Drinkwater, E. J. (2014). Relationships between intuitive eating and health indicators: literature review. *Public health nutrition*, *17*(8), 1757–1766.

138. Henselmans, M. (n.d.). *Chicken in Asian Sweet and Sour Sauce.* MennoHenselmans.com. https://mennohenselmans.com/chicken-in-asian-sweet-and-sour-sauce/

139. Henselmans, M. (n.d.). *The Tex-Mex bowl of awesomeness.* MennoHenselmans.com. https://mennohenselmans.com/tex-mex-recipe/

140. White, M. A., Whisenhunt, B. L., Williamson, D. A., Greenway, F. L., & Netemeyer, R. G. (2002). Development and validation of the food-craving inventory. *Obesity research*, *10*(2), 107–114.

141. Morris, M. J., Na, E. S., & Johnson, A. K. (2008). Salt craving: the psychobiology of pathogenic sodium intake. *Physiology & behavior*, *94*(5), 709–721.

142. Zellner, D. A., Garriga-Trillo, A., Rohm, E., Centeno, S., & Parker, S. (1999). Food liking and craving: A cross-cultural approach. *Appetite*, *33*(1), 61–70.

143. Stanhewicz, A. E., & Kenney, W. L. (2015). Determinants of water and sodium intake and output. *Nutrition reviews*, *73 Suppl 2*, 73–82.

144. Chan, S., Gerson, B., & Subramaniam, S. (1998). The role of copper, molybdenum, selenium, and zinc in nutrition and health. *Clinics in laboratory medicine*, *18*(4), 673–685.

145. Chesters, J. K., & Quarterman, J. (1970). Effects of zinc deficiency on food intake and feeding patterns of rats. *The British journal of nutrition*, *24*(4), 1061–1069.

146. Uchida, T., & Kawati, Y. (2014). *[Rinsho ketsueki] The Japanese journal of clinical hematology*, *55*(4), 436–439.

147. Lofts, R. H., Schroeder, S. R., & Maier, R. H. (1990). Effects of serum zinc supplementation on pica behavior of persons with mental retardation. *American journal of mental retardation : AJMR*, *95*(1), 103–109.

148. Rabel, A., Leitman, S. F., & Miller, J. L. (2016). Ask about ice, then consider iron. *Journal of the American Association of Nurse Practitioners*, *28*(2), 116–120.

149. Nchito, M., Geissler, P. W., Mubila, L., Friis, H., & Olsen, A. (2004). Effects of iron and multimicronutrient supplementation on geophagy: a two-by-two factorial study among Zambian schoolchildren in Lusaka. *Transactions of the Royal Society of Tropical Medicine and Hygiene*, *98*(4), 218–227.

150. DiFeliceantonio, A. G., Coppin, G., Rigoux, L., Edwin Thanarajah, S., Dagher, A., Tittgemeyer, M., & Small, D. M. (2018). Supra-Additive Effects of Combining Fat and Carbohydrate on Food Reward. *Cell metabolism*, *28*(1), 33–44.e3.

151. Hebebrand, J., Albayrak, Ö., Adan, R., Antel, J., Dieguez, C., de Jong, J., Leng, G., Menzies, J., Mercer, J. G., Murphy, M., van der Plasse, G., & Dickson, S. L. (2014). "Eating addiction", rather than "food addiction", better captures addictive-like eating behavior. *Neuroscience and biobehavioral reviews*, *47*, 295–306.

152. Koob, G. F., & Volkow, N. D. (2010). Neurocircuitry of addiction. *Neuropsychopharmacology : official publication of the American College of Neuropsychopharmacology*, *35*(1), 217–238.

153. Michener, W., & Rozin, P. (1994). Pharmacological versus sensory factors in the satiation of chocolate craving. *Physiology & behavior*, *56*(3), 419–422.

154. Orloff, N. C., & Hormes, J. M. (2014). Pickles and ice cream! Food cravings in pregnancy: hypotheses, preliminary evidence, and directions for future research. *Frontiers in psychology*, *5*, 1076.

155. Hollins Martin, C. (2014). Handbook of diet and nutrition in the menstrual cycle, periconception and fertility. *Human health handbooks* (Vol. 7), Wageningen Academic Publishers.

156. Zellner, D. A., Garriga-Trillo, A., Centeno, S., & Wadsworth, E. (2004). Chocolate craving and the menstrual cycle. *Appetite*, *42*(1), 119–121.

157. Hormes, J. M., & Rozin, P. (2010). Does "craving" carve nature at the joints? Absence of a synonym for craving in many languages. *Addictive behaviors*, *35*(5), 459–463.

158. Meule, A., Hermann, T., & Kübler, A. (2014). A short version of the Food Cravings Questionnaire-Trait: the FCQ-T-reduced. *Frontiers in psychology*, *5*, 190.

159. Gilhooly, C. H., Das, S. K., Golden, J. K., McCrory, M. A., Dallal, G. E., Saltzman, E., Kramer, F. M., & Roberts, S. B. (2007). Food cravings and energy regulation: the characteristics of craved foods and their relationship with eating behaviors and weight change during 6 months of dietary energy restriction. *International journal of obesity (2005)*, *31*(12), 1849–1858.

160. Waller, S. M., Vander Wal, J. S., Klurfeld, D. M., McBurney, M. I., Cho, S., Bijlani, S., & Dhurandhar, N. V. (2004). Evening ready-to-eat cereal consumption contributes to weight management. *Journal of the American College of Nutrition*, *23*(4), 316–321.

161. Leahey, T. M., Bond, D. S., Raynor, H., Roye, D., Vithiananthan, S., Ryder, B. A., Sax, H. C., & Wing, R. R. (2012). Effects of bariatric surgery on food cravings: do food cravings and the consumption of craved foods "normalize" after surgery? *Surgery for*

obesity and related diseases : official journal of the American Society for Bariatric Surgery, 8(1), 84–91.

162. Alberts, H. J., Mulkens, S., Smeets, M., & Thewissen, R. (2010). Coping with food cravings. Investigating the potential of a mindfulness-based intervention. *Appetite, 55*(1), 160–163.

163. Forman, E. M., Hoffman, K. L., Juarascio, A. S., Butryn, M. L., & Herbert, J. D. (2013). Comparison of acceptance-based and standard cognitive-based coping strategies for craving sweets in overweight and obese women. *Eating behaviors, 14*(1), 64–68.

164. Forman, E. M., Hoffman, K. L., McGrath, K. B., Herbert, J. D., Brandsma, L. L., & Lowe, M. R. (2007). A comparison of acceptance- and control-based strategies for coping with food cravings: an analog study. *Behaviour research and therapy, 45*(10), 2372–2386.

165. Schumacher, S., Kemps, E., & Tiggemann, M. (2019). The food craving experience: Thoughts, images and resistance as predictors of craving intensity and consumption. *Appetite, 133*, 387–392.

166. Daniel, T. O., Stanton, C. M., & Epstein, L. H. (2013). The future is now: reducing impulsivity and energy intake using episodic future thinking. *Psychological science, 24*(11), 2339–2342.

167. Hollis-Hansen, K., Seidman, J., O'Donnell, S., & Epstein, L. H. (2019). Episodic future thinking and grocery shopping online. *Appetite, 133*, 1–9.

168. Yang, Y., Shields, G. S., Wu, Q., Liu, Y., Chen, H., & Guo, C. (2019). Cognitive training on eating behaviour and weight loss: A meta-analysis and systematic review. *Obesity reviews : an official journal of the International Association for the Study of Obesity, 20*(11), 1628–1641.

169. Henselmans, M. (n.d.). *High Protein, Low Calorie Cheesecake.* MennoHenselmans.com. https://mennohenselmans.com/high-protein-healthy-snack-bodybuilding-cheesecake/

170. Westerterp-Plantenga, M. S., Wijckmans-Duijsens, N. E., Verboeket-van de Venne, W. P., De Graaf, K., Weststrate, J. A., & Van Het Hof, K. H. (1997). Diet-induced thermogenesis and satiety in humans after full-fat and reduced-fat meals. *Physiology & behavior, 61*(2), 343–349.

171. Harvey, J., Wing, R. R., & Mullen, M. (1993). Effects on food cravings of a very low calorie diet or a balanced, low calorie diet. *Appetite, 21*(2), 105–115.

172. Martin, C. K., O'Neil, P. M., & Pawlow, L. (2006). Changes in food cravings during low-calorie and very-low-calorie diets. *Obesity (Silver Spring, Md.), 14*(1), 115–121.

173. Apolzan, J. W., Myers, C. A., Champagne, C. M., Beyl, R. A., Raynor, H. A., Anton, S. A., Williamson, D. A., Sacks, F. M., Bray, G. A., & Martin, C. K. (2017). Frequency of Consuming Foods Predicts Changes in Cravings for Those Foods During Weight Loss: The POUNDS Lost Study. *Obesity (Silver Spring, Md.), 25*(8), 1343–1348.

174. Anguah, K. O., Syed-Abdul, M. M., Hu, Q., Jacome-Sosa, M., Heimowitz, C., Cox, V., & Parks, E. J. (2019). Changes in Food Cravings and Eating Behavior after a Dietary Carbohydrate Restriction Intervention Trial. *Nutrients, 12*(1), 52.

175. Batra, P., Das, S. K., Salinardi, T., Robinson, L., Saltzman, E., Scott, T., Pittas, A. G., & Roberts, S. B. (2013). Relationship of cravings with weight loss and hunger. Results from a 6 month worksite weight loss intervention. *Appetite, 69*, 1–7.

176. Lim, S. S., Norman, R. J., Clifton, P. M., & Noakes, M. (2009). Psychological effects of prescriptive vs general lifestyle advice for weight loss in young women. *Journal of the American Dietetic Association, 109*(11), 1917–1921.

177. Barnes, R. D., & Tantleff-Dunn, S. (2010). Food for thought: examining the relationship between food thought suppression and weight-related outcomes. *Eating behaviors, 11*(3), 175–179.

178. Richard, A., Meule, A., Friese, M., & Blechert, J. (2017). Effects of Chocolate Deprivation on Implicit and Explicit Evaluation of Chocolate in High and Low Trait Chocolate Cravers. *Frontiers in psychology, 8*, 1591.

179. Lampuré, A., Schlich, P., Deglaire, A., Castetbon, K., Péneau, S., Hercberg, S., & Méjean, C. (2015). Sociodemographic, psychological, and lifestyle characteristics are associated with a liking for salty and sweet tastes in French adults. *The Journal of nutrition, 145*(3), 587–594.

180. Holt, S.H.A., Cobiac, L., Beaumont-Smith, N.E., Easton, K., & Best, D.J. (2000). Dietary habits and the perception and liking of sweetness among Australian and Malaysian students: A cross-cultural study. *Food Quality and Preference, 11*(4), 299–312.

181. Wise, P. M., Nattress, L., Flammer, L. J., & Beauchamp, G. K. (2016). Reduced dietary intake of simple sugars alters perceived sweet taste intensity but not perceived pleasantness. *The American journal of clinical nutrition, 103*(1), 50–60.

182. Jamel, H. A., Sheiham, A., Cowell, C. R., & Watt, R. G. (1996). Taste preference for sweetness in urban and rural populations in Iraq. *Journal of dental research, 75*(11), 1879–1884.

183. Zajonc, R. B. (1968). Attitudinal effects of mere exposure. Journal of Personality and Social Psychology, 9(2, Pt.2), 1–27.

184. Riskey, D.R., Parducci, A. & Beauchamp, G.K. (1979). Effects of context in judgments of sweetness and pleasantness. *Perception & Psychophysics, 26*, 171–176.

185. Parducci, A. (1965). Category judgment: A range-frequency model. *Psychological Review, 72*(6), 407–418.

186. Davelaar, E. J., Goshen-Gottstein, Y., Ashkenazi, A., Haarmann, H. J., & Usher, M. (2005). The demise of short-term memory revisited: empirical and computational investigations of recency effects. *Psychological review, 112*(1), 3–42.

187. Deckersbach, T., Das, S. K., Urban, L. E., Salinardi, T., Batra, P., Rodman, A. M., Arulpragasam, A. R., Dougherty, D. D., & Roberts, S. B. (2014). Pilot randomized trial demonstrating reversal of obesity-related abnormalities in reward system responsivity to food cues with a behavioral intervention. *Nutrition & diabetes, 4*(9), e129.

188. Nock, N. L., Dimitropolous, A., Tkach, J., Frasure, H., & von Gruenigen, V. (2012). Reduction in neural activation to high-calorie food cues in obese endometrial cancer survivors after a behavioral lifestyle intervention: a pilot study. *BMC neuroscience, 13*, 74.

189. Buckland, N. J., Camidge, D., Croden, F., Lavin, J. H., Stubbs, R. J., Hetherington, M. M., Blundell, J. E., & Finlayson, G. (2018). A Low Energy-Dense Diet in the Context of a Weight-Management Program Affects Appetite Control in Overweight and Obese Women. *The Journal of nutrition, 148*(5), 798–806.

190. Anguah, K. O., Lovejoy, J. C., Craig, B. A., Gehrke, M. M., Palmer, P. A., Eichelsdoerfer, P. E., & McCrory, M. A. (2017). Can the Palatability of Healthy, Satiety-Promoting Foods Increase with Repeated Exposure during Weight Loss? *Foods (Basel, Switzerland), 6*(2), 16.

191. Martin, C. K., Rosenbaum, D., Han, H., Geiselman, P. J., Wyatt, H. R., Hill, J. O., Brill, C., Bailer, B., Miller, B. V., 3rd, Stein, R., Klein, S., & Foster, G. D. (2011). Change in food cravings, food preferences, and appetite during a low-carbohydrate and low-fat diet. *Obesity (Silver Spring, Md.), 19*(10), 1963–1970.

192. Murdaugh, D. L., Cox, J. E., Cook, E. W., 3rd, & Weller, R. E. (2012). fMRI reactivity to high-calorie food pictures predicts short- and long-term outcome in a weight-loss program. *NeuroImage, 59*(3), 2709–2721.

193. Anton, S. D., Gallagher, J., Carey, V. J., Laranjo, N., Cheng, J., Champagne, C. M., Ryan, D. H., McManus, K., Loria, C. M., Bray, G. A., Sacks, F. M., & Williamson, D. A. (2012). Diet type and changes in food cravings following weight loss: findings from the POUNDS LOST Trial. *Eating and weight disorders : EWD, 17*(2), e101–e108.

194. Gibson, E. L., & Desmond, E. (1999). Chocolate craving and hunger state: implications for the acquisition and expression of appetite and food choice. *Appetite, 32*(2), 219–240.

195. Chao, A., Grilo, C. M., White, M. A., & Sinha, R. (2014). Food cravings, food intake, and weight status in a community-based sample. *Eating behaviors, 15*(3), 478–482.

196. Farrow, C. V., Haycraft, E., & Blissett, J. M. (2015). Teaching our children when to eat: how parental feeding practices inform the development of emotional eating--a longitudinal experimental design. *The American journal of clinical nutrition, 101*(5), 908–913.

197. Altheimer, G., & Urry, H.L. (2019). Do Emotions Cause Eating? The Role of Previous Experiences and Social Context in Emotional Eating. *Current Directions in Psychological Science, 28*(3), 234–240.

198. Schulte, E. M., Avena, N. M., & Gearhardt, A. N. (2015). Which foods may be addictive? The roles of processing, fat content, and glycemic load. *PloS one, 10*(2), e0117959.

199. Temple J. L. (2016). Behavioral sensitization of the reinforcing value of food: What food and drugs have in common. *Preventive medicine, 92*, 90–99.

200. Gorin, A. A., Phelan, S., Wing, R. R., & Hill, J. O. (2004). Promoting long-term weight control: does dieting consistency matter? *International journal of obesity and related metabolic disorders : journal of the International Association for the Study of Obesity, 28*(2), 278–281.

201. Racette, S. B., Weiss, E. P., Schechtman, K. B., Steger-May, K., Villareal, D. T., Obert, K. A., & Holloszy, J. O. (2008). Influence of weekend lifestyle patterns on body weight. *Obesity (Silver Spring, Md.), 16*(8), 1826–1830.

202. Wing, R. R., & Phelan, S. (2005). Long-term weight loss maintenance. *The American journal of clinical nutrition, 82*(1 Suppl), 222S–225S.

203. Marlatt, K. L., Redman, L. M., Burton, J. H., Martin, C. K., & Ravussin, E. (2017). Persistence of weight loss and acquired behaviors 2 y after stopping a 2-y calorie restriction intervention. *The American journal of clinical nutrition, 105*(4), 928–935.

204. Nadeau, J., Koski, K. G., Strychar, I., & Yale, J. F. (2001). Teaching subjects with type 2 diabetes how to incorporate sugar choices into their daily meal plan promotes dietary compliance and does not deteriorate metabolic profile. *Diabetes care, 24*(2), 222–227.

205. Sayer, R. D., Peters, J. C., Pan, Z., Wyatt, H. R., & Hill, J. O. (2018). Hunger, Food Cravings, and Diet Satisfaction are Related to Changes in Body Weight During a 6-Month Behavioral Weight Loss Intervention: The Beef WISE Study. *Nutrients, 10*(6), 700.

206. Legget, K. T., Cornier, M. A., Rojas, D. C., Lawful, B., & Tregellas, J. R. (2015). Harnessing the power of disgust: a randomized trial to reduce high-calorie food appeal through implicit priming. *The American journal of clinical nutrition, 102*(2), 249–255.

207. Mehl, N., Morys, F., Villringer, A., & Horstmann, A. (2019). Unhealthy yet Avoidable-How Cognitive Bias Modification Alters Behavioral and Brain Responses to Food Cues in Individuals with Obesity. *Nutrients, 11*(4), 874.

208. Roberts, S. B., Das, S. K., Suen, V., Pihlajamäki, J., Kuriyan, R., Steiner-Asiedu, M., Taetzsch, A., Anderson, A. K., Silver, R. E., Barger, K., Krauss, A., Karhunen, L., Zhang, X., Hambly, C., Schwab, U., Triffoni-Melo, A. T., Taylor, S. F., Economos, C., Kurpad, A. V., & Speakman, J. R. (2018). Measured energy content of frequently purchased restaurant meals: multi-country cross sectional study. *BMJ (Clinical research ed.), 363*, k4864.

209. Kolaczynski, J. W., Ohannesian, J. P., Considine, R. V., Marco, C. C., & Caro, J. F. (1996). Response of leptin to short-term and prolonged overfeeding in humans. *The Journal of clinical endocrinology and metabolism, 81*(11), 4162–4165.

210. Trudel, R., & Murray, K.B. (2013). Self-regulatory strength amplification through selective information processing. *Journal of Consumer Psychology, 23*(1), 61–73.

211. Champagne, C. M., Bray, G. A., Kurtz, A. A., Monteiro, J. B., Tucker, E., Volaufova, J., & Delany, J. P. (2002). Energy intake and energy expenditure: a controlled study comparing dietitians and non-dietitians. *Journal of the American Dietetic Association, 102*(10), 1428–1432.

212. Besson, T., Lalot, F., Bochard, N., & Flaudias, V. (2019). The calories underestimation of "organic" food: Exploring the impact of implicit evaluations. *Appetite, 137*, 134–144.

213. Vigar, V., Myers, S., Oliver, C., Arellano, J., Robinson, S., & Leifert, C. (2019). A Systematic Review of Organic Versus Conventional Food Consumption: Is There a Measurable Benefit on Human Health? *Nutrients, 12*(1), 7.

214. Koehler, D.J., & Harvey, N. (2004). *Blackwell Handbook of Judgment and Decision Making.* Wiley-Blackwell.

215. Henselmans, M. (n.d.) *Why Diets Fail and "Eat Less, Move More" is Bad Advice.* Paleo f(x). https://www.paleofx.com/why-diets-fail-and-eat-less-move-more-bad-advice/

216. Burger, K. S., Sanders, A. J., & Gilbert, J. R. (2016). Hedonic Hunger Is Related to Increased Neural and Perceptual Responses to Cues of Palatable Food and Motivation to Consume: Evidence from 3 Independent Investigations. *The Journal of nutrition*, *146*(9), 1807–1812.

217. Kroeger, C. M., Trepanowski, J. F., Klempel, M. C., Barnosky, A., Bhutani, S., Gabel, K., & Varady, K. A. (2018). Eating behavior traits of successful weight losers during 12 months of alternate-day fasting: An exploratory analysis of a randomized controlled trial. *Nutrition and health*, *24*(1), 5–10.

218. Monrroy, H., Pribic, T., Galan, C., Nieto, A., Amigo, N., Accarino, A., Correig, X., & Azpiroz, F. (2019). Meal Enjoyment and Tolerance in Women and Men. *Nutrients*, *11*(1), 119.

219. Rolls, B. J., Roe, L. S., James, B. L., & Sanchez, C. E. (2017). Does the incorporation of portion-control strategies in a behavioral program improve weight loss in a 1-year randomized controlled trial? *International journal of obesity (2005)*, *41*(3), 434–442.

220. Zuraikat, F. M., Roe, L. S., Sanchez, C. E., & Rolls, B. J. (2018). Comparing the portion size effect in women with and without extended training in portion control: A follow-up to the Portion-Control Strategies Trial. *Appetite*, *123*, 334–342.

221. Zhu, Y., & Hollis, J. (2013). Appetite control and regulation of food intake: A review of proposed mechanisms. *Nutritional Therapy and Metabolism, 31*(2), 58–68.

222. Wakisaka, S., Nagai, H., Mura, E., Matsumoto, T., Moritani, T., & Nagai, N. (2012). The effects of carbonated water upon gastric and cardiac activities and fullness in healthy young women. *Journal of nutritional science and vitaminology*, *58*(5), 333–338.

223. Rolls, B. J., Bell, E. A., & Waugh, B. A. (2000). Increasing the volume of a food by incorporating air affects satiety in men. *The American journal of clinical nutrition*, *72*(2), 361–368.

224. Rolls, B. J., Castellanos, V. H., Halford, J. C., Kilara, A., Panyam, D., Pelkman, C. L., Smith, G. P., & Thorwart, M. L. (1998). Volume of food consumed affects satiety in men. *The American journal of clinical nutrition*, *67*(6), 1170–1177.

225. Martinez-Brocca, M. A., Belda, O., Parejo, J., Jimenez, L., del Valle, A., Pereira, J. L., Garcia-Pesquera, F., Astorga, R., Leal-Cerro, A., & Garcia-Luna, P. P. (2007). Intragastric balloon-induced satiety is not mediated by modification in fasting or postprandial plasma ghrelin levels in morbid obesity. *Obesity surgery*, *17*(5), 649–657.

226. Geliebter, A., Westreich, S., & Gage, D. (1988). Gastric distention by balloon and test-meal intake in obese and lean subjects. *The American journal of clinical nutrition*, *48*(3), 592–594.

227. Ello-Martin, J. A., Ledikwe, J. H., & Rolls, B. J. (2005). The influence of food portion size and energy density on energy intake: implications for weight management. *The American journal of clinical nutrition*, *82*(1 Suppl), 236S–241S.

228. Veldhorst, M., Smeets, A., Soenen, S., Hochstenbach-Waelen, A., Hursel, R., Diepvens, K., Lejeune, M., Luscombe-Marsh, N., & Westerterp-Plantenga, M. (2008). Protein-induced satiety: effects and mechanisms of different proteins. *Physiology & behavior*, *94*(2), 300–307.

229. Parvaresh Rizi, E., Loh, T. P., Baig, S., Chhay, V., Huang, S., Caleb Quek, J., Tai, E. S., Toh, S. A., & Khoo, C. M. (2018). A high carbohydrate, but not fat or protein meal attenuates postprandial ghrelin, PYY and GLP-1 responses in Chinese men. *PloS one*, *13*(1), e0191609.

230. Bligh, H. F., Godsland, I. F., Frost, G., Hunter, K. J., Murray, P., MacAulay, K., Hyliands, D., Talbot, D. C., Casey, J., Mulder, T. P., & Berry, M. J. (2015). Plant-rich mixed meals based on Palaeolithic diet principles have a dramatic impact on incretin, peptide YY and satiety response, but show little effect on glucose and insulin homeostasis: an acute-effects randomised study. *The British journal of nutrition*, *113*(4), 574–584.

231. Hochstenbach-Waelen, A., Westerterp, K. R., Soenen, S., & Westerterp-Plantenga, M. S. (2010). No long-term weight maintenance effects of gelatin in a supra-sustained protein diet. *Physiology & behavior*, *101*(2), 237–244.

232. Hochstenbach-Waelen, A., Veldhorst, M. A., Nieuwenhuizen, A. G., Westerterp-Plantenga, M. S., & Westerterp, K. R. (2009). Comparison of 2 diets with either 25% or 10% of energy as casein on energy expenditure, substrate balance, and appetite profile. *The American journal of clinical nutrition, 89*(3), 831–838.

233. Bowen, J., Noakes, M., & Clifton, P. M. (2006). Appetite regulatory hormone responses to various dietary proteins differ by body mass index status despite similar reductions in ad libitum energy intake. *The Journal of clinical endocrinology and metabolism, 91*(8), 2913–2919.

234. Lemmens, S. G., Martens, E. A., Kester, A. D., & Westerterp-Plantenga, M. S. (2011). Changes in gut hormone and glucose concentrations in relation to hunger and fullness. *The American journal of clinical nutrition, 94*(3), 717–725.

235. Koren, M. S., Purnell, J. Q., Breen, P. A., Matthys, C. C., Callahan, H. S., Meeuws, K. E., Burden, V. R., & Weigle, D. S. (2007). Changes in plasma amino Acid levels do not predict satiety and weight loss on diets with modified macronutrient composition. *Annals of nutrition & metabolism, 51*(2), 182–187.

236. Bekelman, T. A., Santamaría-Ulloa, C., Dufour, D. L., Marín-Arias, L., & Dengo, A. L. (2017). Using the protein leverage hypothesis to understand socioeconomic variation in obesity. *American journal of human biology : the official journal of the Human Biology Council, 29*(3), 10.1002/ajhb.22953.

237. Morrison, C. D., Reed, S. D., & Henagan, T. M. (2012). Homeostatic regulation of protein intake: in search of a mechanism. *American journal of physiology. Regulatory, integrative and comparative physiology, 302*(8), R917–R928.

238. Efeyan, A., Comb, W. C., & Sabatini, D. M. (2015). Nutrient-sensing mechanisms and pathways. *Nature, 517*(7534), 302–310.

239. Fromentin, G., & Nicolaidis, S. (1996). Rebalancing essential amino acids intake by self-selection in the rat. *The British journal of nutrition, 75*(5), 669–682.

240. Forbes, J.M., & Shariatmadari, F. (2007). Diet selection for protein by poultry. *World's Poultry Science Journal, 50*(1), 7–24.

241. Hu, S., Wang, L., Yang, D., Li, L., Togo, J., Wu, Y., Liu, Q., Li, B., Li, M., Wang, G., Zhang, X., Niu, C., Li, J., Xu, Y., Couper, E., Whittington-Davies, A., Mazidi, M., Luo, L., Wang, S., Douglas, A., … Speakman, J. R. (2018). Dietary Fat, but Not Protein or Carbohydrate, Regulates Energy Intake and Causes Adiposity in Mice. *Cell metabolism, 28*(3), 415–431.e4.

242. Ben-Harchache, S., Roche, H. M., Corish, C. A., & Horner, K. M. (2020). The Impact of Protein Supplementation on Appetite and Energy Intake in Healthy Older Adults: A Systematic Review with Meta-Analysis. *Advances in nutrition (Bethesda, Md.)*, nmaa115. Advance online publication.

243. Griffioen-Roose, S., Mars, M., Siebelink, E., Finlayson, G., Tomé, D., & de Graaf, C. (2012). Protein status elicits compensatory changes in food intake and food preferences. *The American journal of clinical nutrition, 95*(1), 32–38.

244 Bendtsen, L. Q., Lorenzen, J. K., Bendsen, N. T., Rasmussen, C., & Astrup, A. (2013). Effect of dairy proteins on appetite, energy expenditure, body weight, and composition: a review of the evidence from controlled clinical trials. *Advances in nutrition (Bethesda, Md.), 4*(4), 418–438.

245. Long, S. J., Jeffcoat, A. R., & Millward, D. J. (2000). Effect of habitual dietary-protein intake on appetite and satiety. *Appetite, 35*(1), 79–88.

246. Phillips, S. M., Chevalier, S., & Leidy, H. J. (2016). Protein "requirements" beyond the RDA: implications for optimizing health. *Applied physiology, nutrition, and metabolism = Physiologie appliquee, nutrition et metabolisme, 41*(5), 565–572.

247. Henselmans, M. (n.d.). *The myth of 1 g/lb: Optimal protein intake for bodybuilders.* MennoHenselmans.com. https://mennohenselmans.com/the-myth-of-1glb-optimal-protein-intake-for-bodybuilders/

248. Roberts, J., Zinchenko, A., Suckling, C., Smith, L., Johnstone, J., & Henselmans, M. (2017). The short-term effect of high versus moderate protein intake on recovery after strength training in resistance-trained individuals. *Journal of the International Society of Sports Nutrition, 14*, 44.

249. Morton, R. W., Murphy, K. T., McKellar, S. R., Schoenfeld, B. J., Henselmans, M., Helms, E., Aragon, A. A., Devries, M. C., Banfield, L., Krieger, J. W., & Phillips, S. M.

(2018). A systematic review, meta-analysis and meta-regression of the effect of protein supplementation on resistance training-induced gains in muscle mass and strength in healthy adults. *British journal of sports medicine, 52*(6), 376–384.

250. Henselmans, M. (n.d.). *Is protein really more satiating than carbs and fats?* MennoHenselmans.com. https://mennohenselmans.com/protein-is-not-more-satiating-than-carbs-and-fats/

251. Roberts, J., Zinchenko, A., Mahbubani, K., Johnstone, J., Smith, L., Merzbach, V., Blacutt, M., Banderas, O., Villasenor, L., Vårvik, F. T., & Henselmans, M. (2018). Satiating Effect of High Protein Diets on Resistance-Trained Subjects in Energy Deficit. *Nutrients, 11*(1), 56.

252. Li, J., Armstrong, C. L., & Campbell, W. W. (2016). Effects of Dietary Protein Source and Quantity during Weight Loss on Appetite, Energy Expenditure, and Cardio-Metabolic Responses. *Nutrients, 8*(2), 63.

253. Gosby, A. K., Conigrave, A. D., Lau, N. S., Iglesias, M. A., Hall, R. M., Jebb, S. A., Brand-Miller, J., Caterson, I. D., Raubenheimer, D., & Simpson, S. J. (2011). Testing protein leverage in lean humans: a randomised controlled experimental study. *PloS one, 6*(10), e25929.

254. Kleiner, R. E., Hutchins, A. M., Johnston, C. S., & Swan, P. D. (2006). Effects of an 8-week high-protein or high-carbohydrate diet in adults with hyperinsulinemia. *MedGenMed : Medscape general medicine, 8*(4), 39.

255. Sacks, F. M., Bray, G. A., Carey, V. J., Smith, S. R., Ryan, D. H., Anton, S. D., McManus, K., Champagne, C. M., Bishop, L. M., Laranjo, N., Leboff, M. S., Rood, J. C., de Jonge, L., Greenway, F. L., Loria, C. M., Obarzanek, E., & Williamson, D. A. (2009). Comparison of weight-loss diets with different compositions of fat, protein, and carbohydrates. *The New England journal of medicine, 360*(9), 859–873.

256. Leidy, H. J., Carnell, N. S., Mattes, R. D., & Campbell, W. W. (2007). Higher protein intake preserves lean mass and satiety with weight loss in pre-obese and obese women. *Obesity (Silver Spring, Md.), 15*(2), 421–429.

257. Johnston, C. S., Tjonn, S. L., & Swan, P. D. (2004). High-protein, low-fat diets are effective for weight loss and favorably alter biomarkers in healthy adults. *The Journal of nutrition, 134*(3), 586–591.

258. Weigle, D. S., Breen, P. A., Matthys, C. C., Callahan, H. S., Meeuws, K. E., Burden, V. R., & Purnell, J. Q. (2005). A high-protein diet induces sustained reductions in appetite, ad libitum caloric intake, and body weight despite compensatory changes in diurnal plasma leptin and ghrelin concentrations. *The American journal of clinical nutrition, 82*(1), 41–48.

259. Layman, D. K., Boileau, R. A., Erickson, D. J., Painter, J. E., Shiue, H., Sather, C., & Christou, D. D. (2003). A reduced ratio of dietary carbohydrate to protein improves body composition and blood lipid profiles during weight loss in adult women. *The Journal of nutrition, 133*(2), 411–417.

260. Leidy, H. J., Clifton, P. M., Astrup, A., Wycherley, T. P., Westerterp-Plantenga, M. S., Luscombe-Marsh, N. D., Woods, S. C., & Mattes, R. D. (2015). The role of protein in weight loss and maintenance. *The American journal of clinical nutrition, 101*(6), 1320S–1329S.

261. Vergnaud, A. C., Norat, T., Mouw, T., Romaguera, D., May, A. M., Bueno-de-Mesquita, H. B., van der A, D., Agudo, A., Wareham, N., Khaw, K. T., Romieu, I., Freisling, H., Slimani, N., Perquier, F., Boutron-Ruault, M. C., Clavel-Chapelon, F., Palli, D., Berrino, F., Mattiello, A., Tumino, R., … Peeters, P. H. (2013). Macronutrient composition of the diet and prospective weight change in participants of the EPIC-PANACEA study. *PloS one, 8*(3), e57300.

262. Cheskin, L. J., Davis, L. M., Lipsky, L. M., Mitola, A. H., Lycan, T., Mitchell, V., Mickle, B., & Adkins, E. (2008). Lack of energy compensation over 4 days when white button mushrooms are substituted for beef. *Appetite, 51*(1), 50–57.

263. Hess, J. M., Wang, Q., Kraft, C., & Slavin, J. L. (2017). Impact of Agaricus bisporus mushroom consumption on satiety and food intake. *Appetite, 117*, 179–185.

264. Poddar, K. H., Ames, M., Hsin-Jen, C., Feeney, M. J., Wang, Y., & Cheskin, L. J. (2013). Positive effect of mushrooms substituted for meat on body weight, body

composition, and health parameters. A 1-year randomized clinical trial. *Appetite*, *71*, 379–387.

265. Kristensen, M. D., Bendsen, N. T., Christensen, S. M., Astrup, A., & Raben, A. (2016). Meals based on vegetable protein sources (beans and peas) are more satiating than meals based on animal protein sources (veal and pork) - a randomized cross-over meal test study. *Food & nutrition research*, *60*, 32634.

266. Öner, C., Özdemir, M., Telatar, B., & Yeşildağ, Ş. (2016). Does Plate Size Used in Food Service Affect Portion Perception? *Turkish Journal of Family Medicine and Primary Care, 10*(4), 182-187.

267. McCarthy, J. D., Kupitz, C., & Caplovitz, G. P. (2013). The Binding Ring Illusion: assimilation affects the perceived size of a circular array. *F1000Research*, *2*, 58.

268. Rubio-Martín, E., García-Escobar, E., Ruiz de Adana, M. S., Lima-Rubio, F., Peláez, L., Caracuel, A. M., Bermúdez-Silva, F. J., Soriguer, F., Rojo-Martínez, G., & Olveira, G. (2017). Comparison of the Effects of Goat Dairy and Cow Dairy Based Breakfasts on Satiety, Appetite Hormones, and Metabolic Profile. *Nutrients*, *9*(8), 877.

269. Howarth, N. C., Saltzman, E., & Roberts, S. B. (2001). Dietary fiber and weight regulation. *Nutrition reviews*, *59*(5), 129–139.

270. Frost, G., Sleeth, M. L., Sahuri-Arisoylu, M., Lizarbe, B., Cerdan, S., Brody, L., Anastasovska, J., Ghourab, S., Hankir, M., Zhang, S., Carling, D., Swann, J. R., Gibson, G., Viardot, A., Morrison, D., Louise Thomas, E., & Bell, J. D. (2014). The short-chain fatty acid acetate reduces appetite via a central homeostatic mechanism. *Nature communications*, *5*, 3611.

271. Clark, M. J., & Slavin, J. L. (2013). The effect of fiber on satiety and food intake: a systematic review. *Journal of the American College of Nutrition*, *32*(3), 200–211.

272. Capuano E. (2017). The behavior of dietary fiber in the gastrointestinal tract determines its physiological effect. *Critical reviews in food science and nutrition*, *57*(16), 3543–3564.

273. Thompson, S. V., Hannon, B. A., An, R., & Holscher, H. D. (2017). Effects of isolated soluble fiber supplementation on body weight, glycemia, and insulinemia in adults with overweight and obesity: a systematic review and meta-analysis of randomized controlled trials. *The American journal of clinical nutrition*, *106*(6), 1514–1528.

274. Eaton, S. B., & Konner, M. (1985). Paleolithic nutrition. A consideration of its nature and current implications. *The New England journal of medicine*, *312*(5), 283–289.

275. Eaton, S. B., Eaton, S. B., 3rd, Konner, M. J., & Shostak, M. (1996). An evolutionary perspective enhances understanding of human nutritional requirements. *The Journal of nutrition*, *126*(6), 1732–1740.

276. Brand-Miller, J. C., & Holt, S. H. (1998). Australian aboriginal plant foods: a consideration of their nutritional composition and health implications. *Nutrition research reviews*, *11*(1), 5–23.

277. Leach, J. D., & Sobolik, K. D. (2010). High dietary intake of prebiotic inulin-type fructans in the prehistoric Chihuahuan Desert. *The British journal of nutrition*, *103*(11), 1558–1561.

278. Bellisle, F., & Dalix, A. M. (2001). Cognitive restraint can be offset by distraction, leading to increased meal intake in women. *The American journal of clinical nutrition*, *74*(2), 197–200.

279. Hetherington, M. M., Anderson, A. S., Norton, G. N., & Newson, L. (2006). Situational effects on meal intake: A comparison of eating alone and eating with others. *Physiology & behavior*, *88*(4-5), 498–505.

280. Gonçalves, R., Barreto, D. A., Monteiro, P. I., Zangeronimo, M. G., Castelo, P. M., van der Bilt, A., & Pereira, L. J. (2019). Smartphone use while eating increases caloric ingestion. *Physiology & behavior*, *204*, 93–99.

281. Teh, K. C., & Aziz, A. R. (2002). Heart rate, oxygen uptake, and energy cost of ascending and descending the stairs. *Medicine and science in sports and exercise*, *34*(4), 695–699.

282. Hall, C., Figueroa, A., Fernhall, B., & Kanaley, J. A. (2004). Energy expenditure of walking and running: comparison with prediction equations. *Medicine and science in sports and exercise*, *36*(12), 2128–2134.

283. Wagner, D. D., Altman, M., Boswell, R. G., Kelley, W. M., & Heatherton, T. F. (2013). Self-regulatory depletion enhances neural responses to rewards and impairs top-down control. *Psychological science, 24*(11), 2262–2271.

284. STUNKARD, A. J., GRACE, W. J., & WOLFF, H. G. (1955). The night-eating syndrome; a pattern of food intake among certain obese patients. *The American journal of medicine, 19*(1), 78–86.

285. Redman, L. M., Heilbronn, L. K., Martin, C. K., de Jonge, L., Williamson, D. A., Delany, J. P., Ravussin, E., & Pennington CALERIE Team (2009). Metabolic and behavioral compensations in response to caloric restriction: implications for the maintenance of weight loss. *PloS one, 4*(2), e4377.

286. Bradbury, K. E., Guo, W., Cairns, B. J., Armstrong, M. E., & Key, T. J. (2017). Association between physical activity and body fat percentage, with adjustment for BMI: a large cross-sectional analysis of UK Biobank. *BMJ open, 7*(3), e011843.

287. Leung, A., Chan, R., Sea, M., & Woo, J. (2017). An Overview of Factors Associated with Adherence to Lifestyle Modification Programs for Weight Management in Adults. *International journal of environmental research and public health, 14*(8), 922.

288. SEAT. (n.d.). *How has car manufacturing changed?* https://www.seat.se/foretaget/news-and-events/company/changes-car-manufacturing.html

289. Adriaanse, M. A., Kroese, F. M., Gillebaart, M., & De Ridder, D. T. (2014). Effortless inhibition: habit mediates the relation between self-control and unhealthy snack consumption. *Frontiers in psychology, 5*, 444.

290. Wood, W., & Neal, D. T. (2007). A new look at habits and the habit-goal interface. *Psychological review, 114*(4), 843–863.

291. Lally, P., van Jaarsveld, C.H.M., Potts, H.W.W. & Wardle, J. (2010), How are habits formed: Modelling habit formation in the real world. *European Journal of Social Psychology, 40*: 998-1009.

292. Gollwitzer, P. M. (1999). Implementation intentions: Strong effects of simple plans. *American Psychologist, 54*(7), 493–503.

293. Durant, N. H., Joseph, R. P., Affuso, O. H., Dutton, G. R., Robertson, H. T., & Allison, D. B. (2013). Empirical evidence does not support an association between less ambitious pre-treatment goals and better treatment outcomes: a meta-analysis. *Obesity reviews : an official journal of the International Association for the Study of Obesity, 14*(7), 532–540.

294. Dalle Grave, R., Calugi, S., Molinari, E., Petroni, M. L., Bondi, M., Compare, A., Marchesini, G., & QUOVADIS Study Group (2005). Weight loss expectations in obese patients and treatment attrition: an observational multicenter study. *Obesity research, 13*(11), 1961–1969.

295. Grant, H., & Dweck, C. S. (2003). Clarifying Achievement Goals and Their Impact. *Journal of Personality and Social Psychology, 85*(3), 541–553.

296. Foster, G. D., Wadden, T. A., Vogt, R. A., & Brewer, G. (1997). What is a reasonable weight loss? Patients' expectations and evaluations of obesity treatment outcomes. *Journal of consulting and clinical psychology, 65*(1), 79–85.

297. Linde, J. A., Jeffery, R. W., Levy, R. L., Pronk, N. P., & Boyle, R. G. (2005). Weight loss goals and treatment outcomes among overweight men and women enrolled in a weight loss trial. *International journal of obesity (2005), 29*(8), 1002–1005.

298. Gollwitzer, P.M., & Sheeran, P. (2006). Implementation Intentions and Goal Achievement: A Meta-analysis of Effects and Processes. *Advances in Experimental Social Psychology, 38*, 69–119.

299. Carrero, I., Vilà, I., & Redondo, R. (2019). What makes implementation intention interventions effective for promoting healthy eating behaviours? A meta-regression. *Appetite, 140*, 239–247.

300. Milne, S., Orbell, S., & Sheeran, P. (2002). Combining motivational and volitional interventions to promote exercise participation: protection motivation theory and implementation intentions. *British journal of health psychology, 7*(Pt 2), 163–184.

301. Adriaanse, M. A., de Ridder, D. T., & de Wit, J. B. (2009). Finding the critical cue: implementation intentions to change one's diet work best when tailored to personally relevant reasons for unhealthy eating. *Personality & social psychology bulletin, 35*(1), 60–71.

302. Henselmans, M. (n.d.) *3 Reasons You Should Be Bodybuilding*. Paleo f(x). https://www.paleofx.com/3-reasons-you-should-be-bodybuilding/
303. Henselmans, M. (n.d.) *4 More Reasons You Should be Bodybuilding*. Paleo f(x). https://www.paleofx.com/4-more-reasons-you-should-be-bodybuidling/
304. Luszczynska, A., Sobczyk, A., & Abraham, C. (2007). Planning to lose weight: randomized controlled trial of an implementation intention prompt to enhance weight reduction among overweight and obese women. *Health psychology : official journal of the Division of Health Psychology, American Psychological Association, 26*(4), 507–512.
305. Chapman, J., Armitage, C. J., & Norman, P. (2009). Comparing implementation intention interventions in relation to young adults' intake of fruit and vegetables. *Psychology & health, 24*(3), 317–332.
306. Adriaanse, M. A., van Oosten, J. M., de Ridder, D. T., de Wit, J. B., & Evers, C. (2011). Planning what not to eat: ironic effects of implementation intentions negating unhealthy habits. *Personality & social psychology bulletin, 37*(1), 69–81.
307. Adriaanse, M. A., Gollwitzer, P. M., De Ridder, D. T., de Wit, J. B., & Kroese, F. M. (2011). Breaking habits with implementation intentions: a test of underlying processes. *Personality & social psychology bulletin, 37*(4), 502–513.
308. Watson, P. E., Watson, I. D., & Batt, R. D. (1980). Total body water volumes for adult males and females estimated from simple anthropometric measurements. *The American journal of clinical nutrition, 33*(1), 27–39.
309. Dunstan, D. W., Howard, B., Healy, G. N., & Owen, N. (2012). Too much sitting--a health hazard. *Diabetes research and clinical practice, 97*(3), 368–376.
310. Buckley, J. P., Mellor, D. D., Morris, M., & Joseph, F. (2014). Standing-based office work shows encouraging signs of attenuating post-prandial glycaemic excursion. *Occupational and environmental medicine, 71*(2), 109–111.
311. Gibbs, B. B., Kowalsky, R. J., Perdomo, S. J., Grier, M., & Jakicic, J. M. (2017). Energy expenditure of deskwork when sitting, standing or alternating positions. *Occupational medicine (Oxford, England), 67*(2), 121–127.
312. Koepp, G. A., Manohar, C. U., McCrady-Spitzer, S. K., Ben-Ner, A., Hamann, D. J., Runge, C. F., & Levine, J. A. (2013). Treadmill desks: A 1-year prospective trial. *Obesity (Silver Spring, Md.), 21*(4), 705–711.
313. Levine, J. A., & Miller, J. M. (2007). The energy expenditure of using a "walk-and-work" desk for office workers with obesity. *British journal of sports medicine, 41*(9), 558–561.
314. Wansink, B., & Johnson, K. A. (2015). The clean plate club: about 92% of self-served food is eaten. *International journal of obesity (2005), 39*(2), 371–374.
315. Dennis, E. A., Dengo, A. L., Comber, D. L., Flack, K. D., Savla, J., Davy, K. P., & Davy, B. M. (2010). Water consumption increases weight loss during a hypocaloric diet intervention in middle-aged and older adults. *Obesity (Silver Spring, Md.), 18*(2), 300–307.
316. Iyengar, S. S., & Lepper, M. R. (2000). When choice is demotivating: can one desire too much of a good thing? *Journal of personality and social psychology, 79*(6), 995–1006.
317. Greifeneder, R., Scheibehenne, B., & Kleber, N. (2010). Less may be more when choosing is difficult: choice complexity and too much choice. *Acta psychologica, 133*(1), 45–50.
318. Jessup, R.K., Veinott, E.S., Todd, P.M., & Busemeyer, J.R. (2009). Leaving the store empty-handed: Testing explanations for the too-much-choice effect using decision field theory. *Psychology and Marketing, 26*(3), 299–320.
319. Huang, A. L., Chen, X., Hoon, M. A., Chandrashekar, J., Guo, W., Tränkner, D., Ryba, N. J., & Zuker, C. S. (2006). The cells and logic for mammalian sour taste detection. *Nature, 442*(7105), 934–938.
320. Walker, R., & Lupien, J. R. (2000). The safety evaluation of monosodium glutamate. *The Journal of nutrition, 130*(4S Suppl), 1049S–52S.
321. Magerowski, G., Giacona, G., Patriarca, L., Papadopoulos, K., Garza-Naveda, P., Radziejowska, J., & Alonso-Alonso, M. (2018). Neurocognitive effects of umami: association with eating behavior and food choice. *Neuropsychopharmacology : official publication of the American College of Neuropsychopharmacology, 43*(10), 2009–2016.

322. Imada, T., Hao, S. S., Torii, K., & Kimura, E. (2014). Supplementing chicken broth with monosodium glutamate reduces energy intake from high fat and sweet snacks in middle-aged healthy women. *Appetite, 79*, 158–165.
323. Miyaki, T., Imada, T., Hao, S. S., & Kimura, E. (2016). Monosodium L-glutamate in soup reduces subsequent energy intake from high-fat savoury food in overweight and obese women. *The British journal of nutrition, 115*(1), 176–184.
324. Henselmans, M., & Leenman, S. (n.d.). *3 Minute Tomato soup.* MennoHenselmans.com. https://mennohenselmans.com/3-minute-tomato-soup/
325. Feeney, E. L., Leacy, L., O'Kelly, M., Leacy, N., Phelan, A., Crowley, L., Stynes, E., de Casanove, A., & Horner, K. (2019). Sweet and Umami Taste Perception Differs with Habitual Exercise in Males. *Nutrients, 11*(1), 155.
326. Zheng, Y., Klem, M. L., Sereika, S. M., Danford, C. A., Ewing, L. J., & Burke, L. E. (2015). Self-weighing in weight management: a systematic literature review. *Obesity (Silver Spring, Md.), 23*(2), 256–265.
327. Pacanowski, C. R., & Levitsky, D. A. (2015). Frequent Self-Weighing and Visual Feedback for Weight Loss in Overweight Adults. *Journal of obesity, 2015*, 763680.
328. Burnett, K. F., Taylor, C. B., & Agras, W. S. (1985). Ambulatory computer-assisted therapy for obesity: A new frontier for behavior therapy. *Journal of Consulting and Clinical Psychology, 53*(5), 698–703.
329. Harvey, J., Krukowski, R., Priest, J., & West, D. (2019). Log Often, Lose More: Electronic Dietary Self-Monitoring for Weight Loss. *Obesity (Silver Spring, Md.), 27*(3), 380–384.
330. Kaviani, S., vanDellen, M., & Cooper, J. A. (2019). Daily Self-Weighing to Prevent Holiday-Associated Weight Gain in Adults. *Obesity (Silver Spring, Md.), 27*(6), 908–916.
331. Madigan, C. D., Daley, A. J., Lewis, A. L., Aveyard, P., & Jolly, K. (2015). Is self-weighing an effective tool for weight loss: a systematic literature review and meta-analysis. *The international journal of behavioral nutrition and physical activity, 12*, 104.

Chapter 5: How to make working out less effortful

1. Queiros, V. S., Dantas, M., Fortes, L. S., Silva, L., Silva, G., Dantas, P., & Cabral, B. (2021). Mental Fatigue Reduces Training Volume in Resistance Exercise: A Cross-Over and Randomized Study. *Perceptual and motor skills, 128*(1), 409–423.
2. Juliano, L. M., & Griffiths, R. R. (2004). A critical review of caffeine withdrawal: empirical validation of symptoms and signs, incidence, severity, and associated features. *Psychopharmacology, 176*(1), 1–29.
3. van Amsterdam, J., Opperhuizen, A., Koeter, M., & van den Brink, W. (2010). Ranking the harm of alcohol, tobacco and illicit drugs for the individual and the population. *European addiction research, 16*(4), 202–207.
4. Beaumont, R., Cordery, P., Funnell, M., Mears, S., James, L., & Watson, P. (2017). Chronic ingestion of a low dose of caffeine induces tolerance to the performance benefits of caffeine. *Journal of sports sciences, 35*(19), 1920–1927.
5. Gavrieli, A., Yannakoulia, M., Fragopoulou, E., Margaritopoulos, D., Chamberland, J. P., Kaisari, P., Kavouras, S. A., & Mantzoros, C. S. (2011). Caffeinated coffee does not acutely affect energy intake, appetite, or inflammation but prevents serum cortisol concentrations from falling in healthy men. *The Journal of nutrition, 141*(4), 703–707.
6. Smith, A. P., Christopher, G., & Sutherland, D. (2013). Acute effects of caffeine on attention: a comparison of non-consumers and withdrawn consumers. *Journal of psychopharmacology (Oxford, England), 27*(1), 77–83.
7. Goldstein, E. R., Ziegenfuss, T., Kalman, D., Kreider, R., Campbell, B., Wilborn, C., Taylor, L., Willoughby, D., Stout, J., Graves, B. S., Wildman, R., Ivy, J. L., Spano, M., Smith, A. E., & Antonio, J. (2010). International society of sports nutrition position stand: caffeine and performance. *Journal of the International Society of Sports Nutrition, 7*(1), 5.

8. Trexler, E. T., Smith-Ryan, A. E., Roelofs, E. J., Hirsch, K. R., & Mock, M. G. (2016). Effects of coffee and caffeine anhydrous on strength and sprint performance. *European journal of sport science*, *16*(6), 702–710.

9. Richardson, D. L., & Clarke, N. D. (2016). Effect of Coffee and Caffeine Ingestion on Resistance Exercise Performance. *Journal of strength and conditioning research*, *30*(10), 2892–2900.

10. McLellan, T. M., & Lieberman, H. R. (2012). Do energy drinks contain active components other than caffeine? *Nutrition reviews*, *70*(12), 730–744.

11. Kim, W. (2003). Debunking the Effects of Taurine in Red Bull Energy Drink. *Nutrition Bytes*, 9(1).

12. Consumer Reports. (2012, December 15). *The buzz on energy-drink caffeine.* https://www.consumerreports.org/cro/magazine/2012/12/the-buzz-on-energy-drink-caffeine/index.htm

13. Dawkins, L., Shahzad, F. Z., Ahmed, S. S., & Edmonds, C. J. (2011). Expectation of having consumed caffeine can improve performance and mood. *Appetite*, *57*(3), 597–600.

14. Placebo expectancy effect of consuming psychoactive beverages on cognition and mood. Johal, J. (Author). 6 Jul 2015.

15. Moss, S.L., Enright, K., & Cushman, S. (2018). The influence of music genre on explosive power, repetitions to failure and mood responses during resistance exercise. *Psychology of Sport and Exercise, 37*, 128–138.

16. Burket, J.; Eubank, T.; Reed, C.; and Sanders, J. (2014) "The Effect of Music Tempo on Squat Performance," *International Journal of Exercise Science: Conference Proceedings*: Vol. 9 : Iss. 2 , Article 10.

17. Ballmann, C. G., McCullum, M. J., Rogers, R. R., Marshall, M. M., & Williams, T. D. (2018). Effects of Preferred vs. Nonpreferred Music on Resistance Exercise Performance. *Journal of strength and conditioning research*, 10.1519/JSC.0000000000002981. Advance online publication.

18. Henselmans, M. (n.d.). *Is aspartame safe?* MennoHenselmans.com. https://mennohenselmans.com/is-aspartame-safe/

19. Magnuson, B. A., Roberts, A., & Nestmann, E. R. (2017). Critical review of the current literature on the safety of sucralose. *Food and chemical toxicology : an international journal published for the British Industrial Biological Research Association*, *106*(Pt A), 324–355.

20. Ochi, E., Maruo, M., Tsuchiya, Y., Ishii, N., Miura, K., & Sasaki, K. (2018). Higher Training Frequency Is Important for Gaining Muscular Strength Under Volume-Matched Training. *Frontiers in physiology*, *9*, 744.

21. Henselmans, M., & Schoenfeld, B. J. (2014). The effect of inter-set rest intervals on resistance exercise-induced muscle hypertrophy. *Sports medicine (Auckland, N.Z.)*, *44*(12), 1635–1643.

22. Henselmans, M. (n.d.). *Bro splits optimal after all? [New study review].* MennoHenselmans.com. https://mennohenselmans.com/high-frequency-resistance-training-is-not-more-effective-than-low-frequency-resistance-training-in-increasing-muscle-mass-and-strength-in-well-trained-men/

23. Hartman, M. J., Clark, B., Bembens, D. A., Kilgore, J. L., & Bemben, M. G. (2007). Comparisons between twice-daily and once-daily training sessions in male weight lifters. *International journal of sports physiology and performance*, *2*(2), 159–169.

24. Heke, T.O. (2011). *The effect of Two-equal Volume Training Protocols upon strength, body composition and salivary hormones in strength trained males* [Unpublished master's thesis]. Auckland University of Technology.

25. Crewther, B. T., Heke, T., & Keogh, J. (2016). The effects of two equal-volume training protocols upon strength, body composition and salivary hormones in male rugby union players. *Biology of sport*, *33*(2), 111–116.

26. Henselmans, M. (n.d.). *How many times per week should a muscle be trained to maximize muscle hypertrophy? New meta-analysis review.* MennoHenselmans.com. https://mennohenselmans.com/training-frequency-2018-meta-analysis-review/

27. Haun, C. T., Mumford, P. W., Roberson, P. A., Romero, M. A., Mobley, C. B., Kephart, W. C., Anderson, R. G., Colquhoun, R. J., Muddle, T., Luera, M. J., Mackey, C.

S., Pascoe, D. D., Young, K. C., Martin, J. S., DeFreitas, J. M., Jenkins, N., & Roberts, M. D. (2017). Molecular, neuromuscular, and recovery responses to light versus heavy resistance exercise in young men. *Physiological reports*, 5(18), e13457.

28. Stuart, C., Steele, J., Gentil, P., Giessing, J., & Fisher, J. P. (2018). Fatigue and perceptual responses of heavier- and lighter-load isolated lumbar extension resistance exercise in males and females. *PeerJ*, 6, e4523.

29. González-Badillo, J. J., Marques, M. C., & Sánchez-Medina, L. (2011). The importance of movement velocity as a measure to control resistance training intensity. *Journal of human kinetics*, 29A, 15–19.

30. Carraro, A., Paoli, A. & Gobbi, E. (2018). Affective response to acute resistance exercise: a comparison among machines and free weights. *Sport Sciences for Health, 14*, 283–288.

31. Spennewyn K. C. (2008). Strength outcomes in fixed versus free-form resistance equipment. *Journal of strength and conditioning research*, 22(1), 75–81.

32. Wilke, J., Stricker, V., & Usedly, S. (2020). Free-Weight Resistance Exercise Is More Effective in Enhancing Inhibitory Control than Machine-Based Training: A Randomized, Controlled Trial. *Brain sciences*, 10(10), 702.

Chapter 6: How to motivate yourself

1. Vallerand, R. J. (1997). Toward A Hierarchical Model of Intrinsic and Extrinsic Motivation. *Advances in Experimental Social Psychology, 29*, 271–360.

2. Gjestvang, C., Abrahamsen, F., Stensrud, T., & Haakstad, L. (2020). Motives and barriers to initiation and sustained exercise adherence in a fitness club setting-A one-year follow-up study. *Scandinavian journal of medicine & science in sports*, 30(9), 1796–1805.

3. Caudwell, K. M., & Keatley, D. A. (2016). The Effect of Men's Body Attitudes and Motivation for Gym Attendance. *Journal of strength and conditioning research*, 30(9), 2550–2556.

4. Werle, C. O. C., Wansink, B. & Payne, C. R. (2015). Is it fun or exercise? The framing of physical activity biases subsequent snacking. *Marketing Letters, 26*(4), 691–702.

5. Connell, J. P., & Wellborn, J. G. (1991). *Competence, autonomy, and relatedness: A motivational analysis of self-system processes*. In M. R. Gunnar & L. A. Sroufe (Eds.), *The Minnesota symposia on child psychology, Vol. 23. Self processes and development* (p. 43–77). Lawrence Erlbaum Associates, Inc.

6. Ryan, R. M., & Deci, E. L. (2000). Self-determination theory and the facilitation of intrinsic motivation, social development, and well-being. *The American psychologist*, 55(1), 68–78.

7. Niemiec, C. P., & Ryan, R. M. (2009). Autonomy, competence, and relatedness in the classroom: Applying self-determination theory to educational practice. *Theory and Research in Education*, 7(2), 133–144.

8. Ruzek, E. A., Hafen, C. A., Allen, J. P., Gregory, A., Mikami, A. Y., & Pianta, R. C. (2016). How teacher emotional support motivates students: The mediating roles of perceived peer relatedness, autonomy support, and competence. *Learning and instruction*, 42, 95–103.

9. Flack, K. D., Johnson, L., & Roemmich, J. N. (2017). The reinforcing value and liking of resistance training and aerobic exercise as predictors of adult's physical activity. *Physiology & behavior*, 179, 284–289.

10. Fishbach, A., & Choi, J. (2012). When thinking about goals undermines goal pursuit. *Organizational Behavior and Human Decision Processes*, 118(2), 99–107.

11. Perez, D., Van Horn, S., & Otten, M. P. (2014). Coach John Wooden's Pyramid of Success: A Comparison to the Sport Psychology Literature. *International Journal of Sports Science & Coaching*, 9(1), 85–101.

12. Grant, H., & Dweck, C. S. (2003). Clarifying achievement goals and their impact. *Journal of personality and social psychology*, 85(3), 541–553.

13. Dweck, C.S. (2007). *Mindset: The New Psychology of Success* (Upd. ed.). Ballantine Books.

14. Nicholls, A.R. (2010). Coping in sport: Theory, methods, and related constructs.

15. Lagerkvist, C. J., Okello, J. J., Adekambi, S., Kwikiriza, N., Abidin, P. E., & Carey, E. E. (2018). Goal-setting and volitional behavioural change: Results from a school meals intervention with vitamin-A biofortified sweetpotato in Nigeria. *Appetite, 129*, 113–124.

16. Cialdini, R. B., Borden, R. J., Thorne, A., Walker, M. R., Freeman, S., & Sloan, L. R. (1976). Basking in reflected glory: Three (football) field studies. *Journal of Personality and Social Psychology, 34*(3), 366–375.

17. What works for behaviour change? (2018). *Nature human behaviour, 2*(10), 709.

18. Demartini, E., De Marchi, E., Cavaliere, A., Mattavelli, S., Gaviglio, A., Banterle, A., Richetin, J., & Perugini, M. (2019). Changing attitudes towards healthy food via self-association or nutritional information: What works best? *Appetite, 132*, 166–174.

19. Langer, E. J., Blank, A., & Chanowitz, B. (1978). The mindlessness of ostensibly thoughtful action: The role of "placebic" information in interpersonal interaction. *Journal of Personality and Social Psychology, 36*(6), 635–642